GOD, GRACE, HOMOSEXUALS, HETEROSEXUALS

A NECESSARY HEALING

CINDY KRUEGER

First Published 2015

Copyright Cindy Krueger 2015

cindykrueger0402@gmail.com

National Library of Congress

Krueger, Cindy

Includes bibliographical references

ISBN 13: 9780990793311

ISBN 10: 0990793311

Subjects: 1. Religion - Christianity, the Bible, Homosexuality

Cover Design by Shawn A. McAdams

To J.W., Always

And

To Tiffany and Tanya, Josh and Shawn

I Love You All

"TABLE OF CONTENTS"

"To be nobody - but yourself in a world which is doing

Its best, night and day, to make you everybody but

Yourself - means to fight the hardest battle which any

Human being can fight - and never stop fighting."

E. E. Cummings

GRACE: Unmerited and freely bestowed divine assistance, favor and love.

GRACE: Divine influence operating inside of man to inspire virtue.

Grace: "Sinners deserve the verdict guilty. Grace connotes guilt. Mercy connotes misery, the consequence of sin and guilt! Grace not mercy pardons. Mercy not grace binds up, heals, comforts, restores."

R.C.H. Lenski

Grace: "Grace means properly God's favor, or the good-will God bears us, by which he is disposed to give us Christ and to pour into us the Holy Ghost, with his gifts...Nonetheless, grace does so much that we are accounted wholly righteous before God." Martin Luther

Grace: "Grace is an attribute of God, one of divine perfections. It is God's free sovereign, undeserved favor or love to man, in his state of sin and guilt, which manifests itself in the forgiveness of sin and deliverance from its penalty." Louis Berkhof

Chapter 1 A HIGH PRIESTLY PRAYER

"My prayer is not for them alone. I pray also for those who will believe in me through their (disciples) message, that all of them may be one, Father, just as you are in me and I am in you. May they be brought to complete unity to let the world know that you sent me and have loved them even as you have loved me." John 17: 20-21 &23

Jesus prayed for Himself. He prayed for His Disciples. He prayed for all men who had been, who were, and we who were to come after. Jesus prayed a prayer, which as of today, the third petition has not been answered – for all men who love Him to be as *one in Him* as He is with the Father. Jesus defines relationship. It is intimate, it is personal, and it is our life business that we take to God so He can show us what He wants us to do.

You need to ask yourself two questions and answer them with critical awareness.

1. Do you feel a need or want to feel a need to heal the disturbing chasm that exists between the souls of homosexuals and heterosexuals? If no, why not?
2. What are you willing to do to help with the healing?

This I know...

...*Each* of us occupying the tiniest space on this earth has become slaves dedicated to the sophisticated sin of judgment. Sorry, no exceptions. Where are the boundaries, we ask, so we know how far we can take our hate?

...I no longer depend on man alone to show me God; I daily depend on God to show me myself.

...Sexuality and gender identities no longer disturb me.

...At long last I am comfortable living my life with God as who I am, the me He shaped in my mother's womb. He has always understood me and continues to hold His hand over me and work His good in my life in spite of me. I have stopped trying to be something I will never be. I take myself everyday as I am, the whole package, and do the best I possibly can while giving God my everything. My best everything is my heart. Each new day I ask Him to hold it and wash it with Jesus blood. "Ask and ye shall receive." "Seek me and I will find you." I listen to my heart because I trust it in God's divine hand.

Chapter 2 WHO EVEN THINKS TO PREPARE?

"The unceasing anguish in my heart..." Rom. 9:2

The quote by E. E. Cummings on the front page of this book is almost sufficient to become the first one page book ever written. Pain, and everyone is familiar with pain on many levels, is one factor that is a great equalizer. Around the world and maybe even in your own house there are men, women and yes, even young children that have and still do suffer tremendously because people with loud voices work hard to change them into anyone but themselves. They are fighting a hard battle, the hardest battle, and the result is an unnamed civil war in our midst. The most heartbreaking thought is that the fighting may never stop and casualties will forever litter the landscape of our lives.

On one side is a community of people with an iron-clad grip on their faith that they exist and have always existed from birth with a sexual reality that is different from others. In the beginning their childhoods are innocent and full of wonder and questions with no burden of distinctions between one another. Then as they begin to mature they are astounded and thrown into turmoil to recognize others find them disgusting and abnormal and often treat them accordingly. What can that possibly feel like? Maybe like your world has been cruelly pulled from beneath your feet? The modern world labels them homosexuals.

That thought of being no one but yourself when everyone else wants you to become anyone but you creates feelings a majority of people don't know how to pour themselves into. That tiny piece of the puzzle that would allow them to finally say, "I understand" remains MIA, Missing-In-Action. How can I say this with conviction? Just open your eyes and look around yourself with a fearless honesty about what you see. If there is understanding, wouldn't harmony at least be visible on the horizon?

Or maybe others can pour themselves into this, but the angle veers off into a totally different direction and with somewhat different parts. Again, in the beginning we see innocent children, laughing and full of wonder. They see no ugly distinctions among their playmates. But as they mature and become more aware of the world, they are faced with certain diversities they are uncertain how to handle. If their family has strong Christian principles, the moral bar may be set higher than in other families and the final voice of authority is known as God, the Creator of all. They are indoctrinated into a personal Biblical belief that sexual diversity is wrong, sometimes accompanied by the belief that this sin is so far worse than any others the people who share this diversity will go to hell if they don't change. They understand marriage has only one definition, one man and one woman, and these beliefs follow them through the hallways to maturity. The modern world labels them heterosexuals.

The heterosexual youth eventually emerges into a full blown adult world where diversity is everywhere and the powers that be expect him/her to quickly and skillfully dissect their way through each and every unique new position, accept or reject it and get on with life. Their mind says stay true to your own faith in God you have grown up with.

Yet, some of their good friends carry this label of homosexual and confusion arises.

The world with all its' sophisticated knowledge begins to pull you in different directions. On this side one respected group understands God to be saying one thing, but over here this other group, no less respected, understands God to be saying something different. The newly emerged young adult finally finds the courage to make their own position known, one that doesn't seem to necessarily be a death knell to either side. Suddenly they find themselves completely cut off and ostracized from friends, acquaintances, classmates, maybe even a family member leaving them hurt, isolated and confused. What can that possibly feel like? Maybe like their world has cruelly been pulled from beneath their feet.

The thought of being no one but yourself when everyone else wants you to become anyone but you is a position many don't know how to pour themselves into. The world as you understood it growing up hasn't just lost a puzzle piece but has switched puzzles completely and the pieces don't make sense. How can I say this with conviction? I have lived the last eighteen years studying the Biblical puzzle from all angles to hopefully find what was missing for me, so hopefully I could contribute something small but essential for fellow puzzle solvers.

When I began writing this book I gave it the title I thought it would be published under: "Grace, The Middle Ground." When two sides oppose each other, when the rain of pain reaches such torrential amounts that both sides begin to drown in hurt, we must locate a higher MIDDLE GROUND if we are to survive.

I am a Christian, devoted to my God, Creator of all. In these last years He has become my God of Gods in a way words absolutely fail me as I try to describe our relationship. I know it rests on a higher level than I ever thought existed. I've always thought my relationship, my understanding of God was sufficient. Today, my faith in Him alone is such that I trust only Him to hold and rescue all those I love so much.

There is no human, no matter how great and dedicated a leader, no matter how sanctified, no matter on which side of the homosexual/heterosexual chasm he stands with thousands of followers behind him in support, that I would now entrust to hold and rescue my loved ones, myself included. Why? Because God wrote the plan of the game and I have only played it in my bumbling, human fashion.

The World Cup series for soccer, or "futbol" as one American advertisement presents it, is center stage and the eyes of the world are on it as I write this. The association in charge has not asked me to call a single game! I know it. I know it! Not a single game. I have watched it some on T.V. I watched that one guy from Brazil get clobbered from behind and fall to the ground as his vertebrae snapped. Oh, that looked painful. Should he be outraged? Should he turn around and attack or sue the other player? No. It is understood that both sides go all out to win that trophy, those golden hands holding the earth. No one enjoys seeing or feeling the pain, but anyone involved in sports of any kind will tell you it's just the fallout one has to expect. And that is the critical point. Every player on the grid goes in with the understanding he may be the one to fall that day.

Not so in the complex arena of homosexuals and heterosexuals. Not everyone has agreed to be a willing participant to pain and when they find themselves face down in the dirt, grass filling their nostrils and they can't breathe we hear the shout, "foul". And God of heaven help us, the grid sometimes erupts into an emotional and physical blood bath and even the angels weep over our self-destruction.

I am also a mother whose life is wrapped up in the LGBTQ (lesbian, gay, bisexual, transgender, queer) community. My heart is there also because my child is there. I sincerely believe neither of us asked for this. You may believe differently. I am here to tell my story on the "Middle Ground" and ask ahead of time that you forgive my emotions as they travel back and forth across the chasm between sides. Unfortunately when one has a leg in each camp she can be considered a traitor by both camps. No one understands that better than those mothers who have found their lives racked by civil wars; one son in blue, one son in gray, or whatever the colors of that particular war. Both sides could end up calling you traitor. So, it is up to you, your choice if you will, whether you are open enough to want to hear my words.

If the title of this book caught your attention I can only hope you are one other force for truth that would like to experience healing and harmony among the weary of this generation. I know, not all are weary. Some seem to enjoy war and get such an adrenalin surge they look for a new skirmish daily. But as in every war since the beginning of time, perhaps we will someday soon witness the final battle and be able to go home and heal.

This is my story. It describes how I came to find that place where I now reside, my spiritual and emotional home. It reflects the new blueprint of my life, that lets me live and continue to be true to myself and God, standing one-hundred percent firm that no single person can wrestle me away from this safe place where my God has brought me. Why indeed would I follow any man when God has led me to final peace?

The Beginning

When my son came to us, his parents, the first time to reveal he was gay, after the silent but heart rendering scream, "No, please God, don't let this be happening to us", there was shame and heartache. It was followed by days of hollow numbness. And that was just the beginning. How unprepared I was. But we never think to prepare for what we don't believe will ever happen.

Bitter accusations of fault rose up in my mind but they really had no place to go, so they just continued cycling around and around without my permission – no beginning, no end. At some point my brain began to stir and I took what felt like a first breath. I was shocked and scared at how alone I felt. No, not just felt – how alone I truly was. No one had answers to help me understand what to do and how to do it. The truth is some just found homosexuality too offensive to sit down and discuss. Others were equally as lost and ignorant on the topic as I myself was. And that was the first time.

Because I loved my son so much and wanted to help him avoid all the pain that would surely come his way if he continued to pursue this life, my husband and I, as loving parents, sat down with him and tried to convince him he was wrong about his sexual orientation because it was a choice. We shared verse after verse from our Bible trying to explain how God condemns homosexuality, and within our hearts we pleaded with God that our son would understand.

So he tried, and tried hard to be the son *we* wanted him to be. Not just for a few weeks, a few months, but he struggled for years. At times he juggled a duo identity, one for his family and one for himself which is an oppressive and damaging way to live. Why? Without a permanent identity to safely claim, always yearning for freedom, one can wither before its' time like a leaf falling prematurely to its' death, landing in the river of forever and floating to nowhere. Its original potential to shade others in the heat of life and later burst into vibrant color is lost. But what did I know. During those years I dared to hope. I began to relax my guard a little, even a lot, thinking all was settled. But eventually, with a whole new heartbreak, for the second time, now as a young man, my son came to us and said he was gay and must "come out".

The phrase, "come out" refers to walking away from a bleak existence in the "closet" of life which is dark and lonely, and because you can't adequately grow, you begin to putrefy emotionally, spiritually, and finally physically. You so desperately need some fresh air and the light of freedom to help you exist and grow, so you open the door to escape – to "come out", but it jars to a stop as though a strong hand, a malignant hand is pushing you forever back into the closet. "If you are in there we will all be happy" seems to be the message. "You can still be who you think you are, but our lives don't have to experience a huge paradigm shift when we are nicely entrenched in our super social network world and we are happy, happy, aren't we?"

I didn't really grasp the closet world at the time because my own pain took up most of my heart space. How often we see things in relation only to ourselves without fully examining the complete situation from the other's point of view. And quite frankly, as I would later learn, the spiritual eyes of a parent cannot see into the misery of their child when the parent's own heart cannot comprehend it, especially without the Spirit's help. And when we don't see the need for the Spirit's help because we assume we know all we need on the subject, we all end up putrefying in the closet. We just don't realize it!

I was worried for my son physically and spiritually, yet I was bankrupt of knowledge. I really knew nothing about homosexuals except what the media portrayed. No, you just don't get invited to be the spokesperson or call the game just because you have seen some things on T.V. no matter how well informed you may actually believe yourself to be. Because it had never been a topic for study at my church there was no education from that source. So instead, I worried – a lot.

But I can describe a different scene now, one of a lost boy/man, not only fighting the usual difficulties of life that at times are capable of knocking any one of us down, but who had to fight simultaneously on a second front, one of humiliation, and anguish from being despised, marginalized or even invisible to others. I know those are beginning to sound like the battle cry of LGBTQs, but they are worthy words and I will use them.

Even within his small group of gay friends, my son lived with intense isolation, even if he could not recognize it or verbalize it. In one way or another they all suffer isolation initially. My son had spiritual walls slamming against him that not all of his new friends were dealing with as church had never been a part of their lives. But if you and I can stop a moment and really start to listen, a voice will whisper, another will cry, this one will shout, "I don't have anyone to talk to about this." If you choose to listen to their stories, you will begin to hear it over and over and over again, all different voices, all saying similar things.

It wasn't until years later my son was able to describe to me how he felt God hated him. I know in some Christian circles we hear talk about a growing persecution and hate in America from hostile unbelievers that want nothing more than to cut us and the God we love out of this life. Yes, I agree, I do see hostility to the church in our country, but I'm not sure I can comfortably call it actual persecution at this time in America when we are free to live our lives in the way we choose with our creature comforts and our needs met. Is there persecution in our world against Christians? Most definitely. When churches and homes are burned and lives are imprisoned or lost just because they love and serve God, yes, that is persecution. When you lose the right to be *who you are* that is persecution!

But at this time, in America, we are not rotting in mud huts surrounded by electric fences with uniformed thugs carrying automatic fire power and being forced to kill our families to show we are loyal to a leader or else brutally die ourselves. We are not being rounded up and placed in cells where family members are beaten and girls raped by guards. I would humbly share that at least we, as God's children, no matter how bad it gets, and it has room to get worse here, you and I have the comfort in knowing our God fights on our behalf and shelters us beneath the shadow of His power and being. And His will, that mysterious way of His, which man is incapable of looking into and solving, is always working for us according to His plan.

Let me explain. One day my son was a young person struggling with this "thing" in his life that he didn't ask for, and the next, someone that he trusted, his father and I, the parents who have "good intentions" as *they* understood it, confronted him and our words, like a well-honed knife, severed that trust he had built his entire life upon, from the cradle and throughout his daily education in the Christian school he attended.

Our words introduced doubt and misery that grew into actual fears about the relationship he believed he had with God. Was that the affect we intended? Of course not! And had we realized what our actions and words and brought to him, perhaps we might have finally begun to know and understand this raging turmoil in his life. Our sincere efforts were based on our belief system that was taught to us from the beginning of our lives. It really was the alpha and omega of what we knew about homosexuality. We reacted in a similar fashion to Christian parents everywhere who are being confronted with something they have not been equipped to handle, not through the church and definitely not through our society.

I'd like you to stop for a quiet moment and try to envision the anguish of the homosexual who believes God no longer loves them. Stop, shut off the world for a moment and just try. There you are with your head in your hands, all alone, your chest so heavy it hurts. Please try to see it and feel it. Have the Biblical rules suddenly changed toward you? From what the people you trust keep saying, evidently so. For all God's so-called unconditional love and grace, He is actually incapable of lifting a finger of forgiveness your way. Why?

Maybe you misunderstood love and grace. In Sunday School and private school you learned God sent His Son to die for all of us while we were (and still are) sinners. Not a single person on earth then or now has given God much more than grief, but He has overruled our sins and saved us. We don't have to *do* or *be* anything but ourselves to warrant this gift. He only asks us to trust that He was telling the truth and just need and love Him and we will be counted among God's family. Did you somehow not understand this correctly? Why does this suddenly not apply to you?

After finally finding the courage to admit to yourself you are homosexual and that you still love God, now you need Him more than ever. You pray to God; you cry out to God with a tear choked plea because you still want to believe in His promises that He is with you no matter what. You have been taught God hears our prayers and will give us what we ask when it is in accordance with His will. You are still confident in your heart He will change you because everyone has told you only heterosexuals live within the will of God. Since homosexuality is an abomination you have no reason to believe He will not change you. You try to follow your Bible the best you can.

But days pass. How many nights have you called out to Him? You've lost track. Night after night there has only been silence from heaven. Heartbroken, it finally seems your only reality is He doesn't love you anymore because your difference, your sin, is so heinous, God can't or won't help you. He will not be there for you – there will be no guidance or help. You are on you own.

Come back to yourself now. Can you feel it? Can you feel the devastation within you? You love God; He does not love you!

I am a mother with a gay son. I had to decide and then make a commitment within my heart that voices in the homosexual community had something they wanted me to understand, a lot of somethings. So I asked myself, am I God's child? Do I understand unconditional love the way Jesus presented it? If so, I need to listen and hear their stories before I start reacting without adequate knowledge.

When you and I are incapable of walking on the lonely, miserable path of another, or we simply don't want to believe what they are trying to tell us, and our involvement is not crucial because it is not our child – our loved one, we have a tendency to not get entirely involved with our hearts. They desperately want to talk; we don't want to listen because our heart is not committed enough to care.

At this point you have the choice to quit reading right now, or to reach deep and rediscover that initial desire to understand and be a part of the solution and say you are dedicated for the long haul. I hope you choose the long haul with me. God keep us on the middle ground.

Chapter 3 HOW DO I EQUIP MYSELF TO GET INTO THIS GAME?

"Whoever humbles himself like this child..." Matthew 18:4

In life, most people would agree that the need for comfort usually increases with the complexity and desperation of the situation. Our survival instinct to escape pain and find comfort drives us to search for ways to medicate or anesthetize ourselves and at times we turn to those things that damage us further mentally and physically. My son sought comfort for his pain; we, his parents sought comfort for ours. And most of the time the seeking was in solitude, each to his own, void of any warmth or support from one another. We just could not talk to each other about our situation with any clear purpose because my husband and I had no clear understanding of homosexuality, and my son was at a loss as to what he could say to us anymore.

That closeness and ease that so many families with heterosexual children take for granted disappears for those of us who experience the unexpected announcement of "gay" in the family. The confidence and warmth of familial allies is erased to a certain degree. It comes from having no direction, no support network. Over eighteen years ago no one could answer what do we, as a family, accept and what do we refuse? What do we do?

Do I hide these staggering feelings of shame when all I want is to be proud of my son? Do I tell family members or keep their sensitivities protected? How do we handle our future family life? What if he wants to bring his partner (there I've said it) home? What if they want to stay overnight? Do we even let them? Do they sleep in separate beds or rooms for that matter? Will they want to have a commitment ceremony some day or want to get married? How about children, my grandchildren? How can I possibly explain to that child someday why he or she has two daddies and no mommy? Just asking these questions left me physically and mentally drained knowing I had no answers. During my worst days my heart seemed to dissolve into a dark red pool.

During my first year of desperation, so many years ago now, I called a local pastor I respected and asked about any support groups for parents of homosexual children in our city. To my disappointment he knew of none. What a sign of the times. Support groups for anything and everything except the "dirty little secret" called homosexuality. But he did share one thought with me, his knowledge and belief that no child who is disowned or turned away from the love and security of their family ever finds "change".

And here is a key word: *change.* To my ears it was a positive sounding word. From that one word I began to build my plan with little seeds of hope. (Today as I look back I can honestly share what I didn't realize at the time, that someday in my future there would truly be change, but it would not look anything like I envisioned at that present moment.)

Our New Plan

Step 1. My husband and I agreed we would never disown our son and going a step further we wanted to give him the same unconditional love that Jesus gives to His children, the same love the father embraced his prodigal son with in Luke 15:11-31. The very first action that father took the moment he saw his long lost son was to enthusiastically run to greet him. He hadn't spoken a word to his boy yet. For all he knew, there would only be a request for more money. But he kissed him. I see that dad with tears on his cheeks kissing his son many times. He placed a good cloak around those thin, stooped shoulders, put a ring on his finger and new sandals on his feet. My husband and I determined we would try to do the same. Did we understand all we were committing to? No. But we blindly accepted the words of this story as a faithful guide.

I once heard a woman say she didn't go through nine months of carrying her son and deliver him in all that pain to have him turn out to be gay. I began to realize that I didn't carry my son for nine months and deliver him in all that pain to turn my back on him and abandon him just because things get tough and complicated. Besides, what would I be abandoning him to? A society where God is often unwanted and unappreciated would be unthinkable, especially when my son would be cut off from any love or influence we might have on him. But please understand we did not carry out this step perfectly. Far from it. We were still walking in a strange world of shadows and little light.

Step 2 quickly followed. We would allow our son to bring his lesbian/gay friends into our home. What better way could we begin to show our unconditional love, not just to our son but to others who may also need family love. Looking back I'm not saying our son's friends felt totally at ease here with us, but it was a start for us.

You see, somewhere there has to be a start even if it sags in places, doesn't quite come together in others, and threatens to pull apart at the seams occasionally. As a seamstress for over forty years, I remember wearing the first dress I ever made one time only. It wasn't very good. But from that day onward I kept sewing and today consider myself a master seamstress. A beginning is just that, the first step that leads to lots of future steps that eventually move you to a better place that you are working toward.

And please if you notice an overuse of the word "us" try not to judge too harshly. My husband and I had miles to go yet working on just "us" before we could begin to understand how to successfully incorporate "them" in our lives in a way that we also felt would be faithful to God. I never use the words "us" and "them" anymore but they honestly reflect the exclusionary attitude that exists. That is why this book is about a necessary healing.

After that we quickly stalled out. Step 3 was as far out of reach for us as our understanding of how to cure cancer. So, a two-step plan was it. Are two steps enough for a plan? No. Two rules are hardly game plan enough to get from a beginning whistle to the final goal. But I felt a little less lost emotionally than before.

It was during these early heartbreaking days of indecision I discovered and read the official statement on homosexuality from the denomination I married into. I quickly devoured every page, all twenty-nine of them plus lists of resource materials. Afterward, I sat there speechless, eyes glazed over, my heart sinking into my gut. It seemed so vague and wordy. I was searching for specific advice of a day to day guide on what loving a gay son looks like, answering the questions, "What, as a Christian, do I accept into my life and what do I say no to". I craved some beginning step by step details. Was there any such thing? Surely someone has an idea or two. But if that someone existed, I could not find them, and it only intensified my aloneness.

I could not grasp the details being explained by that church document. Clearly it failed to meet all my needs and answer my questions, although I'm sure the leaders of my church felt it was sufficient for guiding a ministry to families of homosexuals. But then no one consulted me, a mother with a gay son who would have told them differently.

One example of my confusion from the document came with the words that Homosexuality does not negate baptism. And yet, then as well as today, so many years later, I don't see those words supported through the actions of many churches. Baptism with all its power instituted by the Word of God, that act recognizing each individual as a member of God's family, has apparently become impotent as baptized homosexuals are totally ignored and disregarded as Christians when Sunday after Sunday we hear homosexuals vilified from pulpits around the world. Baptized, homosexual, Christian – these words have nothing in common in the minds of many ministers.

Those closest to me in leadership who I approached eighteen years ago left me lost and confused. The day after I had a searching conversation with a pastor I was unable to even remember what precisely had been said to me. I'm not trying to lay blame. I'm trying to explain how complicated finding help was and how hopeless I felt when everything and everyone continued to fail me.

At some point in those early months of my confusion those twenty-nine pages were misplaced so that I could not find them as the years continued to shuffle past. It seemed they were not to be the source of help for my journey. Looking back I now truly believe God wanted to strengthen my faith, my spirit, and my heart by simply having me reach for His hand alone. He knew how to take me deeper into His Word and build the field of faith that I needed. God's love had already begun to pour caring grace on me and a surer, stronger woman would eventually emerge.

The Past Affects My Today

In order to start gathering the equipment to get me into this game of healing, there were some rooms in the past with various items that I needed to revisit and claim. Perhaps you will find a similar necessity in your own life if you are with me today on this page because your own child or loved one is gay.

During my own childhood, Jesus was such a natural part of my life, an extension of who I was. My friends and I were so fortunate as we lived, loved and were nurtured in the innocence of God's perfect love for us. Life was beautiful whether it was going to Sunday School, summer camps, or my best friend Patti and I going home with one another after church spending the entire afternoon together. It was so hard to stop playing to get ready for church on Sunday night. (Interestingly enough it is this same friend, Patti, who gave me the courage as an adult to step forward in this overwhelmingly scary faith journey and know that God would not let me go. She was the first truly dedicated child of God to demonstrate that not all Christians believe the worst about the LGBTQ community and that in fact God loves each one of us the same. I want to grow up to be like you. I love you my friend.)

The first room I revisited was from a lifetime ago. I was a little four year-old girl silently asking Jesus to please not return to earth until I was saved. I knew being saved was essential to joining Jesus in heaven someday, and though I didn't completely understand everything that was involved in being saved, I knew I needed to be baptized and I knew I really wanted to go heaven when I died. Oh yes, and I would love to be able to eat that little cracker and drink grape juice out of that tiny glass in the church service sometimes. It all seemed so grown-up like. I talked to Jesus frequently. That memory is clear and permanent in my mind. Fortunately, even though churches disagree on the specific theology of baptism, God's arms are wider then all of man's theological interpretations combined.

So I told my little four year-old self the only truth I understood, I hadn't walked down that long church aisle by myself yet, but at four, people didn't seem to expect that of me, so I wasn't concerned. I may not be "saved" but it was safer and easier just to talk to Jesus on my own. The truth that my ability to even call upon God's holy name could only come from God Himself working His will, His very grace, inside my heart was a truth still in my future waiting to be discovered. This room

18

was necessary to revisit so I could understand the strong place I came from spiritually.

This next room helped me understand that humans have legitimate questions about God and teachings we don't understand in the Bible that sometimes go forever without being answered.

God created some of us to be movers and others are granted the gift of stillness. I was a mover. But while my little body wiggled in my chair my ears were open and I heard and I learned. For instance, one particular Sunday morning our four year-old lesson was on Martha who frantically cleaned the house and prepared a meal for Jesus, and Mary who wouldn't help. The latter quietly sat at Jesus feet listening to His stories. When my teacher asked who chose to do the better thing that day I confidently chose Martha.

For years at the dinner table, swirling my green peas into my mashed potatoes so I couldn't taste them as much, I'd listen as Mom and Dad occasionally shared stories of the hardship during the depression years of my parents and grandparents, and how hard work was a virtue, an absolute necessity if one was to survive. So yes, of course, Martha beamed brightly in my mind as I gave my answer nice and loud during that Sunday School class that particular morning.

Let me tell those of you who are unsure, four year-olds can and do get embarrassed. I will never forget the teacher telling me I was wrong. Mary's choice was wisest that day and I still hold that memory in my heart. It is as clear today as the paper leaflet I received fifty-nine years ago with Martha, Mary, and Jesus pictured on the front. And it was my first powerful revelation that God does not always think or act in a way I understand or can predict based on what I hear and see around me, and it would revisit me repeatedly as I matured.

Pulling On The Game Shirt Of Grace

Some of us can live a lifetime without much need to contemplate where our lives are heading. There are those who might say we are lucky that life has been so simple. But there are others who might see a different story and will say we are to be pitied for lacking the type of challenge that would draw one right up to God's Holy side for help. But life can be so fragile; can be torn apart at any time. When it is, things are exposed you never wanted to see, never dreamed of having to deal with.

The contented little girl trusting Jesus to wait for her to be saved before He returns to earth, with her tightly held picture leaflet of Martha and Mary is only a soft memory now. In her place lives a wife and mother of two who finally understands she cannot close her eyes to the harder lessons of truth; that she, after all, will not be spared the fight, the challenge that has her crawling up to God's side for help.

So one spring when I desperately needed answers so I could begin to equip myself to deal with this foreign concept of homosexuality, my adult daughter was there for me and suggested I read *The Ragamuffin Gospel* by Brennan Manning. Here was a man who had his own painful secrets that he willingly shared with the world. He was open and receptive to the dirt and raw places of people's lives, wanting to help them, hoping that other Christians would also be open and receptive to the same dirt and raw places, willing to risk a part of their lives for the love of Jesus to help those who are hurting.

In my mind Brennan Manning was a humble soul whose own gritty life harvested compassion, grace and merciful insight rather than bitterness, entitlement and blind arrogance. In his own words, he was an alcoholic. And while reading those very words about him it hit me that my life is full of mess and sins also. I could pretty much safely say almost every sin in my life has been committed as a Christian, a child of God.

This insight didn't just blitz and then quickly disappear. It took root deep into the walls of my heart and soul and began to grow. This was another room that I was required to revisit if I wanted to heal. I looked down at my sins now cracking the mortar trying to hold my spiritual life together and it fully dawned on me if all the sins of my lifetime were rolled together, the size of the bundle would leave me breathless and heartbroken – impossible to shoulder. And for a time my world stopped and I visualized that picture and meditated on that ugly truth. And it wounded my heart, the one I had so happily and eagerly given to God as a young child.

Why God used this man with his amazing awareness of grace and sin to shake me awake I have no answer for. I can only believe this particular reality was something God knew I was ready to see, not just in a Sunday morning kind of way, but in a life-jolting kind of way, and in His Holy wisdom knew the time had come for the unveiling. It was my time to learn about a new gift from God called grace, a word I had heard mentioned in countless sermons, but one that was now about to be introduced in a truly three dimensional way. I would not just hear or read about it, I began to feel its presence and I would begin to sharpen my wit by it and live it. The true and miraculous gift from God this word represents would turn my world inside out and be my safety net time and again as the coming months unfolded.

The day grace becomes a living element within us, growing with tendrils throughout, we will at last no longer hold in ignorant awe those educated seminarian "superstars" empty of humility, legal moralists, (more in chapter 8) intent on changing others so they will receive the credit, who blast those humble seminarians who preach more like John, the gospel story of love and grace.

Manning helped me see the church will no longer be able to set herself as a first class saint, over "those who can't possibly be Christians", second class sinners. It's because grace destroys that erroneous judgment and replaces it with the truth we now have from God, eternal life, not by our merit or our right by what we have done, but by God's pure gift, freely given, is for all mankind. But for those who insist on first class church members versus second class homosexuals sinners, if they are considered a class at all, indicates quite clearly this will not be a simple journey.

So here I sat with a big fat scarlet letter "S" for sin on my chest, all dressed up and no place to go. I sat and waited. My life had reached a critical point. There was hardly a day that went by that I didn't obsess about the pain in our lives; this relationship, now truly abnormal because we weren't relating at all. One night, I finally cried, realizing I could no longer pretend to fully live life while I was only going through the motions. In my misery, I decided I would do whatever it took, go wherever I must go, endure whatever I must endure, good and bad, to end this ugly cycle. I didn't know if I would have to walk along hell-fire and brimstone to face down this monster, but the desire to resolve was greater than the extreme fear of this unknown journey toward the game now shaping up.

When my kids were both in high school, I went back to complete my college education with a degree in Registered Nursing. After graduation I couldn't wait to go on a medical mission trip. Life was still very unsettled with my son but I was still trying to exist in those days. The national offices of our church's denomination had outfitted an eighteen wheeler, half medical, half dental, and it was presently in Kazakhstan to bring physical help to the people who needed it. Shortly after graduation I was being introduced to a strange but alluring country that was nothing like America.

During our stay, it was time to move the mobile "office" to a new location, to the city of Narynkal located in eastern Kazakhstan. What made it unique from other cities we had seen was a completely fenced eastern border that overlooked "no man's land", a region stretching from this struggling country to the powerful regime of China. This is a no nonsense piece of real estate requiring you to pass through a security check point before the armed guards will raise a barrier allowing you access to the road that continues up to Narynkal. As we drove through I glanced behind only to see the barrier fall back into place blocking the way out. I felt like there should be a sign saying,

"ENTER AT YOUR OWN RISK".

When at last we arrived, we stopped our vehicles outside the edge of town, stepping out to inspect a sight several of us had never witnessed before. Stretching as far as our eyes could see was dirt, tall grass and scrubby trees that traveled miles until at last butting warily up against a continent of contention. I couldn't actually see China, but I knew it was out there somewhere. In that moment of quiet, I wasn't sure I could process all my feelings, and there was certainly more than one swirling in my head.

I wondered if I climbed over that fence was someone nearby waiting to shoot me? If I wasn't shot, would I be allowed to climb back into safe territory or ordered to stay separated? Was there any way to survive out there?

I hope you can sense my uncomfortable, uncertain feelings, because through these shared memories you will begin to get a glimpse into my own "no man's land" I felt I was about to face if I ever hoped to understand God, myself, and homosexuality.

I silently asked, "Is this desolate place where you're going to teach me the rules of the game, Lord?" One day I realized God had heard me because it seemed a quiet answer was filling my spirit. I knew I wasn't alone anymore. It felt like Jesus was saying, "I will take you into this unknown land and you will not be alone. I want you to take my hand and become a little child and follow me." And I answered, "Okay, I will." I would somehow rediscover the essence of my childhood for Jesus.

A Child's DNA

Manning captured it well when he said, "The child doesn't have to struggle to get himself in a good position for having a relationship with God; he doesn't have to craft ingenious ways of explaining his position to Jesus; he doesn't have to create a pretty face for himself; he doesn't have to achieve any state of spiritual feeling or intellectual understanding. All he has to do is happily accept the cookies: the gift of the kingdom." 1 Manning.

His little unpretentious self just shows up. He is an all ways humble. The child of Jesus' day emptied himself of nothing before coming to laugh and play at the side of the gentle Teacher, for it never crossed his mind anything of consequence or value existed in him to be emptied! Beyond any doubt that child perceived a loving and reassuring authority in that man, Jesus. And whether or not he mentally understood it, he was never afraid to put his life in the gentle Teacher's hand with a trust that went beyond reason. How sweet and uncomplicated that sounds. I am weary of struggling against the over ambitious objectives and expectations our adult world thrives on. The trust of a child is what I need.

My daughter, a teacher of PK 4 year olds for years, has given me ample opportunity to observe little children by substituting for her in the classroom. I find they are innocent in the hyper-awareness of their own private world, one that we as adults can't always see, yet they can interrupt themselves immediately to pick up on the drama around them, especially the fascinating news from the adult world in their vicinity. Somehow they acknowledge, if only to themselves, there are many unknowns they need to master, and so much the better if they snag the "prize" before their neighboring friend. They can endure hurt one moment only to forget and later swear undying loyalty to the previous antagonist. They manage to live in the now, yesterday is forgotten, tomorrow too invisible to waste energy on. Maybe that isn't such a bad way to live.

Doug Pollock writes, "Anyone whose world is dominated by dogmatic certainty – whose mind and heart are closed to any other reality – is living a life without wonder. It's easy to end up 'wonderless' in a world that seems to prefer answers over questions and certainty over mystery." 2 Pollock. I don't want to be a 'wonderless' old codger. I want to believe life and God still have a few mysteries left to reveal. I began to grasp the essence of my little child before God. Having every single answer is not what it is about.

"Because we never lay hold of our nothingness before God, consequently, we never enter into the deepest reality of our relationship with him." 3 Manning.

Now I understood about that huge bundle of sins incapable of being carried. Through the years I had managed to discard their nagging memories, and in doing so self-goodness took their place. I belonged to God and Sunday after Sunday I was told how special that was. Yes, being God's child is to be cherished, but it's not because of anything I've done myself out of goodness. The failure to own the sinfulness that still exists and wars within my flesh every day can produce a selfish denial of who I am in connection with every single person on this earth, whether they are God's children or not. I needed to locate and accept the shoes of humility. I needed to lay hold of my "nothingness before God."

When we finally decide to reach deep down into our hidden places and grab a firm hold onto our nothingness we can begin to discover how to enter into the deepest reality of our relationship with our God. I had to stop stuffing my past history of sins out the window of my consciousness and begin to recognize my ongoing state of sinfulness, which would be the secret to open the door and shed light on how to become a tool of compassion to others. The word compassion actually means to stand with others in their pain. My son was in pain; I was in pain. Perhaps I was finally getting somewhere.

Jesus knew all about sin and pain. He entered the world not to condemn those considered the least important but to save them. His sandals crossed miles of Hebrew "no man's land" to touch, talk to, eat with, laugh with, and love sinners, downtrodden and oppressed. I could see an American "no man's land" consisting of LGBTQs that "good" people don't want to touch, eat with, talk to, laugh with and love.

Late that night in my bed I was ready to lay my "child" before God. I prayed what may seem like a strange prayer to you, but I want to share it with you anyway.

"If I crawl up in your lap, Abba, I will be safeguarded. If I bathe myself in your Holy Word I will be shielded. If I cover all of me in prayer with you, Satan cannot penetrate that barrier. My trust in you, Father, is all I now own. This one offering, my trust is sacrosanct, inviolate of all evil. It is the only safe place where I can rely on that every whisper is yours. This is where I begin a new birth. It is you, Father and me, Cindy. No church, no learned leaders, just you and me. It is a risk worth taking. Now let me accept your grace, God, as I learn to become a new student and a risk taker. Amen"

Chapter 4 ENTERING NO MAN'S LAND WITH JESUS

"Call to me and I will answer you and tell you great and unsearchable things you do not know." Jeremiah 33:3.

The next day I picked up my Bible, some commentaries, my "Ragamuffin Gospel", "Romans" by Luther, and I thought C.S. Lewis might also want to keep me company. This was a short list that multiplied many times over the next three years of study.

My first lesson in the great and unsearchable things began. I personally believe one of God's first loves is for us to know Him personally in a one-on-one relationship, as unequal as it may be. "Come to me, all you who are weary and burdened, and I will give you rest. Take my yoke upon you and learn from me, for I am gentle, and humble in heart, and you will find rest for your souls. For my yoke is easy and my burden is light." Matthew 11:28-30.

The day this verse jumped out to me was like God saying, *"Cindy, look at me with new eyes."* I couldn't argue I had been weary and burdened for a long time. This was His promise to me that I would find the rest I needed. He alone is capable of teaching me and He would do it gently and humbly so that at last my soul, no matter what the outcome of my search, would stop hurting. God's yoke is the easiest and His burdens are such as to appear light in weight for the downtrodden. He only had to say it once. I would now follow my Heavenly Father to the ends of the earth for such a rescue.

In the midst of this great hope a little word snuggled down among the others but I found it. God, our Holy Magnificent King, just told me He is *humble* of heart! Have you ever gone on a treasure hunt where there are clues you have to solve along the way before you can find the treasure? I was so excited because I felt like I had just found the answer to a clue I didn't even know I was looking for. I had prepared myself for this journey searching for my humility of sinfulness and on finding it was humbled by who I really am. Now I was struck beyond amazement that God showed me He is also humble in heart. Imagine that.

I don't know if that affects you in the least. I wondered how this great God of Heaven could ever be humble in any way because we humans give humility such low status in our lives, but my chest swelled with thanksgiving. For the first time I was washed in the reality that God who created me is my real Father. It wasn't just head knowledge any longer. He wasn't just God, the Creator of heaven and earth, but He had become my personal Abba Father in a newer, deeply intimate way. I really was awestruck. He established an extremely human and personal link with lowly me and I truly felt at long last that I could believe I have been created in His image. He truly is everything we are not and we are everything created in His image. In this monumental moment He personally took my hand, my sinful hand currently curled and bent with confusion, hurt, and anger and covered it with His grace infused holy hand.

Then He quickly and gently led me to Matthew 28:16-19 and He continued to expand my bewilderment. "Then the eleven disciples went to Galilee, to the mountain where Jesus had told them to go.

When they saw him, they worshipped him; but some doubted. Then Jesus came to them and said, 'All authority in heaven and on earth has been given to me. Therefore go and make disciples of all nations...And surely I am with you always to the end of the age.'" And Mark 16:19 brought it full circle. "After the Lord had spoken to them, he was taken up into heaven and sat at the right hand of God."

This has got to be the *greatest* example of faith in the entire Bible. Hebrews 11 has some amazing faith stories which most Christians probably consider to be the greatest faith stories of the Bible. But that day God showed me a different one which overshadows them all. Jesus trusts me, lowly, sometimes doubting me, to love the rest of the world for Him, and somehow, with His help, guide them toward Him so He can establish the relationship they were created to have with Him.

And I am amazed by those words, "...they worshiped, but some doubted." I do not in my life recall a Bible class or sermon that ever presented those words of doubt to me in the context of the followers of Jesus. How reassuring for me that Jesus reveals the imperfections of the apostles so like my own. And now I felt I had a link to a new set of brothers. My family is growing. My Lord's faith in me is overwhelming.

Jesus has so much faith that I can do my small part to move this mammoth job forward, to move the mountain of the masses just the slightest bit closer to Him, that He goes all the way back home to our Father, in heaven, perfectly assured the one thing He asks of me, of you, of all of us will be done. He understands I will have doubts, we all will have doubts, about what we should be doing sometimes, but that doesn't seem to concern Him.

In all of this, He has not asked me to *fix* anyone. God has not asked me to hate the sins of people on His behalf, to hold the malignancy up to their faces and tell them I am doing this because I love them. Nor has He once expected me to change the heart and life or even the sexuality of anyone. That's the job of God's Spirit as He chooses, not mine. He wants me to fully comprehend that. He has simply entrusted a tiny measure of His grace into my hands to share with those I come into contact with so maybe they might also desire a unique relationship with God.

When Scripture is understood from God's point of view it is so simple and pure. It almost puts those long chapters of complex theological interpretations in those large, impossibly heavy books bound by leather to shame. And as I unroll my fingers to reveal this small, light-weight measure of grace, I find the examples of "unmerited and freely given favor and love", "underserved pardon", and the "virtue" such acts can inspire in the lives of men who receive these gifts. I find the grace that pardons guilt. It bursts into a galaxy of light in my heart and mind and after receiving it I can now generously show it to others.

The day I rediscovered Matthew 25:14-30 I began to feel the excitement of God's Spirit nudging me. The servants of a noble master each received talents. Before leaving his homeland the nobleman instructed each servant to put the money to work. After a timely absence he returned and called the workers before him for an accounting. One man had turned his five talents into ten. The second turned his two into four. The third was afraid to risk anything fearing punishment if the risk didn't pay off. So he hid his talent away and had no treasure for his master. The master was angry, took the man's one talent and gave it to him who had ten. The servant with nothing was called worthless by the master and thrown outside into the darkness. This entire story is about risk and what we are willing or not willing to do for God when it seems scary to jump into the unknown or the difficult. Who would have thought God would teach me something from this particular verse that would assist me in learning about sexual and gender diversity?

Understanding The Risk And Why I Should Care

I knew there would be risk involved and that was important to understand. When we risk we are vulnerable and we become an easy target to the barbs and arrows flying from the bows of insecure people or those too proud to admit they might have something to learn from a simple, humble person who has and is fighting the good fight. Trying to discover if God really loves and accepts homosexuals as equal to heterosexuals is certainly not going to make me popular with those who believe there is nothing to uncover. For some, cruel and taunting jests are a hobby rather than a defense mechanism, and they practice it constantly and effortlessly, tallying up their points to proudly exhibit to equally heartless gamers. Yes, it's important to understand the risk, even though at the onset we never realize just how rough the game can actually get. We jump with both feet assured we will slay the hard-hearted dragons of society, ignorant of the countless times we will sink requiring God's faithful hand to pull us back to sanity and safety and life.

In Genesis 39, Joseph risked telling Potiphar the truth about his wife's intended seduction of Joseph and it landed him in prison for years in Egypt. (One mark under the negative column for "RISK".) In the fullness of God's time Joseph was released to oversee the greater task of saving and feeding all of Egypt and small outlying countries during the famine. (One mark under positive risk.) However, as the responsibility rose, the risk rose. (Positive or negative? My teeth are grinding.)

In Exodus 4, Moses chose the risk of returning to Egypt to free God's people facing his own possible death in that land. (Second mark under negative.) David risked his life day in and day out against the enemies of God for years. Saul wasn't the only one who wanted to kill David. (Third mark under negative.)

I know for sure not everyone understood or agreed with what these Biblical leaders were doing. No doubt many positioned under their care spoke poisonous words behind their leaders' backs, and maybe to their faces. There was probably more than one dignitary in Egypt who felt Pharaoh had made a bad decision allowing the alien, Joseph, to be his right hand man. How many times did the people following Moses grumble their desire to give up and just go back to the security of what was, even though they had been mistreated slaves? (Fourth mark under negative.)

In hindsight how thankful we are they took the risks Yahweh called them to. (Huge positive mark just wiped out all the negatives.)

We call these Old Testament legends leaders. I could be wrong, but I think maybe they saw themselves simply as *followers*, of Yahweh. Joseph was the boastful next to youngest son of his father, sold into slavery and later spent years in an Egyptian cell. Moses was raised in royal Egyptian privilege, killed a man and had to flee from his princely life, and later tried to persuade God he wasn't up to the task of confronting Pharaoh. David, the youngest son, a wisp of a shepherd boy, grew to assume a throne and spent the next years running from his enemies and at times from God. They were so aware of their own sins and limitations, yet I believe that is exactly why they were so valuable to God. And that is why their stories are now so valuable to me. For the most part, they had no illusions of who they were. None of them saw themselves as infallible. And because they willingly risked so much for God, He loved them and we love them.

For people who refuse to risk, even at the Master's instruction, "He or she limps through life on childhood memories of Sunday School and resolutely refuses the challenge of growth and spiritual maturity. Unwilling to take risks, this person loses the talent entrusted to him or her." 1 Manning. To dare to grow leads to spiritual maturity and the willingness to take risks for God's greater glory to continue to grow the church on earth, even in the face of hostility, is a calling worthy of God's children. That is the essence of being a little child who has emptied herself before God.

Can we sacrifice too much for the sake of the kingdom? Is the walk alone with God too risky to venture, especially if new knowledge reveals a different view from the masses? The truth is, our greatest risk will always appear too small. And yet, there will be nights that no matter how sincere we plead to God, the quiet continues to enfold us and

God's presence seems so distant. For the Christians who choose to set aside the warnings and condemnation of homosexuals we have been taught and have grown up believing, and decide to risk our reputations to find out for ourselves whether or not God truly loves LGBTQs, is to walk barefoot on a rock strewn uneven ground. Tender feet will cut and bleed and at times God will seem far away. But after the journey we will feel His presence that made truth and grace possible to heal all wounds.

David Kinnaman writes in *You Lost Me,* "What happens to the transference of faith, when the world we know slips out from under our collective feet? We have to find a new process – a new mind – that makes sense of faith in our new reality." 2 Kinnaman. I believe that homosexuals and their honest need to be accepted by a heterosexual world, with their civil rights granted would constitute the world as we know it slipping from under our feet, a least for a lot of people. So, we can either ignore risk, hide our talent and face the Master's wrath over what He asks us to do, or we can find a new process – a new mind – that makes sense of faith in our new reality of the sexual and gender diverse world now emerging.

Homosexuality certainly doesn't represent the first quaking ground the church has experienced requiring us to find a new process that makes sense of our faith in a new reality. If you have any understanding of the history of the church you see this very thing over and over again. Each time the church has undergone a paradigm shift that her leaders perceive will threaten the essential base of our faith, we start to unravel. We shout, we fight, at times we lose our identity as peacemakers, and even our dignity, and unconditional love for all mankind pretty much gets trampled under the cry, "Save the Church and Save the World."

And yet, time and again God's presence, filling one-hundred percent of the world maintained a solution, and rather than shrivel, the church grew stronger. Was it simple and effortless? No. But with each rethinking, relearning and restructuring of men's minds they stayed faithful to the eternal truths of God's word because God showed them how. And the best part, our understanding of God expanded, and God Himself became a "bigger, Holier God". The key was looking at God and His eternal truths with new eyes. She will squirm, she will shout, she will raise her fist in protest against the "oncoming evils" of the day, but the church does not like to re-examine God's truths with new eyes. It shakes the foundation, and the once upon a time of our secure eternity feels threatened because we don't seem to actually trust that God will lead us and never forsake us exactly like He promised He would. In times of insecurity we too often rely on the words of men rather than the faith promises of our God and Father.

Starting To Dig Deeper With New Eyes

Mark 4:26-29 was short and sweet but unforgettable. Yes, I had studied this alongside a multitude of verses before, but the difference for me was seeing them through the eyes of an eager student – a clean notebook waiting for God to fill.

In this parable written beside others describing the Kingdom of God, the man in these verses scatters his crop seed over his field. The days and nights pass and those tiny seed start growing, "...*though he does not know how.*" The process is pictured as first the stalk, then the head, and last the full kernel. It grew in stages. It didn't mature overnight. But scratching his head, the farmer fails to grasp that priceless pearl of wisdom, that it is *solely God's desire* for the seed to grow and ripen and be harvested that makes it all possible. The power to change and grow His children is God's alone, not mine.

Yes, the dirt, the fertilizer, the rain, the sun assist in the growth being as they are all tools from the fingertips of Our Father. But without God's *desire* that it happen, that a seed is planted and grows, all hope for a crop is impossible. All hope for even a single stalk of wheat is hopeless. The church, the minister, the people in fellowship, the sermons and songs all assist in the growth. But it is solely God's *desire* for growth to happen that first places the seed itself into the heart of a man, woman or child where it can begin to germinate.

Do you believe that when God desires a relationship with His creatures, it is His hand alone that places the seed to germinate into the heart of a person, even a homosexual person? How can they grow in Him without His careful tending to their lives? I know many LGBTQs that love God. Therefore, God must love them and choose them equally to their heterosexual brothers and sisters. Otherwise, how could they even call upon His name?

In the next field over the hill, Matt. 13:24-30, the owner sowed good seed but when the family was sleeping the enemy came and threw bad seed in with the good. The wheat began to grow into stalks, but to the owner's vexation he noticed tares mingling with the good growth. This is an actual fact in the agricultural world, as the stalks begin to grow, wheat and tares look alike.

So Jesus tells His parable to His followers and all the crowds. "The disciples' request to their Master to have this parable expounded to them; (v36) 'Jesus sent the multitude away' and it is feared many of them went away no wiser than they came; they had heard a sound of words, and that was all. It is sad to think how many go away from sermons with the word of grace in their ears but not the work of grace in their heart." 3 Henry.

Now, only the landowner in this story, who the Bible identifies as God, can infallibly identify between the two, wheat versus tares. "Note, it is not possible for any man infallibly to distinguish between tares and wheat, but he may be mistaken; and therefore such is the wisdom and grace of Christ, that he will rather permit the tares, than any way endanger the wheat." 4 Henry. Here we witness the grace of God and his love for what he sows. He doesn't allow anyone to carelessly ruin His harvest.

The discerning job of gathering could only be done by chosen harvesters. When Jesus identifies them as angels, He gives us a glimpse into actual life being revealed through the story of the parable. God will one day send His angels to harvest the wheat from the tares in our world. In the parable special harvesters had the ability to do this work for the owner that the other servants, no matter how long they had worked for him, could not.

Who are these other servants? You and me. "Note, the over-hasty and inconsiderate zeal of Christ's servants, before they have consulted with their Master, is sometimes ready, with the hazard of the church, to root out all that they presume to be tares: 'Lord wilt thou that we call for fire from heaven?'" 5 Henry. We are at times so prideful of our positions as God's children that we assume the leadership as His "right hand man". We know what we believe, it must be true, so call down the scorching flames of heaven to destroy what we will not tolerate on God's behalf. Ah, but is it what God actually wants?

God, as owner, will someday allow His angels to reap the earth as He instructs. But as His most trusted and loyal servants, you and I, His children, will never be called on to judge another human being for any reason or assume to know another human's value in the sight of God. Even if I, or you, mistakenly perceive that the fruits of "those others" could not possibly be good, we cannot positively know whether or not the end harvest will reveal them as wheat or tare. "The tares, if continued under the means of grace, may become good wheat; therefore have patience with them." 5 Henry. God's growing season is a long and patient one. This is God's job and this earth is God's fields. He alone has the omniscience to see into the hearts of all men. It is neither my job nor your job to uproot what God has chosen to grow under His season of grace! Only He can see the heart of my son and any other LBGTQ on earth.

The reason these verses were so important to me is because I saw my own confusion that I had carried for years about wheat and tares in the world. I had seen it as my duty to pull homosexual tares from the society I moved within. The concept that "those people" could possibly love God, let alone as much as I did, was a foreign one that I had not begun to think about until these last years of critical self-inspection. Could sinners such as those produce any fruit on God's behalf? Surely LGBTQs couldn't be considered Christians!

It has recently come to my attention that we in God's family seem to be divided into either primarily grace focused or sin focused people. Let me explain. Are you aware that from Romans throughout each letter in the New Testament, words in the introductions leave no doubt that each letter was written to the church – the followers of Jesus? Go back and take a look. Before really noting this truth I would at times earmark certain verses as written for unbelievers having nothing do to with me as a good Christian. But that is not true. Every word in the Bible has been written for the benefit of God's people.

When I forget that every word in the Bible was written for the church, was written for me, when I want to inform others just how wrong they are as sinners, I slip into a sin focused personality. The problem is that my sin focus is a laser I project onto others for the sole purpose of destroying the tumors of sin in their lives. That is called judging others. The laser is rarely if ever turned upon myself disclosing my awareness that I'm not living up to God's expectations.

You see, somehow in my years in church, I had grown to misunderstand my job. I had been taught that if I loved God it was my duty to make others see they are sinners who need to repent and make a one-eighty degree turnaround. That is in total opposition to the definition of grace which is "Divine influence operating inside of man to inspire virtue." I am not Divine. My job is to walk with compassion, sharing God's grace in the hope that some will hear His Spirit calling their name and respond. This is the truth God wrote on my slate that day. If you don't readily agree with me, I hope you will at least be willing to think about this and conduct further Bible study on your own. Take the time to ask yourself what do you believe and why do you believe it? If you can't put it into words you have some work to do.

"True wisdom is confident in knowledge yet humble in awareness that there are limits to our knowledge. Only God is God – a fact that should lead us to trust in Him rather than in our own rightness on any given topic." 6 Kinnaman. We won't always have all the answers nor does God require us to have all the answers. Don't get tangled up in a myth. Because the man who insists on knowing all the answers lies with self-pride at the end of the day.

St. Augustine, in his book, "On Grace and Free Will", talks about when the stone heart is made soft to receive the truth of His Spirit, God is revealed as Holy. It requires the holy hand of God to soften the heart of any and every man. And only when the heart is softened do the eyes see God's holiness. Faith comes before repentance. Each of these lessons matched up with those verses in Matthew. I now proceeded with the logic that whatever heart God softens and turns toward Him in faith will be made heirs unto eternity, anyone, and that includes homosexuals or heterosexuals because God removed any superior differences between people, sexual or otherwise.

I know this because of Colossians 3:11. "Here there is no Greek or Jew, circumcised or uncircumcised, barbarian, Scythian slave or free, But Christ is all and is in all." Wham! In one stroke God has removed all the previous barriers between all people everywhere. And Galations 3:28 adds that now that faith has come there is neither male nor female. In simple child-like faith I now also add there are no homosexual or heterosexual differences in God's eyes because God himself has canceled out any differences among people of the earth. There is simply no distinction in His eyes. For me, this is a huge discovery! God sees no differences! So why do we? And why in our ignorant humanity do we try to put words into God's mouth that says he cannot and will not accept homosexuals? As we are all sinners, why do we put into God's mouth the words that heterosexual sinners are saved and homosexual sinners are not?

Cain and Abel were the same in God's eyes. As a young girl this story just would not make sense to me. I couldn't understand why Cain's offerings of animals were not as good as Abel's offerings of grain. The crucial part about Cain's *heart* not being in sync with God, unlike Abel's heart in sync with God, was a missing link in my early days of Sunday School. Cain's obligatory offering given from an empty heart was rejected by God because Cain had rejected the seed God had set to grow in his heart. The sin of murder and revenge was then only a short step away from finding its way into Cain's life because his heart was not protected by God. "God is no respecter of persons, hates nothing that he has made, denies his favor to none but those who have forfeited it..." 7 Henry. I was going to discover so much about those that forfeit God's blessing down the road.

C.S. Lewis wrote, "Religion is God's statement to us of certain quite unalterable facts about his own nature." 8 Lewis. So the Holy Spirit helps us to see, hear, and to accept the mystery that is God's nature and assists our imperfect nature in responding to Him. God's Spirit helps us discern the seed growing in our hearts, helps us hear God's voice calling us to Him and He does it without distinction of persons.

A Hard Truth

We are, if nothing, enthusiastic and spend so much time in church meetings planning bigger and better things to bring people into the church. We sometimes spend so much busy time for God that we forget something close to God's heart – *His own humble heart in sync with ours*. "The sacrifices of God are a broken spirit, a broken and contrite heart, O God, you will not despise." Psalm 51:17. No, that verse was not written to sinners who need God in their life. That verse too, like all the rest of Holy Scripture, was written for God's own children, because we, His children are the ones who are concerned with our suitable sacrifice to Him. Suitable sacrifices are not sought by unbelievers.

Matthew 22:1-14 tells a thought provoking story about people, kingdom people, and those not considered kingdom people. It is a story for all of us who love God.

The king was giving a wedding banquet for his son. He sent out beautiful invitations to his people but when the feast day arrived all those who had been invited refused to come. The king tried again to get his people excited by telling them everything he had planned to make this banquet unique, one like they had never attended before. But the people were just too preoccupied with all the things on their lists of important things to be done. The king became angry, so he sent his servants into the street corners to "invite to the banquet anyone you find." So they obeyed. They went and "gathered all the people they could find, *both good and bad*." These new guests didn't personally know the king before that day but:

> When the poor in the city, (those who tried to live "good" lives and those who flat out lived " bad" lives) were approached in sincere kindness and told how it would please the king if they came to his banquet to celebrate his son's wedding, their humble hearts opened with a need and desire to be with the king. Amazed as they were by his offer, *they believed* the king really would open wide the exotic pearl inlaid doors of his palace to them. They trusted he would offer them the best wine from gold and jewel encrusted goblets and be served off of gold plates with foods they rarely if ever tasted. But mainly they were wild with anticipation over meeting the king's son and becoming his friend. Hours later, one of the original invited guests, so proud of his life and accomplishments, changed his mind at the last minute. He was returning home after an event

he had arranged and attended with other original invited wedding guests, and casually dropped by the shimmering banquet hall. Standing there in his sport shirt, shorts and athletic shoes he insulted the king by not being properly dressed – properly covered before the king. Immediately, without explanation, the arrogant guest was escorted out by palace guards.

Grabbing my attention in this section of scripture is a little three letter word, "bad" which I promise I don't ever remember seeing before I began my deeper study, located in verse 10. I looked at it like this. It seemed those people the king normally dealt with, were prioritizing their own agendas even if their good intentions were to further the prosperity of the kingdom in their own way.

So the ruler sent His servants to the lowly, the poor of spirit, the others, the townspeople. These people had a natural knowledge of things good and things bad, but they didn't hyper-dwell on it all the time. Some went about their daily lives, loving their families, helping their friends, perhaps even being kind to strangers passing through their town offering them meals and shelter. Some helped comfort the sick.

Some liked to gossip about others while filling their water jars at the well. Some preferred thievery to an honest day's work, or maybe in addition to. Some lied to manipulate and further their extortionist schemes. Some were drunk all day. Some were up to a romp in the hay or maybe the vineyard with another's wife. But none were recognized as the king's special people. Are you still with me here? The turning point came when:

#1. They were approached with some really good news where no mention was made of how wrong and "*sinful*" they were, or how they never went to church, and

#2. The good news that the king wanted them by his side to share his meal at the the wedding of his son which allowed their hearts to open and accept his astounding offer.

Notice, there is no point #3 that belabors a long converting process, of being ashamed, getting a bath, lots and lots of reading on etiquette rights and wrongs at the palace, running out to Salome's Latest Fashions for new clothes. Why are these important steps left out? Why are these essential elements the church has always held as the follow-up to accepting Christ's atoning work for salvation not included here?

Perhaps it is because the Father of the Bridegroom had already received the one and only essential element from the poor of spirit in His city, an element the original invited guests lacked. Their response was immediate joy rising up from humble lives; a spontaneous faith quickly responding to the King's invitation. Their hearts became in sync with his. There were no second thoughts of "things" that needed to be put before the King's summons. His summons was the "thing". And that was all He required. It was His pleasure to take care of everything else, and the party began – *PERIOD.*

Sometimes without "a broken spirit, a broken and contrite heart" we can't see what God sees and He can't help us see the bigger picture because we won't slow down and listen. We don't stop during our day and get quiet so we can focus our hearts on Him or pray through our pain at His feet. So we come up short of being attuned to His will. Sadly, I looked back on previous years in my own life that fell into that category, and still occur on some days in my life now.

The story king, God, was not afraid to bring the forgotten people, *good or bad* unto Himself. It seems no one else was going to bring them to His attention. His special people were too busy with their lists. The *things* they were doing for God were never going to be a substitute for spending pure one-on-one time with those who needed to see God's love at work on their behalf. The lesson from God that few saw, and few still see, anyone with a broken and contrite heart receptive to His simple, uncomplicated invitation can have a relationship with Him. That takes personal love, not programs.

God does not call us to a denomination, a budget, or activities, but to the person of Jesus Christ. It's all about God. And when we forget that, not only do we ourselves slip outside of the action for Christ, we may miss one single opportunity to love another, an opportunity delayed or entirely gone forever as "another" walks away not even knowing God's Spirit, ready to offer them full pardon was nearby. God's Spirit living in me connecting with God's Spirit filling the universe releases His holy power like a pure cloud around other individuals with the gift that might revive them like a cup of water.

"The emphasis is not on what man does in appropriating the grace of God, but on what God does in applying it." 9 Berkhof. It's all about God. But we are here to assist Him. We can make His job a little lighter when we love someone first, fact-to-face with God's love. It opens a door, a window, even a tiny crack for the Holy Spirit to move through on the wind of God's breath.

I slip my small hand into His own, so warm and sure, and add a little skip to my step. I like the sound of happy feet clacking on the road. "Well, that wasn't as bad as I thought it would be", I say. He smiles down on me as He steadies the yoke across His shoulders so far above mine. Suddenly, "no man's land" doesn't' seem quite as scary as before.

Chapter 5 WHOSE SINS HAVE BEEN FORGIVEN?

"If you confess with your mouth, 'Jesus is Lord', and believe in your heart that God raised Him from the dead, you will be saved...Everyone who calls on the name of the Lord will be saved. Romans 9:9 & 13

This chapter deals with the sin we all have in our lives. Some identify it by the name "original sin", that state which we are naturally born into due to mankind's fall away from God in the garden. It is a state our bodies in the flesh cannot escape from. This chapter is not here to identify homosexuality as a sin or any other act in our lives as sins. It is here because it is the instrument I found that best humbled my pride of self-goodness.

Another Day, Another Lesson With Me And God.

Today I tried to form my words into questions that sincerely puzzled me. "If homosexuals were born that way, and they love You and are glad You died for their sins, why do so many people keep saying they must change for You to love them or else they are going to hell? Weren't their sins forgiven? I was born a heterosexual and there are sins in my life, the kind where my flesh always seems to win out over what my heart wants. Am I going to hell? Are my sins forgiven? Some people believe homosexuals aren't born gay, they just choose to defy You, and live the 'lifestyle.'" I need to think for a moment.

"If they aren't gay, but they believe they are born gay and no matter how many prayers they have said or how hard they have tried, they can't stop being homosexual, but they love you and need You in their lives, are their sins forgiven? What about the man in church who doesn't make a lot of money and has children that need clothes but he can't always avoid spending money on alcohol and only has a little left over for his kids, are his sins forgiven? Then there are those people who are always hurting others by the gossip and harsh words coming out of their mouths, are their sins forgiven? Whose sins have been forgiven?"

"The problem of the origin of evil that is in the world has always been considered as one of the profoundest problems of philosophy and theology...It is a matter of daily experience in the life of every man." In the end, of the many solutions man proposes to explain sin and God, "...the problem of God's relation to sin remains a mystery." 1 Berkhof. And God does not require us to have all the answers.

Apparently, it is due to the profound problem of explaining God's relation to sin that some people do not believe sexual and gender diverse people could possibly love Him and need Him enough to ask God into their heart, and be recognized as a Christian, the same as you and me. I have to believe such thinking is wrong because it cancels out what Paul says in Romans 9 that calling on the name of God with a sincere heart is the only "doing" one must "do" to be saved. Our ability to "do" a one-eighty degree change in our lives comes solely from an intimate witness of God's presence in our life. Our spirit bursts alive with the feeling of Him.

45

I lift my eyes up to God's and just have to share with Him that church people love to talk about that one-eighty degree change in our lives when we become His children. I lean closer to His breast and tell Him, "I don't care for that analogy anymore because one time I believed it was true, but when I began to see I couldn't stay changed, I thought I was a hateful failure to me and You. My 'lifestyle' change is more like one-hundred degrees away from my old self, fifty degrees back to it, sixty degrees away from, eighty degrees back to and I just flip-flop like a fish struggling to breath out of water." I pick up my pencil drawing a fish struggling to breathe. I feel the Father's eyes look into mine with love and understanding and I sit back and sigh, the sad tension leaving me.

"We are all, equally, privileged but entitled beggars at the door of God's mercy!" 2 Manning. Part of healing is to want all men to love God, and to personally be able to understand that God actually has His own plan to accomplish this. Equally important for our healing is to realize that we, at times, can get in the way of His plan when we misunderstand God's purpose at any given moment and try to manipulate things our own way because that's what we've been taught or want to believe. We are all beggars at the door of God and yet, when we receive our mercy in our sack, like Halloween candy, and we quickly walk away, we too easily pick up our same old habits afraid to risk anything new apart from our safe world of lazy knowledge. We willingly accept God's grace as beggars, but hold back that same grace from other beggars whom we judge as "not good enough."

How many times do I as an individual hinder God's work with my inaccurate judgment of another person that I impulsively act on in a negative way? It takes a monumental effort to break the cycle of relying strictly on what others have fed my mind, and instead, trusting God to teach me a new way to interact with people. It takes a monumental effort only God can achieve within our minds to understand there are times we do have His permission to walk away from "fixing" others to suite our own misguided vision of "saving" people. It takes a divine monumental effort to stand down and finally realize with all your mind, heart and soul, that God is one-hundred present in our world and in our intimate lives with Him – that He is still working to achieve His final goal in His world – in spite of our attempts at "good intentions" to make the world "good" for Him.

What Does God Want From Us?

Does God want our all and nothing less even though our sins are paid for in full? Absolutely! I know that because as Jesus took our place, only His *all* was enough to pay for us. God demanded that only holy lifeblood would adequately pay for sin and Jesus willingly paid it with His own. Isn't it this "account paid" stamped across our lives that which makes it possible for God to overlook man's sins through His appointed grace to fulfill His plan on our behalf? And isn't it that blood tainted cross that strikes my heart with the greatest desire to be everything for Him that He desires, even when my flesh won't allow my heart's desire?

It is that deep life changing dimension of sudden realization that one really does want and desire Jesus as a Savior, Brother, and Friend, that starts that never-ending circular turn around in a life. You and I can't make that happen by our "well-intentioned" words and works unless God has breathed His power into the moment. Far too often, our most powerful and effective tool, prayer, is lost along the way when we set out to accomplish something in His name.

Yes, sin is confusing and all our sins are against God. None of us are capable of not sinning and God understands this better than we do. Berkhof explains there is no doubt that God has absolute control over the free actions of His moral creatures in that *God on behalf of His own purpose overrules evil for good* to achieve His will according to His eternal plan. I want to stop here a minute because there must be some who haven't heard such words before, that God overrules evil for good.

There is a good possibility that God loves His creatures more than He hates sin. It's only a guess but I figure a clue is that He wouldn't have thought grace into existence otherwise. If sin had a higher priority, I don't think God would be willing to overlook sin for the benefit of His plan for reconciling us back unto Himself.

That is part of what grace is all about, overruling evil for good. "Blessed are they who by grace are freed from the burden of iniquity, namely of the actual sins which they have committed. That, however, is not sufficient, unless also their 'sins are covered' that is, unless the radical evil which is in them, is not charged to them as sin. That is covered when, *though still existing*, it is not regarded, considered and imputed by God; as we read: 'Blessed is the man to whom the Lord will not impute sin.'" 3 Luther. I would ask you to read Luther's words over several times and let this truth sink in. While our sins still exist, while we still sin each and every day, they are no longer held against us when we love God. And our heart's desire to please Him, straining toward perfection and striving not to sin, comes from our relationship with God. Not from anything we can do on our own.

What About Free Will?

A close family member of original sin is the perplexing problem of free will. C.S. Lewis gives an example in his book *Mere Christianity* that might help us. A mother tries to teach her little children that at the end of the day they need to clean up their playroom. It is her own free will that determines she is not going to force them to do it. One evening after supper she goes up to the room and toys are scattered about, paint is drying on the table, paper and books are in disarray everywhere. She prefers that her children clean up each night, but it is her free will that allows the children to be messy. "That is not what you willed but your will has made it possible...Because free will, though it makes evil possible, is also the only thing that makes possible any love or goodness or joy worth having." 4 Lewis. Free will, sin, and grace are bed partners, possibly a new idea to some. Perhaps God thinks my free will and my son's free will is the only thing possible that makes love, goodness or joy worth having from us, imperfect as it is. Maybe He is good with that.

Where Does Virtue Come From?

And then we trip over virtue. "Virtue" is defined as moral excellence, effective or commendable quality, chastity. "Grace" is defined as unearned Divine influence operating inside of man to inspire virtue. Many believe virtue is like a skill that if we try hard enough we will obtain.

Although we pay lip service to grace, we live our lives relying on "personal discipline" and "self-denial" to transform us into the perfect moral being God wants us to be. We think we, the emphasis on we, can change our wounded lives in the same way those hoping to stop smoking put on a patch to take the desire away. And God is somewhere up in His heaven keeping score, busy with who knows what. Brennan Manning has opened my eyes to many myths in my life.

Virtue comes from God. He inspires it within us so we can share it beyond ourselves. Do you understand how, far too often, some churches have influenced their members to think they can "do" something that will bring favor with God? And when those who are more pragmatic than others, watch themselves fail more times than they succeed, they eventually lose faith in the church and more importantly the very Word of God and leave religion behind. Yes, we're known by our fruits and faith without works is dead. But we don't create the virtue ourselves and that desire to accomplish good works doesn't materialize from our broken selves. God originates this impossible desire inside of us and the victory of the "doing" belongs to Him alone. We, as clay cups, have never filled ourselves with the cold water that slaked the divine thirst of any man. And in spite of what some may think, being known by our fruits and faith without works is dead, is not to be used as a tool to judge another. If anything, it is the plumb line for each individual to look inward to his own self to determine where he is in relation to God.

Sins Or A Sin

Who in the Christian church, and even outside the church, have not heard of the Ten Commandments? We are told that if we love God we will turn away from sin. I can't tell you the number of sermons I have heard on these commands. I have also heard numerous sermons describing how God turned away from Israel because the people wouldn't stop sinning. Their sins were many against God. So why did God turn away from Israel and abandon them to their enemies? Why couldn't grace cover their sins?

Because there is a difference between those sins inherent in us, that we are born into, that we try hard to conquer but fail at so often that God in His divine grace chooses to overlook, and the sin of complete and willful rejection of God. If we look closer at the Old Testament stories, God's grace flowed like new wine into Israel's drinking cups for hundreds of years. God was their coach. The scoreboard was stacked in their favor. But the tension, the strife, and finally the seduction of so-called other gods won their hearts and they willingly moved from under God's protection.

Let's go back to the garden for a moment. I was taught as a little girl that Adam and Eve *disobeyed* God and were cast out of the garden forever and the world was never the same. I was taught what they did was a sin. But on becoming an adult it became obvious they didn't simply commit sin in the nature of "original sin". They didn't struggle against what their hearts wanted and their sinful flesh won out as will happen many times over with original sin. Instead, their hearts turned in a direction away from God. They willfully chose to turn their backs on

God, to disregard what He told them because they wanted to be *like* Him. They wanted His great knowledge; His amazing power over life and death. They coveted all the answers. They wanted to be gods themselves. So they ate the forbidden fruit of the Tree of Knowledge.

In the end, not only did they not become gods, but they lost their purest source of freedom. "But man did lose his material freedom, that is, the rational power to determine his course in the direction of the highest good, in harmony with the original moral constitution of his nature...He is not able to apprehend and love spiritual excellence, to see and do spiritual things, the things of God that pertain to salvation." 5 Berkhof. We lost the perfect beauty of what life could be, we lost our innocence, and we lost the most important thing of all, man's perfect relationship with his Creator.

Impressionable children have greater abilities to remember than we credit them with. To teach them that Adam and Eve simply *disobeyed* God is a great injustice to children in Sunday Schools everywhere. Why? Because they grow up thinking to sin, to disobey God, will get you thrown out of the garden, thrown out of the family and you can't go back again. It teaches hopelessness, whereas Jesus teaches us something quite different. In Him is complete hope in spite of our sinful selves.

We think we need to teach kids lessons on their level; within their limitations of understanding. There's nothing wrong with that – unless we reduce the lesson to a half-truth that will lead them in the wrong direction as they grow older. Some who go to Sunday School as children never return as adults. They retain what was watered down for them as children and it misses the mark in adulthood when they would be taught a deeper, more thorough lesson had they stayed in church. In some ways we underestimate the abilities of children and hurt them by not giving them the bigger truth. Even if they don't totally understand it as a child, if that is the one opportunity for them to ever hear the truth then they need the *complete* truth. The seeds of truth will stay with them and bloom into full understanding later with the Holy Spirit's help.

A half-truth will just remain a half-truth.

Why is it essential to understand the difference between original sin that torments us through our daily weaknesses even when our hearts fight against it, versus turning one's back on Jesus and completely disavowing Him as Adam and Eve demonstrated by coveting the forbidden things of God and succumbing to Satan's suggestions? Because when original sin, *something we didn't choose, were born into and we can't escape* in this lifetime, is equated to consciously turning our backs on God and His grace, something we choose from empty hearts, it allows us to wrongly condemn people to an eternity in hell. Therefore it condemns us all to hell. The elusive "good heterosexual Christian" whose original sin tally is no different from the gay Christian man's original sin tally, falls into the same category. So to condemn them is to condemn ourselves. We all live flawed lives – not lifestyles – lives.

In chapter one I mentioned the feeling that our world has slipped out from under us. I shared Kinnaman's words previously, but would like to reinforce them here. "What happens to the transference of faith, when the world we know slips out from under our collective feet? We have to find a new process – a new mind – that makes sense of faith in our new reality." 6 Kinnaman. I know of only one way to find that new mind, and it requires letting go of the dogmatic "old laws" that no longer enslave us and seeking God's Spirit to fill us with His new wine, grown and harvested throughout the New Testament. It requires new eyes to see and accept the Gospel truth, which in some unhealthy ways has been unbalanced and over-shadowed by the old covenant for too long.

"The time is coming, declares the Lord, when I will make a new covenant with the house of Israel and with the house of Judah. It will not be like the covenant I made with their forefathers when I took them by the hand to lead them out of Egypt, because they broke my covenant, though I was a husband to them. This is the covenant I will make with the house of Israel after that time, declares the Lord. I will put my law in their minds and write it on their hearts. I will be their

God, and they will be my people." Jeremiah 31:31-33.

Can The Actions of God Speak Clearer Than His Words?

If we travel back into the Old Testament when God called Israel out of Egypt and set them apart to be His people we will begin to find the building blocks of one of the strongest examples of making sense of faith in a new reality. Leviticus is frequently punctuated by the words, "I am the Lord" and continues on to say, "I will put my dwelling place among you, and I will not abhor you. I will walk among you and be your God, and you will by my people." Lev. 26:11-12. God made a very specific and detailed covenant with Israel because that's what the world needed to see in order to understand God's holiness.

We mustn't think this appointment to be God's people came from something they earned. St. Augustine revealed that God called Israel to be His people for *His own name's sake*, so the heathen will see and know that He is God. God has chosen this way to begin to reveal to the world, in a new and different way, all about who He is. God does not choose the Hebrew tribe because of their good merits. Scripture plainly reveals not only were their merits not good, but they were exceedingly evil before this. "In those days Israel had no king; everyone did as he saw fit." Judges 21:25. "So I poured out my wrath on them because they had shed blood in the land and because they had defiled it with their idols. Ezekiel 36:18. Note the connection with idols, those false gods mankind has and does worship. God the Creator is always concerned with the ultimate sin of worshipping false gods, the sin, that in refusing to be turned away from, will forever separate man from his Creator.

Mankind desperately needed to understand about holiness as it specifically applied to God. God chose to use sinful people to demonstrate His holiness in contrast to the sinfulness of all mankind. God's people and all those Old Testament Laws that guided their daily lives were to be the standard reflecting His holiness to the godless tribes of that day so they too could begin to understand who God is and what His pure holiness is all about. They were set aside to be so different by the laws they were called on to follow at that time, that others couldn't help but see a huge difference between themselves and "God's people". The story is all about God. It always has been.

So, God goes on to warn Israel that He alone is their God and their faithlessness to Him will bring heartbreaking consequences. These people of the house of Israel were singled out among all other men on the earth as God's very own and the Old Testament faithfully records their story. It also accurately records their *faithlessness* to Him and the resulting destruction of their kingdoms and lives. Yes, they struggled with the original sin in their lives, that's why God instituted sacrifices at that time in the world, and they daily struggled with over six-hundred laws called the Holiness Code. But their downfall, God turning away from them in anger, was solely determined when they turned their backs on their Holy God in relentless pursuit of other gods. Those building blocks once standing high now lay scattered across the world.

But, the story does not end here for God had a plan of grace to bring His people back to Himself, one that included another group of people living hundreds of years later. Their name was Gentile, old enemies of the God of heaven. Through the words of this story God shows us how to pick up those blocks and begin to reconstruct a life that makes sense of faith in a new reality.

God chose to initiate His plan during the time of Jesus – a time we call New Testament Gospel. We can only imagine how those complacent Jews who heard the new covenant words of Jesus were suddenly stumbling over a new reality that felt as if their world was slipping beneath them. For those who could not process the absolute free will of God their faith was stretched to the breaking point, unfortunately. They could not reconcile these new actions of God with the covenant words previously belonging to them. They were the chosen seed of God! But their questions of "How can He do this to us?"

were met with, "But who are you, O man, to talk back to God." Romans 9:20.

"I will call them 'my people' who are not my people; and I will call her 'my beloved' who is not my loved one, and, it will happen that in the very place where it was said to them 'you are not my people,' they will be called 'sons of the living God.'" Romans 9:25-26. During the generations of Israel's Old Testament Covenant with God the Gentiles were pronounced His enemies. They had no acts that were pleasing to Him because they did not worship Him as Lord. Yet, on the exact same ground that God originally opposed the Gentiles they were now called "sons of the living God." As a Gentile, my family is a member of the one-time enemies of God. No doubt many of you are also. There is not enough gratitude within me that can equal the love God has shown to this world of sinners.

My point is who in the entire family of God from Adam up to the time of Jesus could have possibly predicted the situation the Jews found themselves in. Who dreamed the time would come making it necessary to find a new process to make sense of their faith in light of this new reality? Israel, who God called and loves, were set aside to be disciplined by his anger, and those whom He did not love, Gentiles, were now the recipients of His grace. "What then shall we say? Is God unjust? Not at all! For He says to Moses, 'I will have mercy on whom I have mercy, and I will have compassion on whom I have compassion.'" Romans 9:14-15.

Quietly writing on my tablet beside Jesus, I gasped. It is the parable of Matthew 22 coming to life.

Approaching the Deeper Places With God

God had already put on my heart the need to understand the risk I would be taking in this No Man's Land with Him. There's nothing simple about writing a book that you hope will bring two outspoken, at times bitter and angry opposing teams onto the middle ground playing field. It's tricky because you find yourself sharing your new beliefs and when someone hears them for the first time they may immediately reject them instead of patiently letting new thoughts simmer through their hearts and minds with God at their side. How quickly the Pharisees outright rejected the words of Jesus without praying through their confusion.

I think what I risk saying now could be one of those difficult, easy to dismiss without thinking through moments. If prayers can be tossed into the universe and later captured in the needed moment, then please know prayers are caught between these pages.

God gladly grafted the Gentile nation onto His tree, the source of all life. We in this century can't appreciate what a seemingly unbelievable act on God's part that was to the people of that time. "After all, if you were cut out of an olive tree that is wild by nature, and *contrary to nature* were grafted into a cultivated olive tree, how much more readily will these, the natural branches, be grafted into their own olive tree!" Romans 11:24. You can almost hear the voices echo through the centuries, "That's the dumbest thing I've ever heard," in response to Paul's words to the Christian church in Rome. "Everyone knows you can't graft the wild branch onto the weakening cultivated tree. You have to graft the cultivated branch onto the wild tree hoping for a new burst of life." But are they really dumb words or just not within the Pharisees and even our own immediate understanding as mortal clay vessels? What was God doing that mankind couldn't comprehend?

First of all, it's contrary to nature for the wild shoot to be grafted onto the natural or cultivated shoot as we see God's hand was unnaturally cultivating and which Paul explains in his letter. The natural shoot, weakened for some reason hopes for a new burst of life by being grafted into the stronger wild shoot. God was doing it backwards by grafting in the wild (Gentile) shoot onto His cultivated tree of life. But God had a plan hoping that one day the natural shoot, Israel, would in the future, want to be re-grafted. He hoped they would see the necessity of grafting in the wild shoot He was currently planting.

I'd like to draw your attention to the words *contrary to nature.* Paul plainly says that by doing this, God is acting totally against nature. I'll share more on this in chapter 8.

The people are amazed by this act. Some are absolutely confused and others are outraged, enough to begin plotting to kill the Messenger. But Paul continues to say, "...for God's gifts and his call are irrevocable. Just as you who were at one time disobedient to God have now received mercy as a result of their disobedience, so they too have now become disobedient in order that they too may now receive mercy as a result of God's mercy to you." Romans 11:29-31. The Jews, God's chosen, became disobedient so God could show His mercy to the unloved Gentile. God doesn't go into detail about those words, 'became disobedient *so* God could show His mercy." The word *"So"* that means "in order that, provided that, for that reason" allows us to read it as, the Jews became disobedient providing the reason so God could now show His love to the unloved Gentiles.

God doesn't reveal more about His actions or feel obligated to tell us why. "For my thoughts are not your thoughts, neither are your ways my ways declares the Lord." Isaiah 55:8. Make no mistake. God reveals His will to us. We just don't always see it at first or follow His logic, and some choose to never try to understand it.

Let's say in your mind you equate homosexuals with the enemy Gentiles of God. God shows us at least one instance where He has no problem going against "nature", at least as we understand it, to graft enemy Gentiles into His tree of life in spite of all their imperfections and sins. Why would it be impossible to think that God would and could once again graft anyone He chooses onto His tree of life today? You may see homosexuals as God's enemies. I have come to believe He does not. He will graft in and have mercy on anyone He chooses.

We live in an age when huge quantities of heterosexual men and women have turned their backs on God's blessing of marriage. They have abandoned their walk with Him in this area. His desire for their lives concerning marriage is not important to them. They have turned their backs on God's original plan for mankind. So I ask you to wrestle with this question – based on what God did in the New Testament, what would stop Him, if He desires, from once again grafting the wild shoot, homosexuals, into the natural shoot of marriage? Who's to say God will not act contrary to "nature", again, as we understand it, by blessing the union of two men or two women if He chooses? There are lesbians and gays who long to follow God into this household of faith. We brag nothing is impossible with God, but in those areas where we don't understand God's actions, we prefer to tie His hands rather than risk that He might be trying to stretch our faith toward understanding a new reality. And God alone answers to staying faithful to Himself.

Sometimes we must learn to wrestle with what God's truth actually holds for a dynamic world. Like Jacob, sometimes we must wrestle on our own for a great length of time to understand new blessings from God. Jacob laid his concerns and fears before God. In an attempt to lay hold of God, God reached down and lay hold of him. They began to wrestle. Was God in opposition to Jacob returning to his homeland, the inherited land which by law should have gone to Esau as firstborn? "Note, strong believers must expect divers (various) temptations, and strong ones. We are told by the prophet (Hosea 12:4) how Jacob wrestled: he wept and made supplication." 7 Henry. (Parenthesis mine.)

He wrestled spiritually as well as physically that night. And what was the resulting success? "Jacob kept his ground...this discouragement did not shake his faith, nor silence his prayer. It was not in his own strength that he wrestled, nor by his own strength that he prevailed, but in and by strength derived from Heaven...We cannot prevail with God but in His own strength." 8 Henry. And Jacob received his blessing even if in his body he suffered by his hip placed out of joint by one touch. And yet through this act of a misplaced hip that we still don't always understand

and wonder about, Jacob never forgot God's prevailing and holy power, and the lesson that when we are weak we are strong through Jesus.

It really bothers us sometimes to not get our answers like we want. God instead says, *"Let me give you a story, an example to wrestle with, and then go on your way relying on Me alone for strength"*. God our Father does not always reveal His reasons to us.

LGBTQ coalitions work to see laws passed that would bring the same benefits to gays that heterosexuals take for granted and even casually disregard. Each time a court overturns the ban on same sex marriage, hundreds and thousands quickly line up to obtain a much coveted marriage license and ceremony.

Tony Campolo a writer and speaker who seeks to heal the breach within the church, has been spoken of harshly and in cases been rejected by certain church bodies and Christian individuals. He says, "I call upon the church to stop making same gender eroticism into some kind of supersin that somehow warrants parents throwing away their children or barring people from the church. I plead with the church to join in efforts to grant full civil rights to gay men and lesbian women and to make the church into a safe place where no preacher will issue denigrating rhetoric or ignorant generalizations to hurt them." 9 Campolo. Mr. Campolo issued this plea in 2004. It is now 2015 and God alone knows why a plea goes unheeded still in so many places.

The first printing of *What the Bible Really Says About Homosexuality* was in 1994. Helminiak has this to say, "Thirty to forty percent of the youth living on the streets are teenagers who were thrown out of their homes because they were homosexual. Thirty percent of teenage suicides are among homosexual youth." 10 Helminiak. Coming out of the closet in a hopeful bid for understanding and acceptance, they were instead thrown out of their homes or felt no alternative but to leave under unbearable circumstances. Helminiak has been ministering to lesbian, gay and bisexual Catholics and their friends since 1977 through a group called Dignity, doing what he can to fill the wounded gap inflicted by obstinate, "good people".

Thirty to forty is an outrageous percentage of homeless youth thrown out like garbage or who left home due to difficult circumstances. Our world is so full of distractions pulling at us for our attention we lose the ability to be touched in our souls by such statistics. We may want to be sensitive to others, but sometimes we run on burn out or become totally desensitized. I know because I feel this way a lot. I think I can't take on one more world crises or donate to one more needy cause. It's everywhere, all the time.

But I'm not asking you to send money. I am asking you to set aside a small portion of your prayer time to ask God, in faith, how to discover a new mind for this new reality of the homeless and rejected. And if you get a chance to touch someone's life for a moment or two, accepting them for who they are shouldn't necessitate an act of charity, it should be an automatic act of compassion, one we don't need to think about. The warmth of a kind word and a smile really doesn't take much from any of us, but the benefits can be enormous. But not charity; never charity. LGBTQs don't want your charitable kindness, they want equality, kindness and respect because they are just like anyone else.

Three years ago I met with six lovely LGBTQs at my son's home. They opened their hearts to me and let me ask any question I wanted and generously gave me answers. One question I had was, "What is the worst thing that's been done to you by a Christian?"

Angel: "Thrown out of the house."
Brandon: "Yeah. I was thrown out of my house. My sister told me that I would never be able to be around her children – that she could not have that influence in her children's lives."
Amanda: "My parents lie to my brother about who we are. (She and her partner, now her wife.) They say we're just roommates. He's fifteen."
Brandon: "See, I think that would probably be even more hurtful if they (family) act like it didn't exist."

Angel: "That's like Shirley's brother. He's never spoken one word to me. Ever...well, once he found out we were together."

Shirley: "I think that's the most hurtful thing, that it's not one event, it's an ongoing event. I was extremely close to my brother and it hurts me that we don't have a relationship. I mean, we can have a relationship about neutral things, but not about meaningful things."

These are sensitive people like you and me who sometimes face tremendous obstacles that we can't begin to understand as they try to live normal lives but are cheated out of by ex-families and ex-friends.

Helminiak continues to paint the bleak picture of people who lose their jobs due to their gender identity. Parents courageous enough to come out as lesbian or gay lose custody of their kids or even the right of visitation. People are evicted from their apartments, homes are burned, and humans are brutally beaten and murdered just because they have one small difference in their lives from the majority of others. Leaders publically abuse men and women with their loud comments, critically ill individuals die alone because their loved ones are not allowed into their rooms and the list goes on. What are we doing? Are these the actions of good people who see themselves as compassionate and full of mercy? That was a difficult question for me to honestly ask and force myself to face a true answer, "Indeed, what am I doing?" Where has the confusion of understanding God's relation to sin driven us?

God's Solution To Sin

The previous words I shared in Isaiah 55:8 were followed by these, "Let no foreigner who has bound himself to the Lord say, 'The Lord will surely exclude me from his people.' And let not any eunuch complain, 'I am only a dry tree.' For this is what the Lord says: 'To the eunuchs who keep my Sabbaths, who choose what pleases me and hold fast to my covenant – to them I will give within my temple and its walls a memorial and a name better than sons and daughters; I will give them an everlasting name that will not be cut off.'" Isaiah 56: 3-5. Eunuchs were forbidden by the old Hebrew laws, laws instituted by God, to enter the Tabernacle of the Lord.

God continues in Isaiah, blessing foreigners, those once considered outcasts alongside the eunuchs. If they love Him and serve Him, those He will also bring to His holy mountain and His house will be called a house of prayer for all *nations*. God's not just talking about tribes of people. We know "nations" is a term designating all types of people everywhere by the inclusion of eunuchs, a "type" of person once not permitted before God's holiness in the tent of meeting in the desert.

But now we see in Isaiah God is rescinding the law for a new way. We see the similarity today when some say LGBTQs shouldn't be allowed in a church to actively participate on the same level as Christians. Enlightened by these verses, why would we draw that conclusion? Perhaps there are more than just the so called "six Biblical references" that apply themselves in a critical way to homosexuality and we just have failed to recognize them.

As far back as the Old Testament prophet, Isaiah, God told us He was going to throw open His doors of sanctuary to anyone and everyone. Thousands of years later we still can't accept His word or all of His people. God will have mercy on anyone He chooses to have mercy and He will have mercy today as well as yesterday. There is room for all who profess their love for Him in their hearts at God's holy alter. And whether it is for a union, a marriage or some other reason, who are we to say this cannot be done? Sometimes God's actions speak louder to us than words.

Jesus opened the way for all people to come to Him, yet there doesn't seem to be a record of too many in the temple crowd who fell on their knees to beseech understanding of a world that seemed to be slipping beneath their feet. I don't recall too many Hebrew leaders begging God to fill their heart with His truth and help them understand what God was doing that seemed so out of character. I' m not bad mouthing the Jews of old because evidently we are still unwilling to throw ourselves into prayer begging God to help us understand where He might be trying to take us today. I held out for years before I caught on there was be a need to be healed concerning my judgmental attitude toward gays.

The Temple leaders weren't interested in understanding what Jesus was saying. Instead they dug in their heels ready to fight to continue life their way, to their advantage. It was comfortable. "There is one vice of which no man in the world is free…There is no fault which makes man more unpopular, and no fault which we are more unconscious of in ourselves. And the more we have it ourselves, the more we dislike it in others. The vice I am talking of is Pride or Self-Conceit: and the virtue opposite to it, in Christian morals, is called Humility." 11 Lewis.

If you think accepting LGBTQs today is difficult, we can't begin to conceptualize, to feel, to put into words, what the Jews of Jesus' day were going through when they started hearing rumors the Gentiles were being brought into God's holy family. And not just upstanding Gentiles. Jesus was including prostitutes, tax collectors, thieves, adulterers, all types of sinners who were willing to put their hearts in Gods' hands. There was no prayer the synagogue leaders could pray that was big enough to break through the icy glaciers of their hearts to make sense of this, because they didn't want to pray. They didn't want to make sense of this. Pride is a huge obstacle.

"God, who knows the heart, showed that he accepted them by giving the Holy Spirit to them, just as He did to us. He made no distinction between us and them, for He purified their hearts by faith." Acts 15: 8-9. If anyone is able to call on the name of God, He demonstrates His acceptance by sending the Holy Spirit into their lives. Jew and Gentile, homosexual and heterosexual, for God there is no distinction.

But mankind loves distinctions. Without them how do we determine who to "love" and who to "disdain"? My son-in-law was recently telling me about the sexual harassment review meeting in his work place. He accurately pointed out that people want to know just where acceptance ends and harassment begins so they can push the sexual harassment envelope as far as possible and not get in trouble. Likewise, we want to know the Biblical degree required governing acceptable treatment of LGBTQ's so we can justify excluding them from our clean spiritual lives. We prefer to not apply the Good Samaritan to this situation because we might have to realize God really does mean love your neighbor as thoroughly and completely as you love yourself, even your homosexual neighbor. "Who is my brother?" God didn't give a direct answer. He told a story about a Good Samaritan that gave an example. *"Rely on me to make you strong when you are weak."*

The Jews had their distinctions. Gentiles were considered dogs. There is a story of a Canaanite woman who knelt before Jesus and asked for his help. She begged Jesus to heal her daughter. At first Jesus was silent as though to ignore her. That doesn't seem like the Jesus we know and love. But Jesus, the Divine Teacher had something He wanted all within hearing distance to learn. By His silence He draws in the listeners. When Jesus does answer her the words seem so unlike Him. Jesus told her it wasn't right to take the food from the children and toss it to their dogs. Oh yes, everyone knew Gentiles were considered dogs. This answer everyone could understand. Look around this village street and you can see the Jews nodding in agreement. But she countered Him saying, "...but even the dogs eat the crumbs that fall from their master's table." Matthew 15:27.

Jesus heard her words of desire, of hope and even expectation. His praise for her was recorded for men of all generations to hear and be in awe of her faith. Because all others had failed her, she opened her mind and heart in faith and appealed for any favor Jesus might cast her way. She was willing to wrestle in faith, like Jacob, for blessings. She was persistent enough to give Jesus everything she had and let Him know she was ready to accept anything, no matter how small, He might give her. Her faith was of the magnitude that she would not underestimate Jesus due to the pre-conceived ideas of those around her!

We have a tendency to believe that new plans, seen as inferior to old plans, will destroy the chosen "us" we know and understand. But Jesus took Jewish security that day and toppled it in favor of His own new way. Can you imagine those people grumbling, "That's not the way we do things. We must cling to the old Law; it is safe." Isn't that exactly what we are doing, clinging to safety, when leaders say "gay marriages will completely ruin the family unit as God intended?" Aren't we afraid to risk everything as this woman did, when we opt to keep God in a pre-conceived box rather than free His Spirit to fill us with where He wants to take us regarding new realities?

The first problem I have with the prediction that gays will ruin the "family" as God ordained it, is that it has come thousands of years too late. In the first generation, Adam and Eve managed to ruin God's original plan when they chose themselves over Him to lead their family. By the second generation, Cain readily killed Abel, and if that's not ruining the family unit I don't know what is. It really is senseless to blame LGBTQs for what heterosexuals have fouled from the beginning of time.

Let's no longer delude ourselves into thinking the family unit hasn't always been tittering on the brink of ruin due to original sin. With critical honesty, look around you. Are we really so blind that we will fail to acknowledge that the only way any family has remained intact is solely due to God's intervention of grace in the lives of each and every one of us? Are we so lost in our own pride that we take credit for any good thing that happens in our lives? Do we believe the "family" as we understand it exists in its glory because we have done something right in and of ourselves apart from God's will within us?

Second, when God chose inferior Gentile "dogs" as new family members, that action of His contrary to what many believed "natural", it successfully resulted into what you and I have today, our faith in God and the privilege to be called His children. I don't hear anyone complaining about that in the modern church and society.

I don't know if it's because we have failed God in every other respect that we feel we must cling to the "creation order", one man and one woman, as if it were the super-command above all other commands and desires of God, when clearly even it has been tainted by adultery, divorce, multiple marriages and concubines since the very beginning of time. While some proud voices lead the way stating marriage is between one man and one woman, in part, because they themselves have demonstrated such a marriage, their retort blows itself out as barren lip service when compared to the statistics of second, third, and fourth marriages and living outside of marriage. And even if those marriages are between one man and one woman at any given time, it's certainly not the life-long committed marriage God originally intended in His "creation order". To believe remarriages, punctuated by living with a person of the opposite sex in between marriage, is God's concept of one man and one woman is clearly a twisting of "creation order".

Can God's actions demonstrate His words better than mere definitions and interpretations? I know that God went against "His nature and creation order" by granting Israel divorce "out of the hardness of men's hearts." Isn't there just a possibility that today God might again go against "His nature" by granting lesbian and gay marriage, this time out of the love in their hearts? When do we finally say, *"It is not my job to instruct God. It is time to step aside and let God be God."* "To praise and glorify God means for us to be silent (before Him), not to extol ourselves, (our good works), but believe that we are lost sinners." 12 Luther. Will you be the first in your family or in your church to glorify God by your silence, recognizing your state of sin rather than preening yourself over what you have "done right"?

That there is inconsistency in the way we have lived God's plan is the least ugly way to put it. None of us have all the answers or solutions, but God does and He is capable of one-hundred percent holding His world together until the day of Christ's return. The best any one of us can do is to pay attention to our own lives, get our uncontrolled carnal thoughts out of the bedrooms of others and remember, "When you judge the law, you are not keeping it, but sitting in judgment on it. There is only one Lawgiver and Judge, the one who is able to save and destroy. But you—who are you to judge your neighbor?" James 4:11-12.

As part of my own healing process I have recognized the need to ask for God's help to find a way to process my faith in the light of a new reality. Perhaps you still can't accept certain areas of equality, say for instance marriage for LGBTQs as your reality. It's not a simple process to re-examine the interpretation of Biblical sexuality that you have always taken as God's truth and begin to see it in a new light. There were times when a new concept on gender orientation was presented to me I would mentally draw back asking myself how anyone could creditably accept it as a truth. Each and every time I had to lay it before God. It has taken me over three years of hard work and long hours, sometimes deep into the night, to get to my place of peace today. And the only way I got there was with God 100% by my side, filling my heart and mind by His own hand.

To expect you to process all that I am presenting and make it your own in the time it takes to read one book would simply be unreasonable. Actually, the only thing I am asking is that you take everything you are being exposed to and prayerfully lay it at God's feet. I am encouraging you to begin a relationship with God that builds your full reliance on Him alone rather than solely on the words of men. I am challenging you to begin to think for yourself in the presence and by the power of the Holy Spirit, relying on Jesus to intercede for you before the Father in heaven, and to trust His ability to work in your heart and mind with His truth. I am asking you to choose God's perfect omniscience over man's imperfect interpretations to lead you into the future that might eventually recognize that homosexuals have the perfect right to live life equally to heterosexuals.

" God really is working in human history...As history progresses, God guides the process and things really do change. There is development and novelty. According to this understanding, religion is not locked into its first-century form." 13 Helminiak. Man is no longer locked into first-century life. We live in the twenty-first century with a vibrant and interested God who shares our days with us and guides us through the undeniable changes of life.

Undoubtedly, there are people afraid to accept the possibility that God works in the changes of life because Hebrews 13:8 refers to Jesus as the same yesterday, today and tomorrow. They wrongly define yesterday, today and tomorrow being that which is the same and unchangeable, rather than the message that Jesus is the same eternally. Just as we project our own limited understanding of love and hate onto our image of who God is, we also limit Him, insisting He work His plan according to our finite understanding of those words, "Jesus is the same". Unfortunately our human minds can't begin to understand God's omniscience and His faithfulness to Himself as He carries out His plan in our ever-changing lives. He is the same yesterday, today and tomorrow. He doesn't change. But that never meant we were granted the full insight of exactly how He would continue to move and work throughout the days of this time on earth.

The books of the Bible may now be closed to any new additions, but God did not retire. He did not sit back and say, *They have the Bible now. My one-hundred percent presence to fill every crack and crevice in the universe is no longer needed. They can read can't they?* So long as man is at odds with himself or others, as long as he lifts his heart to the Father for help, as long as God responds to our needs to bring us closer to His side, the story is not finished. New chapters of God and man are being written daily. So again, I ask the question, "Whose sins have been forgiven?" Those of all mankind. And we are mankind devoid of any and all distinctions in God's eyes.

The Kingdom of God

*"The primary idea of the Kingdom of God in Scripture is
that of the rule of God established and acknowledged in the
hearts of sinners by the powerful regenerating influence of
the Holy Spirit, insuring them of the inestimable blessing of
salvation, - a rule that is realized in principle on earth, but
will not reach it's culmination until the visible and glorious
return of Jesus Christ." Louis Berkhof*

*All through history this and other doctrines have been
disputed, debated and re-defined many times. We ask, does
that mean men are trying to rewrite the Bible? We answer,
of course not. In every generation men seek to discover a
fuller understanding of just what his relationship with God
is by exploring, or like Jacob, wrestling, to find the truest
definitions of the language of the Bible.*

CHAPTER 6 A NEW PRIEST – A NEW COVENANT – NEW WINESKINS NEEDED

"So They Pour New Wine Into New Wineskins, and Both are Preserved."
Matthew 9:17

From the moment LGBTQs came out of the closet and realized one small identity difference had immediately extinguished many of the civil rights they had previously possessed, they questioned the word "freedom" that our country likes to boast about so loudly to the world, and they began to take steps to reclaim what is rightfully theirs. Why is it rightfully theirs? Because civil rights belong to everyone based on the simple fact that we are humans, citizens, existing in the United States of America. Civil rights aren't ours because we are "good" versus "bad", "righteous" versus "sinner". If so none of us would be eligible. That is not hard to understand unless one obstinately chooses not to understand.

From that same moment, as the interpretation of "marriage" became a major hinge of those civil rights, many have felt threatened that their faith and God's Word was being tampered with. Words like sin and abomination took the limelight and one little verse, Leviticus 18:22 became known to everyone. I know this very intimately because my world used to run on this spiritual gas.

If you are a Christian who never questions what imperfect men teach from the classroom or pulpit, who never takes the time for deeper self-study with God so you can be convinced in your own mind what you believe, Leviticus 18:22, "Do not lie with a man as one lies with a woman" is probably deeply rooted and can only be interpreted one way, and that one way has come to mean "homosexuality" with an extremely narrow translation. You are convinced of it because educated, God-fearing yet imperfect men went to schools taught by other educated, God-fearing yet imperfect men, and you trust every word out of their mouths. The sermon sounds right so you never bother to enter into the deepest relationship you have with God to see if He agrees also. Honest, God-fearing, imperfect men make honest mistakes. We are so ready to become mankind's puppet if it suits us; yet so opposed to being God's.

I'm not saying we can't rely on and trust our ministers. I rely on and trust mine. Those who are called by God He will lead. My point is that even ministers are not infallible. The result is that sometimes the only place we can find the truth for ourselves is to sit alone with God and wait for His voice, His advice, and it will be based on His promises. There are times in life where situations, problems, and pain can only be solved between you and God. Such was the case with my gay son, my church's beliefs, and my personal faith struggling to understand what I positively believed. If you don't feel comfortable that you can hear God's voice, you are afraid He won't speak to you or you won't hear His voice, then I gently suggest you have some work to do and urge you to begin this faith relationship which you will never regret.

Let me share a little story to explain my thoughts. "The story is told that a collier (coal miner) was asked what he believed. He replied: 'What the church believes.' Asked what it is that the church believes, he did not know, was perfectly satisfied not to know, and replied: 'I do not know but nevertheless believe what the church believes.'" 1 Lenski. At times we are content to let the institution or the church we attend be a

71

substitute for our true, inner faith. Do you dare to not only ask yourself what you believe but also why you believe it? Could you risk the belief that God is bigger than even the church and the mistakes we make? If our Biblical interpretations involve anything less than perfect love for all men, our mistaken interpretations must be laid at our sinful door; whether our home door or our church door, but never at the foot of God's heavenly throne. A change in long held beliefs requires faith; it requires a faith in God that is greater than faith in man. Sometimes that is all we have to rely on.

If you're honest with yourself, you might admit that when you start reading all those wordy laws in Leviticus it's confusing about which laws we need to observe today and which ones don't matter anymore. Perhaps you fear that if your long held interpretation of Leviticus 18:22 means something on a different level and of a different nature to the Hebrew nation of that day than what it means to us today, you will begin to doubt your faith or even other references in the Bible. Please let me assure you this is simply not true. Understanding words of a verse with greater accuracy and meaning does not negate the rest. Scholars are still trying to accurately interpret passages of the Bible, even today.

If my toe needed amputating I would need to take positive action right away, and be glad for the intervention that might save my life. I certainly wouldn't go around believing next I will have to amputate my foot, then my leg, my knee, and then my thigh. There is no sane reason to believe that. If you have diabetes and need your diet adjusted, that is a positive move toward good health. It doesn't mean all food is bad and of no further use to you.

"Thoughtful conformity to Christ – not unthinking conformity to either contemporary culture or textual prohibitions – should be our unchanging reference point." 2 Rev. Steve Chalke. Understanding what God has done for us and closely mimicking the deeds of Christ rather than allowing the Bible to become man's sin scorecard should be our starting point each day. One brings freedom, the other brings dread and death.

Please hear what this chapter has to say.

When wine was stored in the skins of animals, unlike our fancy bottles of today, one simple fact ancient winemakers understood is that you cannot pour the newly harvested wine into last years' wineskins. As the new wine fermented, expanding the skin, it would rip apart and only the dry earth would taste the new wine. What a terrible loss to all. No one would receive the benefit of God's harvest blessing.

It is a tragedy when God's new blessings spill upon the earth and we never get to enjoy them because we are afraid to risk a new spiritual wineskin. Jesus encourages us to find new wineskins, hoping we will open our hearts and minds to a new way. Jesus wants to expand our spiritual lives to include the new love, grace, ideas, and laws He brought and demonstrated. But we so unsuccessfully try to stuff them into old wineskins, Old Testament wineskins, and we lose them. We lose what God wants to bless us with.

Colossians 2:13 says, "When you were dead in your sins and in the uncircumcision of your sinful nature, God made you alive with Christ. He forgave us all our sins having canceled the written code, with its regulations, that was against us and that stood opposed to us; he took it away, nailing it to the cross." Paul's reference to "written code" refers to God's divine hand that wrote the commands and laws for Moses on God's holy mountain, the same God whose presence we cannot see face to face and live. (Exodus 33:20).

"Completely and utterly against us was this handwriting which no man in the world could face and live. God blotted it out, cancelled, and annulled it completely! Remember that this handwriting contained all the demands God made upon us. The cancellation wiped out all of them." 3 Lenski. "Since you died with Christ to the basic principles of this world, why, as though you still belonged to it, do you submit to its rules..." (Colossians 2:20). Well, that is a good question I thought to myself. Lenski is expanding our understanding of the words in Colossians 2.

"Not only the writing was stricken out, the very document itself perished on the cross! Christ was so nailed to the cross, and in him the law was nailed to it; Christ, when he was nailed up, died; so did the law. Christ rose again, but *not* the law. Christ rose because his death killed the law forever. If the law had not died in the blood of the cross, Christ could not have arisen." 4 Lenski. Just think what message Lenski is trying to give us. He is not making up some illusive argument to pass the time of day or purposely mislead Christians.

God constructed the old covenant knowing all along its purpose was for a limited time as it was only the shadow of what was coming. Through 600 plus laws God was trying to teach men about holiness and therefore about Himself. When the Reality, Jesus, appeared and began His ministry, the shadow was no longer necessary. Lenski goes so far as to introduce the truth that if 600 plus laws had not perished in the blood of the cross, Jesus would never have arisen from death. It doesn't take more than that single reality to convince me Leviticus is long dead, because my Jesus is alive! I am not a slave to Levitical laws. I am free from them.

During my months and years of digging, I suppose that very vivid sentence did the most in helping me visualize the death of the old Laws. I kept seeing Christ whose skin hung in strips of flesh and trails of blood from the thorns on His head and the nails in His hands and feet. And then I saw pages and pages of laws nailed with Him and the trails of Jesus blood made the pages redder and redder until they hung as limp as His own body after He finally released His Spirit to God. As they took Jesus' body down the soaked pages began to rip and tear apart, and finally in tiny tatters, they blew away in the wind, no longer to be seen. Since that time if I've read this verse once in the Bible, I've read it multiple times and together with the book of Hebrews, there isn't much room to misunderstand the message here. The Old Testament Levitical Laws are dead to those who love and trust Jesus, including Leviticus

18:22. It's time to let it RIP, (Rest In Peace).

We can't un-ring the bell and we can't put New Testament truth into Old Testament wineskins carrying the old Laws. God's plan is always in forward motion, even when we, even when the Pharisees and Sadducees, even when other religious sects simply can't or won't see changes on the horizon. Change scares us. We mustn't fear that because we don't have a written road map after the Book of Revelation that we can't trust our hearts to lay hold of God, the Master planner, as He navigates us around a curve He has already prepared for. Am I saying around the curve God doesn't care if we sin? Absolutely not. I'm saying around the curve Jesus brought two new laws and only two to simplify our spiritual lives, and perhaps we don't fully understand that God has given us permission through His own Son to let go of hundreds of old Laws to embrace two new ones. If we never give another thought for a single Old Testament command, following Jesus' new laws of love for God and all men is sufficient. Why? Because the two new laws of Jesus have sufficiently covered us by devouring all the old Laws within themselves and are therefore sufficient to stand alone.

We are to love the Lord our God with all our heart, our soul, and our mind, and the second law is to love our neighbor as ourselves. "For he who loves his fellowman has fulfilled the law...and whatever other commandment there may be, are summed up in this one rule: 'Love your neighbor as yourself." Romans 13:8-9. "Jesus replied: 'Love the Lord your God with all your heart and with all your soul and with all your mind.' This is the first and greatest commandment. And the second is like it: 'Love your neighbor as yourself.' All the Law and the prophets hang on these two commandments." Matthew22:37-40. Jesus Himself tells us all the Old Testament Laws and teachings of the prophets are contained in these two laws. Jesus has indeed blessed us by ridding our lives of all the confusion and controversy that came with the old way.

Paul's Fight To Preserve The Balance Of The Gospel

"When law observance is demanded by present day legalists, the gospel is upset and we must fight as Paul does in Galations... But when certain observances, rules and regulations are attached to the gospel, which are said to produce a much safer and superior Christianity, we must fight as Paul does in Colossians, scorn this fictitious safety and superiority with the absolute completeness and superiority of the gospel, with the infinite supremacy of the God-man, the utter fullness and completeness of his saving work, and the fullness he has bestowed on us." 5 Lenski.

I see two things here in Lenski's quote. One, we can stop resurrecting Leviticus to live our lives by when Jesus' resurrection makes those laws "obsolete". Second, some may think that including legal marriage for gays in the civil rights now being withheld is like attaching something new to the Gospel that God didn't intend. Those leaders in Colossians were afraid to risk letting go of their laws. They preferred to hedge their bets so to speak, by dragging the past into the present and future. They would be superior because they kept the ceremonial laws alongside the new. They wanted a foot in both worlds and Paul said no!

As the apostle's began to teach and build on what Christ began, there emerged a group of people known as Christian Judaizers, like those mentioned in Colossians, who felt superior to Gentile converts. They were trying to combine the New Gospel with the old Laws and ceremonies feeling this would be a superior way to worship. What it did was unbalance the Gospel; water down its truth and power to stand alone in its saving grace through faith alone. If "legalists" today feel the need to follow the Levitical Laws of old, even those considered the moral laws, they produce the same imbalance, once again watering down the truth and power of the Gospel. We can't have it both ways. Remember, Jesus did rise from the dead.

Please do not get me wrong or twist the true intent of my words. God does not allow or disallow according to our wants. I am not putting rules in God's mouth for Him to abide by. I am asking you to take a look with Spirit filled eyes at who God was and is, at what He did and does now, and from these two, expand the possibilities of how the Creator might use His power and wisdom in our lives today according to New Testament scripture. And while we don't have an absolute key to follow, such as a new Biblical letter from Paul, living by faith alone can help us put God back on His throne and out of the little boxes our minds have forced Him into.

Divorce, not a part of the creation order, never halted God's plan for moving all men forward. He overlooked the hardness of men's hearts because He had bigger and better plans for us and He needed to keep us moving. If God had allowed Israel to sit down – just stop and stagnate over hate in their marriages, arguing in their preoccupation with this one issue which at that particular time threatened the strict family hierarchy that pointed to God as the patriarchal head – do you, with critical honesty, believe that would have helped? God knew how important a single, lifelong, devoted marriage was and is, and yet He allowed grace to overrule the sin and instituted divorce. You can't move forward when you sit in stagnant waters. You simply begin to mold and decay.

God could have left Israel to continue in hate filled marriages according to the creation plan of "no divorce", destroying peace and harmony among His chosen people, leading to who knows what as relationships continued to fester. He could have. But He didn't. He chose a solution of His own for mankind, divorce, not a part of creation order, nonetheless His decision for His creatures.

Now I ask you to wrestle as you ponder the question – by His actions concerning divorce, did God set His own precedence that could lead to His making necessary adjustments to problems in the future lives of men when and as they materialize on mankind's horizon? Can you begin to apply this to our present day stagnating arguments over marriage for homosexuals? God made a decision to employ His grace to overlook hard hearts and grant divorce. Is it at all possible God can make a decision to employ His grace, once again, to overlook something, not in the creation order, to move His personal plan for His creatures forward? Could He not choose to bless, through marriage, the love between two men or two women, therefore continuing to move forward His personal plan of grace that benefits all mankind?

At times, God's actions speak to us more accurately than the ancient words we argue over. St. Francis of Assisi said, "Preach the gospel at all times and when necessary use words." 6 Assisi. Perhaps some of God's greatest sermons to us are through His actions.

How well God know us. Better than we know ourselves. God wants our focus to be heavenward where His blessings pour out to anoint us. How can sinful, obstinate children focus heavenward when their souls are rife with earth-bound fighting to be right, especially when we tell ourselves our best intentions (born through our pride) are on God's behalf? Sometimes God has to take control. It's our job to seek to understand how He wants us to listen and respond. We do that by individually emptying ourselves out like a little child, going to Him, falling on our knees before Him for His Holy Spirit's guidance alone. And there are those times when we must wrestle all night only to have our pride painfully knocked out of joint first before receiving the blessing of assurance we seek. He promised He would find us and reveal great things to us. Do we not believe Him?

The truth is we may never reach a consensus across the board about marriage between two men and two women. But for me, when two people seek out God's will through faith and believe with all their hearts that He will bless their marriage, how does any man set himself up to judge what took place in their private, spiritual relationship and worship with God that led to their decision? Sometimes we don't have all the answers and sometimes with God's blessing we are to simply step aside and let Him be the Creator God. To realize this, is to realize there can be healing if we really desire it, even if it's not the way we expected.

Paul believed in his mission. Jews and Gentiles could come together and form a new church under Christ Jesus. What is so difficult in believing heterosexual Christians and homosexual Christians can't also come together on the middle ground of God's grace, stop the bickering and restore the former glory to the church? I guess I use the words "former glory" to represent a church that at one time was a sanctuary, specifically a place of refuge and protection for sinners. All people were welcome to worship God in the individual way God Himself placed into their hearts. It didn't depend on "Godly" rules overseen by men. Well, maybe that church never existed; never actually found its place in time and space. Maybe that church is also waiting to be fulfilled like the third petition of Jesus High Priestly Prayer.

"Believe me, woman, a time is coming when you will worship the Father neither on this mountain nor in Jerusalem…Yet a time is coming and has now come when the true worshipers will worship the Father in spirit and truth, for they are the kind of worshipers the Father seeks. God is spirit, and his worshipers must worship in spirit and in truth." John 4:21 & 23.

I edge a little closer to His side seeking to place my hand in His. Whose truth, I quietly ask God?

"The Holy Spirit also testifies to us about this. First he says: 'This is the covenant I will make with them after that time, says the Lord. I will put my laws in their hearts, and I will write them on their minds.'" Hebrews 10:15 & 16. We have echoes of Jeremiah 31. When God writes His truth in our hearts and minds, I don't think we have to worry anymore about whose truth we should follow. It is His truth and we know it beyond a doubt. God has brought us full circle. First were the righteous truths from creation which He originally set our eyes upon and put in the hearts of mankind. These eventually led to the written word which evolved into 600 plus laws that were set to be used for a

79

specific timeline until the Savior of the world would come to do just that, save us, since 600 plus laws never could or would be able to. And those 600 plus have now dwindled to two whose fullness of understanding God has imprinted, once again, upon each individual heart and mind.

But Father, I have another question. If your words are true, why do some men insist that the only true way to worship is their way? Do they think people can't hear the Holy Spirit give them the correct way to be with You in their own heart? Do these people not trust You to do what You said You would? I'm just thinking if someone told me they were going to give me an infusion of blood that I needed and I turned around and started looking for other people to give me their blood, that first person would probably get hurt and ask me why I didn't trust them. I'm satisfied that what You have put in my heart is good enough to make You happy and I don't need to keep looking for anything better. And I think if I start getting it wrong the Holy Spirit will correct me and get me right again. I don't like these other people who don't seem to trust You and they are making me mad. Did I hear a quiet laugh and feel a gentle hand tussle my hair? *Don't get angry my child. You don't have to fight My fights. Not everyone has faith on the same level as others.* That was something to think about.

What Do We Need?

"We need communities where it is safe for people to talk about their deepest, darkest concerns, where expressing uncertainty is not seen as abnormal or apostate." 7 Kinnaman.

If you think you are a member of such a safe community, perhaps you might conduct an experiment by introducing a dark topic and express your uncertainty about it. What do you think the result might be? Or just cut to the chase by making a bold statement concerning the equality of homosexuals in our world, including the right to marry. See how quickly and in which direction the topic takes off. If your church, if you yourself are not a safe place for gays, why would they seek to worship God where there is no common fellowship? And if they are not safe and whole in your presence how does Jesus prayer that we all become one in Him finally get answered?

"For he himself is our peace, who has made the two one and has destroyed the barrier, the dividing wall of hostility by abolishing in his flesh the law with its commandments and regulations." (Ephesians 2:15). We certainly have a dividing wall of hostility today. Christ was crucified destroying a barrier that we have turned around and rebuilt. Must we re-crucify Him because we would rather argue and be right? We have taken blocks of "good intentions", mortared them with the blood of Christ so once again we can have a dividing wall where conflict exists between hurting and hostile people on both sides of the wall. Healing is not found there.

"In the same way also, man sinks into a spiritual idolatry of a finer kind, which today is spread far and wide. Ingratitude and love of vanity (of one's own wisdom, or righteousness, or as it is commonly said, of one's good intentions) pervert man so thoroughly that he refuses to be reproved, for now he thinks his conduct is good and pleasing to God." 8 Luther. Has man's "good intentions" perverted our minds so thoroughly that we believe our conduct is pleasing God in this quagmire of wills? Is your "good intention" to change homosexuals into heterosexuals by quoting an obsolete law and failing to hear anything God's Spirit may be trying to tell you about Scripture "perverting you so thoroughly that you refuse to be reproved, because you are convinced in your own mind that your knowledge is superior to others and absolutely pleasing to God?" Have we sunken into a "spiritual Idolatry of a finer kind?"

Testing Our Wineskins

The new wineskins of people with open attitudes and minds willing to hear about a New Way were the only way the Gospel of Christ could be preserved. In the same way, an open attitude and mind on your part may be the new wineskin needed to hear what the Holy Spirit may want to teach you about Jesus' New Covenant laws and what they do or don't say regarding homosexuality.

"If perfection could have been attained through the Levitical priesthood (for on the basis of it the law was given to the people), why was there still need for another priest to come – one in the order of Melchizedek, not in the order of Aaron? For when there is a change of the priesthood, there must also be a change of the law." Hebrews 7:11-12. I don't know how else to understand these words. When there is a change of priesthood, when a new priest comes, there must be a change of the law! When, if ever, was the last time you heard this explained to you? Changes of civil and religious laws have been observed in every conquering nation since time began. A new ruler automatically means new laws. And in each and every generation God has preserved His people and taken the bad, in whatever form it came from these new rulers, and turned it into good for His living, forward moving plan even if it didn't resemble "good" at the time.

"But the ministry Jesus has received is as superior to theirs as the covenant of which he is mediator is superior to the old one, and is founded on better promises." Hebrews 8:6. I want to follow the superior covenant in my life that is based on better promises. We are not waiting for the promise to be fulfilled like in Abraham's day. We are no longer burdened by laws we can't keep. It is the heart and only the heart that keeps the laws, and when it becomes hardened toward God, laws mean nothing. So when one asks you, "How do men know how to live their lives?" the answer is God Himself has taken care of that by placing His laws with His own hand into our spiritual selves. And concerning those that break the laws, it's not because they never read them or didn't know them, but rather their hearts didn't care to follow them due to their cold, hardened state. The fault lies not with Jesus two New Testament laws, but those who care nothing for God.

"It will be a testament without ceremonial, ritual, civil, and formal laws. All outward regulations will be discarded." 9 Lenski. The law is no longer a wall of legal restriction that watches our every move, waiting to catch us and shame us before God and demand we pay a penalty. The scaffolding has been removed because the laws have been disassembled to make way for the new. The New Testament sees a complete fulfillment of all God's promises through Christ. Rather than be coerced or legally forced, once we begin to live in God's love we find we want to please God because His Spirit and Word shines within us.

It becomes personally intimate. It's all about God, and His personal work through our hearts. Each and every man, woman, and child, who loves God can now freely kneel before Him and privately worship God with the private, personal and spiritual matters between them and the Father. It doesn't involve me or you. Just two are needed; the child and His Father.

"If the blood of goats and bulls and the ashes of a heifer sprinkled on those who are ceremonially unclean sanctify them so that they are outwardly clean, how much more, then, will the blood of Christ, who through the eternal Spirit offered himself unblemished to God, cleanse our consciences from acts that lead to death, so that we may serve the living God." Hebrews 9:13-14.

In his commentary, Lenski points out some essential lessons here. By including the blood of goats and bulls and the ashes of a heifer, the writer of Hebrews is including *all* the sacrificial ceremonies of Israel to cleanse the priests, the entire Tabernacle assembly, and also the individual. None are omitted. Christ's atoning sacrifice covers all this and so much more. Not only are our bodies cleansed but the conscience of mankind is purified from dead works. They include the original sin we are born into which initially became our death sentence, separation from God.

The blood of animals were spilt on the Holy of Holies alter. Jesus carried His pure blood up to the holiest altar of all – the feet of God's throne. Again I emphasize even our consciences have been cleansed from dead works. We are free. Death no longer holds us. Each and every homosexual and heterosexual who has a faith relationship with the Father, Son, and Holy Spirit, now stands purely cleansed in thought, word, and deed before the throne of heaven. We stand shoulder to shoulder in our sameness. There should be no coercion or legal bullying against any man. Each and every one of us are the sum total of our entire being. God does not focus on the small green lint on the white jersey. Why do we? He looks at the heart that longs to be all things for God, obtaining the righteousness our flesh cannot.

An Expired Priesthood

The evidence that the days of the Levitical priesthood have ended is scripturally overwhelming.

Galations 2:16&19 says, "...know that a man is not justified by observing the law, but by faith in Jesus Christ...For through the law I died to the law so that I might live for God."

"Now that faith has come, we are no longer under the supervision of the law." Galations 3:23&24. The law which should have been our death knell upended when instead God showed overwhelming mercy and unmerited forgiveness to men. Paul spent the remainder of his life trying to share a new plan based on the New Covenant Laws of Jesus.

"Christ is the end of the law so that there may be righteousness for everyone who believes." Romans 10:4.

"Therefore, there is now no condemnation for those who are in Christ Jesus, because through Christ Jesus the law of the Spirit of life set me free from the law of sin and death." Romans 8:12.

"When you were dead in your sins and in the uncircumcision of your sinful nature, God made you alive with Christ. He forgave us all our sins, having canceled the written code, with its regulations, that was against us and that stood opposed to us; he took it away, nailing it to the cross." Colossians 2:13&14.

There is more than enough weight in these verses to totally throw the scales off against the one verse in a covenant law no longer valid to us. Leviticus just doesn't have the power to oppose what the larger volume of scripture points to. "The law is only a shadow of the good things that are coming – not the realities themselves." Hebrews 10:1. Do you get it yet? The entire Old Testament Covenant was a *shadow*, to point the way to God. It was never established to be the reality because Christ Jesus is the reality and He established a New Way with two new laws and only two that successfully cover the others.

What is supposed to be a positive revelation to us about who God is, as we've discovered the Bible is God's way to reveal who He is to mankind, has instead become a negative enforcer of "thou shalt and thou shalt not" and once again the focus is on us rather than God. We must hang onto this this thread as we visit the revelation of a new wine that teaches us what to do with the commands first written by God's own hand.

During the holidays I was at the grocery store check-out and I smiled and said, "Hi, are you shopping?" to a little girl probably around twenty month's old. She answered me by shaking her head "no". Her mom said, "We are trying to get her to learn to answer "yes" as she gently took the little girl's head in her hands and moved it in a "yes" nod. Most of us have probably laughed at the joke about the child who thought his name was "No, no" until he was five. And here we pick up a true fact of life – even as tiny children we gravitate to things which we shouldn't do or might be dangerous. That word a little child learns, sometimes before even saying "Mom" or "Dad", is the word "No".

As parents, we understand we aren't trying to give life a negative or unhappy meaning, but "No" is the quickest and the most effective way to get a child's attention so eventually he or she can grow to understand their lives are full of good and positive experiences when they finally conquer common sense and safety. The adult grasps that a child will quickly respond to "No, no", whereas a discussion about electrical outlets causing a painful shock or hitting another child doesn't build friendships has no meaning yet for an eighteen month old.

God understood what it would take to get His children's attention so He could move mankind toward a good and positive life. As mankind was still living in the shadowland of time, The Reality, Jesus, having not yet appeared on earth, God started out with "Thou shalt not" or "Don't do this", or "No, no", and in doing so began to reveal His holiness to the world in perhaps the best way for men to understand it at that time. I think it's fair to say God found a way to reveal His absolute holiness by contrasting it with man's natural inclination to wound himself and others. Our Father told us "No, no" because Jesus had not yet redeemed us by paying the price for our sins. He told us "No, no" because as all children, we are drawn toward self-destructive acts.

God, most of all, understood man would never be capable of keeping all those "Thou shalt nots". I don't believe He ever intended to use them as a daily scorecard against us, because the reality, if you've broken one law you have broken them all, (James 2:8-12) leaves us with a pathetic score of zero, now and forever. The score against us is off the charts.

I believe God's reason for these often guilt inducing commands was so man would finally fall down on his knees before God and say, "*I can't do this. I'm a failure, and at times, the harder I try to follow the rules the worse I act.*" And the God of love answers, "*No, you're right, you can't. Since you are unable to keep them, you must find one who can, one who can take your place and pay the price my holiness demands so you will be freed from the consequences of your guilt.*" Then with tenderness He says, "*I am your Father and I provide for you. I know someone who is willing to take your place. It is my own Son, and He will willingly die in your place to make you mine."*

Now, that's a plan. That scenario makes sense to me in view of the words of the entire Bible when they are taken as a whole. So what do we do with the Ten Commandments? We live by the two new Laws given to us by Jesus and use this list as our guide on how to fulfill love for God and man with our whole hearts, understanding the body, at times, will never be able to fully comply.

"The little word, 'law', you must not take here in human fashion, as a teaching about what works are to be done or not done." 10 Luther. Luther goes on to say that this is the way human laws work. We do lawful works by our body having nothing to do with our heart. But God judges according to what is tucked deep in the heart, and for this reason, *His law makes its demands on the heart* and can't be satisfied with works of the body. Therefore any works that don't come from a pure heart are considered as hypocrisy and lies.

When I do good deeds for other people, share, donate, if I do it grudgingly it can't satisfy the demands of God. That is why if a LGBTQ is taught he can only satisfy God by living a life that is not his own and is not from a pure heart, if he struggles in resentment and pain to live a heterosexual life, giving up his freedom to be who he believes God created him to be, it becomes a hypocritical lie which I don't see could ever satisfy God's business with the heart. With everything we have read, how could it?

"Then he adds: 'Their sins and lawless acts I will remember no more. And where these have been forgiven, there is no longer any sacrifice for sin.'" Hebrews 10:17&18. We are then called to persevere in a life that pleases God, relying on Jesus' intercession for our help. "Therefore he is able to save completely those who come to God through him, because he always lives to intercede for them." Hebrews 7:25. That holy language between Father and Son is beyond our imaginings. Let's stop thinking we understand it and let God be the judge.

Two New Laws for Us

"Teacher, which is the greatest commandment in the Law?" Were these Sadducees and Pharisees thinking Levitical Law? "Jesus replied: 'Love the Lord your God with all your heart and with all your soul and with all your mind.' This is the first and greatest commandment. And the second is like it: 'Love your neighbor as yourself.' All the Law and the Prophets hang on these two commandments." The Law and Prophets include the words of the Old Testament leaders. Matthew 22:36-40. Why strip away the powerful truth from Jesus' own mouth that two laws are all we need for life and instead revert to obsolete laws to satisfy our human insecurities?

I am one hundred percent convinced after all the hardship, all the strict laws that led to death – meant only to be a shadow of His coming, all the shed animal blood literally smeared on an altar with the daily ongoing sacrifices, all the harsh years of Pharisaic oppression, that Jesus embraced His humility by becoming an "outsider" and accepted the road to the cross to simplify the pathway to God for us. God, a jealous God, wants His creation for Himself, back where it started before the fall, and He does not take lightly to loosing even one child He would claim as His own. *They are mine and I will have them if they only say, "Yes, I will come to You." "It is finished."* There will be no more sacrifice, no more penalty to pay because Jesus paid our sin-tab in full, and in a single act of faith our sins, even tomorrows sins, completely vanish – they don't exist. Do you believe? Don't worry about what any others believe. Do you believe?

Do we, like the Pharisees, keep asking the questions that only circle the parameter of life? What about divorce Jesus? How come you're walking so far on the Sabbath? Why do you heal on the day of rest? Why do you not wash your hands before you eat? And speaking of food, what are you eating? Why do you enter the homes of sinners and eat with them? Jesus eventually lost patience with them because their hearts were not interested in really understanding Jesus with a focus on life through faith, but rather on death through laws. Their interest was a malignant intent focused on His death.

Are we today also only concerned with rules circling the parameter rather than cutting to the core of the needs of people, in particular homosexuals? In our Bible classes are we being trained to address the complex spiritual, emotional, and physical issues of our generation? Are we learning how to approach, accept, and love sexual and gender diverse people without putting them on the defensive, a place they are already too familiar with?

Or do we blunder right across a would-be friendship because that's what we believe the Bible says about sin and we must vocalize our superior insight? Do you feel compelled to let gays know in the first few lines of introduction to them that you don't agree with their "lifestyle"? They've heard it so often they don't care what you think. And why should they? How much love have you invested in them that gives you the right to judge them by stepping into God's place? What cross did you bear to allow yourself such superior words?

"The law indeed made a difference between Jew and Greek, giving the Jews on many accounts the pre-eminence: that also made the difference between bond and free, master and servant, and between male and female, the males being circumcised. But it is not so now; they all stand on the same level and are all one in Christ Jesus; as the one is not accepted on the account of any national or personal advantages he may enjoy above the other, so neither is the other rejected for the want of them; but all who sincerely believe on Christ, of what nation, or sex, or condition, soever they be, are accepted of him, and become the children of God through faith in him." 11 Henry. There is nothing that can be said to convince me LGBTQs are not welcomed in God's embrace.

Jesus Himself simplified our way to the Father and we see it immediately on His cross, and everything we believe hinges on that splintered tree on Calvary. It all changed that day. The thief hanging by Jesus just asked to be remembered by Him when Christ came into His glory. In an instant, full redemption moved from theory to reality when Jesus pronounced, it is done. That very day one man, a thief, sinful through and through became, in a single heartbeat, God's own. It has never gotten simpler than that. Grace doesn't just outweigh sin on the scales of God's justice. Grace profoundly outweighs sin.

When we at last put sin in the proper hierarchy of our lives with God's love through His Son at the top we will finally be able to look up and see the face of God. It's all about God. Wouldn't it be better to seek the face of God and learn to pray continually for grace? When we do our hearts will take over longing to please our Father, and sometimes our bodies will willingly follow along – but not all the time.

The Wailing Wall Of Legalism Renounced

There has been testimony after testimony, in books, on videos, at meetings, of men and women who have tried to become heterosexual. The have participated in untold numbers of counseling sessions, have repeatedly prayed to be changed, and have gone to conferences designed to help people come out of their "sinful lifestyle." One man was so determined he went to the same conference doing all the prescribed work afterward three different times amounting to three years of his life and it failed.

I just hurt for some of these tortured souls that resort to such extremes to find God's peace in their lives by what they have been told they must "do". They have repeatedly heard only by becoming heterosexual or being a homosexual whose life is void of any sexual contact, (our sexuality being one of the strongest, natural, God-given impulses known to man, by the way) is the only way to please God. We have totally striped away any sign of the New Covenant of faith and run back to the desert, to be penalized by what we do and don't do. In the end LGBTQs come away with lost hope when they cannot achieve man's goal dressed up to look like God's goal. Some come away with no hope and end their lives. I want to scream and rip my clothes in mourning because the "Bride of Christ" refuses to rely on her "Bridegroom".

LGBTQs are being constantly told their conduct and lives are not following Jesus, and if they fail to change, no one can help them, God included. And these leaders, assured of their own wisdom, strip away God's very own holiness into one apparently without any power or grace, and the sacrifice of Jesus death into a useless act, only to be resurrected when the need applies to their own personal, sinful lives.

An ever increasing population of experienced counselors, researches, doctors and yes theologians are now saying that whatever else, homosexuality is definitely not a choice. Will you hear them? Will you listen even though LGBTQs, the very people who should be the authority, have been saying this very thing until their voices grow hoarse? By continuing to ignore intense scholarly research, and years of experienced counseling, we are telling the sexual and gender diverse they are only throw-away people, since obviously they can't try hard enough to be saved by making "good choices", so they may as well save time and jump into hell right now.

My relationship with my Abba Father is not a group effort. While I appreciate the prayers and support of other Christians, in the end they cannot fix what the world may think is wrong with me. They cannot grow my faith, forgive me of my sins, or even stop my reactions to my sinful nature; no friend, no enemy, no minister, no family member. Jesus allowed many people the liberty to walk away from Him. He still does. We seem to forget that or perhaps we can't understand what Jesus was doing by letting them walk away. Not all LGBTQs will desire to bring their hearts to God just as not all heterosexuals do. But their relationship or non-relationship decision doesn't include me and you. It's between them and Jesus. And sometimes we just have to stand with Jesus and watch them walk away. If they won't listen to Jesus, what superior words do we possess that would make them listen us? So we pray instead.

We as Christians also have the liberty to wrestle with our beliefs according to our faith in God rather than faith in a religious institution. When I come to God now, I ask what do I need to bring forth today to be living in a kingdom walk with Him? What is permissible for me in light of Jesus death and resurrection and in accord with His New Covenant? Each and every LGBTQ has the liberty to ask those very same questions assured the Holy Spirit will hear and answer them as individuals. It's not a group effort.

"Let no debt remain outstanding, except the continuing debt to love one another for he who loves his fellowman has fulfilled the law. The commandments, 'Do not commit adultery,' 'Do not murder,' 'Do not steal,' 'Do not covet,' and whatever other commandments there may be, are summed up in the one rule: 'Love your neighbor as yourself.' Love does not do harm to its neighbor. Therefore love is the fulfillment of the law." Romans 3:8-10. And when our neighbor is of a different sexual or gender orientation than ourselves, we are without excuse to ignore this law of Christ's. When we fail to love, resulting in harm to others, we ourselves will be judged by our hardened heart.

In *unChristian* Kinnaman tells us only one percent of Christians pray for homosexuals. In a survey of over one thousand with the majority citing homosexuality as a problem, when asked what they would suggest to address the "problem" only one single individual suggested prayer. Can we heal if we don't care and how can we care without God's help?

"Now if the ministry that brought death, (ten commandments) which was engraved in letters on stone, came with glory, so that the Israelites could not look steadily at the face of Moses because of its glory, fading though it was, will not the ministry of the Spirit be even more glorious? If the ministry that condemns men is glorious, how much more glorious is the ministry that brings righteousness? For what was glorious has no glory now in comparison with the surpassing glory. And if what was fading away came with glory, how much greater is the glory of that which lasts?" 2 Corinthians 3:3-6. Simply said, everything new that

Jesus brings for our new wineskins is more glorious and greater than the old and it is here for the duration of time.

Aaron, Israel's high priest, entered the Holy of Holies with the nations of Israel on his breast (ephod). The even greater High Priest, "Christ appeared before God as the representative of His people, and thus reinstated humanity in the presence of God...Through the Atonement Christ met all the just demands of the law so that no legal charges can justly be brought against those for whom He paid the price." 12 Berkhof.

There are only two groups of people in the Bible, believers and non-believers. There is no third group, believers in Christ who are going to hell because of a sin they supposedly choose. If that were a possibility, Jesus' promise of salvation by faith is void! It is empty! It is ashes running through our fingers and the cosmos is laughing! Our failure to understand what multiple verses point to, that *all* people, no exceptions allowed, are God's own by the simple words born of the heart, "Yes I believe" amounts to our desperate clinging to a halfway belief. What good is that to any of us?

"The Lord has sworn and will not change His mind: you are a priest forever in the order of Melchizedek." (Psalm110:4). All you have to do now is ask yourself is Jesus my new priest?

Jesus, with His two new laws has fulfilled the Old Testament to the Father's satisfaction. The new has come and I personally rejoice! My new wineskin is holding just fine. I hope yours is also.

CHAPTER 7 THE TRUTH ABOUT SODOM AND GOMORRAH – THEN, LET'S MOVE ON

"His Way is in the Whirlwind and the Storm, and Clouds Are the Dust of His Feet." Nahum 1:3b

"The whole land will be a burning waste of salt and sulfur – nothing planted, nothing sprouting, no vegetation growing on it. It will be like the destruction of Sodom and Gomorrah, Admah and Zeboiim, which the Lord overthrew in fierce anger. All the nations will ask: 'Why has the Lord done this to this land? Why this fierce, burning anger?' And the answer will be: 'It is because this people abandoned the covenant of the Lord, the God of their fathers, the covenant he made with them when he brought them out of Egypt. They went off and worshiped other gods and bowed down to them, gods they did not know, gods he had not given them.'" Deuteronomy 29:23-26.

When was the last time you remember hearing that Sodom and Gomorrah is about homosexuality? When was the last time you read this verse in Deuteronomy? Deuteronomy is rarely the reference for a sermon topic. When did the announcement that, "Next week we are beginning a Bible study on the amazing book of Deuteronomy ever get your spiritual juices flowing? I won't be surprised if you've never read or heard of this verse. I hadn't until about a year ago. I put it alongside the Genesis account and found no smoking gun that points whatsoever to homosexuality as defined in our present culture.

Where do these misleading theories come from? "I don't know; that's what I was taught." Those were my words exactly. I never even thought to question this "fact" until my whole world fell out from under my feet. When the real choice becomes find the truth or shrivel up and quit living, the truth seems a better option. Even if the truth isn't something I want to hear, peace can come with truth. The alternative is to never have confidence in knowing your personal beliefs which leads to having no public voice on the things you care about. You will continue to believe all others are "smarter" – they must have the right answers, and you cast aside the joy to speak freely and intelligently about matters of your heart.

Let me share, as simply as I can, the truth about Sodom and Gomorrah; not my truth, God's truth according to His words.

New Facts – Five Cities Not Two

Have you ever heard of Admah and Zeboiim? I hadn't until I came across this verse. Later I found out more about these cities from Josephus, *The Jewish War,* Book IV. It's a description of Lake Asphalitis and the Dead Sea. "Next to it lies the land of Sodom, which in olden days was a land rich in crops and in the affluence of its various cities, but now entirely incinerated. It is said that it was burnt up by thunderbolts due to the impiety of its inhabitants. Indeed, there are still marks of the fire from heaven and faint outlines of five cities to be seen. The fruits which grow there still contain ashes; they have all the appearance of edible fruit, but when plucked with the hand, break up into smoke and ashes. To this extent the legends about the land of Sodom are confirmed by visual evidence." 1 Josephus.

Let me stop here a second and call your attention to the fact that without Josephus I might never have identified who or what Admah and Zeboiim were. Originally, I was at a loss when I read Deuteronomy about what I guessed were towns, but wasn't for sure. That is what happens with Scripture at times. We do not have an accurate explanation and sometimes nothing we do to research ancient manuscripts will hand us the truth we are looking for. But sometimes outside sources stimulate our need to keep looking, and after looking into Genesis 14 so much came tumbling out.

Now I can tell you there were five cities, not two, not four, but five, the fifth called Bela. They were richly prosperous cities and each had their own king. Clearly they would be sought after by invading armies looking to enrich their coffers.

While the story of Sodom and Gomorrah with the unanswered question "why" is in Genesis 19, and the answer to that "why" is in Deuteronomy 29, the entire background on the abominable acts of these men actually begins in Genesis 14. The widely popular belief for generations is that Sodom was a town where homosexual men were so wicked the word "sodomy" was coined from the town's name.

God's own words tell us He destroyed Sodom and Gomorrah because they were towns run by completely *godless men* who rebelled against their Creator. Godlessness is the sin that brings destruction to godless people. There is the proof, as plain as can be written for anyone who wants to know the truth. "It will be like the destruction of Sodom and Gomorrah..." Not just the burnt, wasted land would be like Sodom, but the fierce burning anger of God would also mirror Sodom and Gomorrah. The nations will ask why and the answer is, "...this people abandoned the covenant of the Lord." They were adulterers toward God making them idolaters. To believe anything else is to not want to see what God is saying. Everyone in the town except Lot and his family detested God.

Now for a little background lesson. All five kings from Sodom to Bela went to war in the Valley of Siddim, against the king of Elam and three other kings. Five kings against four, Sodom lost and Elam totally ravaged their camps taking all their goods including families who were with them. Abram's nephew Lott suffered as a prisoner of war. When Abram found out he took 318 trained men and pursued the victorious armies as far as Dan where he recovered all people and possessions that belonged to the five kings of Sodom's community.

Returning as a victor himself, Abram meets the king of Sodom to give back everything. "Then Melchizedek king of Salem brought out bread and wine. He was priest of God Most High, and he blessed *Abram* saying 'Blessed be Abram by God Most High, Creator of heaven and earth. And blessed be God Most High who delivered your enemies into your hand.'" Genesis 14:18-20. We understand the bread and wine were distributed by Melchizedek between those of Abram's tribe and those of Sodom's communities in recognition of what God had done for them.

 The king of Sodom says he only wants his people back and told Abram to keep the possessions. Being forced to accept their own possessions from Abram the victor's hand, reveals the extent of pride in the kings of Sodom's five communities. They did not want to be indebted to anyone, especially anyone who worshiped God. But being nudged by the Spirit of God, Abram refused saying he had made an oath to God that he would accept nothing, "not even a thread or the thong of a sandal, so that you will never be able to say, 'I made Abram rich.'" Abram listened to what God gave him and leaned not unto his own understanding.

Can you see how this begins to set the stage for Genesis 19? The king of Sodom resented Abram and his God. Melchizedek called it accurately. He nailed the situation. On God's behalf he praised Abram for his faithfulness to God. Men who covet and maintain self-pride end up condemning themselves before God. The king of Sodom not only lost the war and ran away to the hills, he was now forced to accept everything he had previously lost from the hands of God's conquering faithful, Abram, and he felt humiliated, resentful and angry, and seethed on a slow burn. He wallowed in humiliation instead of seeking the humble heart of God, thankful for all God had restored to him and the four other kingdoms that day.

At this time in the book of Genesis, the father of nomadic family units or kings of cities fulfilled the role of "priest" before God, laying the sacrifices for man's sins on God's altar. These men knew about their Creator. They knew about the needed sacrifices to atone for their sins. We learn that from Genesis 14. But in Sodom and Gomorrah they just couldn't be bothered to care. But if you need the words a little more specifically: "… he condemned the cities of Sodom and Gomorrah by burning them to ashes, and made them an example of what is going to happen to the *ungodly*…" 2 Peter 2:6. One more time, the Bible spells out the proof, these men were idolaters, God haters, and it seems their idolatry may well have been the worship of themselves.

Before we pick up Genesis 19 let's make one more short stop, this time in Genesis 18. God's own angels were being sent to Sodom by Him because the outcry of the humbler people in that town had reached God's ears. Genesis 18:20-21. Never does the Bible waste words on what is not important. I want to focus on "outcry" for a moment. These words tell us there were people, families, being severely mistreated. Someone or many someones, those obviously in power and control, the kings and leaders were abusing the humbler families of these cities. This wasn't a little problem where people gathered on the square and whispered their discontent. There was an outpouring of heinous wrongs loud enough and long enough that God heard and would no longer patiently wait for men's hearts to change. Genesis 18:20 & 21.

God's heavenly messengers arrive at the town gate and what happens next is what many believe to be the "sin" that in and of itself brought God to His judgment. Out of an entire city of men, Lot was the only one who offered a safe place for these "men" to pass the night. To remain outside the city gate throughout the night risked exposure to nature, wild animals, and wicked men that could result in death. The need to provide hospitality to travelers was more than a nice gesture. It was an act of life or death. Yes, hospitality is important to God, but there is something here even more important to God.

The men are taken to Lot's house and receive a meal, company, perhaps even prayers. But before they snuff out the lamps and lay down to sleep, "...all the men from every part of the city – both young and old – surround the house." Genesis 19:4. They demand Lot hand over the two visitors so they can "have sex with them." (vs.5). Since, "all the men from every part of the city" were involved do you actually believe this city had only homosexual men living there? Or maybe you use that label on anyone who performs the act even if they are heterosexual. It is important for you to understand there is a difference between a heterosexual male who engages in a vengeful homosexual act and those who are trying to live their lives loving others and serving God who fall under today's cultural "label" of homosexual.

There were families and children living in this city. Both the young and old men are specifically pointed out to have participated. How often do these two specific age groups find themselves coerced into following the instructions of stronger, more ruthless men? These leaders were heterosexual men who had turned their lives away from God and worshiped worthless idols. They were wicked, they were out of control, and believed they were accountable to no one but themselves.

Their city was rich and affluent, and in their minds it was successful because they had made it so, their blessings having nothing to do with God. They liked their city the way it was and I imagine Lot's life, more respectful toward God, tarnished their self-images in more ways than one. Seeing Lott honor God's law of hospitality brought to a boiling point the memory of that long ago day when Abram refused to be condescended to by Sodom's king.

From Lot's doorstep they did not request the "men" be handed out so they could have a sex party. These were warriors (if just in their own minds) who owned their town. They didn't like the memory of losing that previous battle to the kings of Elam and running away into the hills. They didn't like being "out-warriored" by Abram, a man of God, so they had to grow large in their own eyes. No doubt they enjoyed the king of Sodom's blessings over their conquer-all attitudes. How else would the king keep his throne? These city leaders were afraid of nothing and no one (especially when they had a large group of "yes" men at their backs).

So as "conquering warriors" on this night, they wanted to celebrate their strength by defiling, dehumanizing, and profaning, these "good men". It would be a warning to lesser kingdoms to have no doubt to their place of subordination should they visit the glorious lands of Sodom.

This sexual penetration between heterosexual men was an act of ultimate shame that a victorious soldier would force on one who was conquered. It was an act that meant you are a possession or a slave like a weak woman who has no recourse over her owner. That's what they were interested in. Sadistic, egotistical men who are "gods" in their own eyes want the power to make all others subservient before them, "to lie with a man as one lies with a woman."

Daniel Helminiak wrote about those days of war and the explicit act of anal penetration to debase, dehumanize, or 'de male' another man. It was a huge insult to treat men like soft women who were considered little more than inferior pieces of property by most men at the time.

Every conquering army throughout the Bible and those who have come later have raped and ravaged their way to victory. They wanted to rape these "men" – angels of the Lord God of Heaven. When Lot offered up his daughters it didn't interest the raging crowd because they weren't interested in sex. They weren't there for a huge sexual orgy. Sex would never satisfy the appetite for destruction these animal-like men of Sodom were bent on obtaining. They wanted to conquer in their own godless fashion by totally desecrating the law of hospitality the Creator set down for men to follow. They wanted to do it their way just like Adam and Eve and all of us ever since.

Even that much later coined word "sodomy" can't do justice to this reality.

If you think the only important message in this report in Genesis is a sexual act between men you have totally missed the point. Not only are God's words crystal clear, the story finally makes total sense when seen through God's lens of accuracy. This Biblical text has nothing to do with homosexuality.

Then Let's Move On

I Corinthians 6:9-10 is another frequently used verse against homosexuality. "Do you not know that the wicked will not inherit the kingdom of God? Do not be deceived: Neither the sexually immoral nor idolaters nor adulterers nor male prostitutes nor homosexual offenders nor thieves nor the greedy nor drunkards nor slanderers nor swindlers will inherit the kingdom of God." (New International Version).

I'd like to address the elephant in the room/verse, the word "homosexual" in the NIV version. I have found nothing in my day to day, month to month, even year to year study of the entire Bible to support the inclusion of this twentieth century coined word in this verse or any other verse.

The NIV uses very modern words in translation as seen above and includes the word "homosexual" which first appeared in our Bibles during the "ancient" days of 1946. This is opposed to other translations, "...neither the immoral, nor idolaters, nor adulterers, nor sexual perverts..." and "...neither fornicators, nor idolaters, nor adulterers, nor voluptuaries, nor pederasts...". Voluptuaries are people who will do anything to pamper themselves and supply their every sensual need;

anything whether morally right or not. Pederast easily leans toward pedophilia and the abusive act of a grown man forcing a young boy into a sexual act against his will. In New Testament cities at that time, there was nothing "ill-legal" in this act as long as the younger boy was not an actual citizen. The Apostle Paul seeks to straighten out their confused immoral views as he writes his letters to New Testament churches.

In *Jesus, The Bible, And Homosexuality* by Jack Rogers, I want to share an incident that supports my thoughts. In the Presbyterian Church they have what is called the *Book of Confessions,* from the Heidelberg Catechism. This particular story involves a special edition for their four-hundredth-anniversary translated in the early 1960s. A woman by the name of Johanna Bos noticed something different about this translation as compared to the ones she had studied as a girl in the Netherlands where she was from. "Bos said that, despite all of her study in the Netherlands (in the Dutch reformed church) she had never heard any mention of homosexuality." 2 Rogers.

This caught Roger's attention and he began to investigate. He went back to the Heidelberg Catechism as far as 1586 and moved forward to consecutive editions and never found a reference to "homosexual perversion". The 1961 translations was the first time in their church history it had been used. Eventually Rogers found who had written the new translation and contacted him asking why he had used this particular wording.

The gentleman first answered that since it was the beginning of the sexual revolution those who he worked with thought it was better to be more specific in language. Rogers also became more specific asking why insert the particular phrase "homosexual perversion"? The gentleman answered, "We just thought it would be a good idea." 3 Rogers. "A good idea" the man replied which immediately begs the question, "For whom?"

Can you begin to understand how significantly misappropriated words can and do affect our lives. Substituting "homosexuality" for the words "voluptuary" and "pederast" or even "sexual perverts" has no valid reason to be printed into our Bibles, especially when you add in what we have learned so far by looking at the Bible as a complete story rather than trying to translate and understand a verse as it stands isolated from the others. Common sense becomes overrun and a piece of scripture that was once orderly and easily discerned, on the "good intentioned whim of a good idea" becomes an uncontrolled tool used to shovel people right into hell.

"So I tell you this, and insist on it in the Lord, that you must no longer live as the Gentiles do, in the futility of their thinking. They are darkened in their understanding and *separated from the life of God* because of the ignorance that is in them *due to the hardening of their hearts*. Having lost all sensitivity, they have given themselves over to sensuality so as to indulge in every kind of impurity, with a continual lust for more." Ephesians 4:17-19.

The "futility of their thinking" leading to "hardening of their hearts" is the only hell-bound route ever identified by God. Their lives have no boundaries or control so they lust for anything and everything that can satisfy their sexual appetites and are preoccupied with the greed of money to get these sexual gratifications no matter whose innocent lives they may ruin. But it's not just about sexual appetites. "Giving themselves over to sensuality" can be attributed to any of the senses including but not limited to thoughts, tastes, eyes, ears, and emotions. This is a direct result of idol worship, God's absence from their lives! The absence of God is the condemning factor.

I'd like to take a moment to return to "pederast" or pedophilia. The category of pedophile maintains its own restricted type of individuals, and they are overwhelmingly known, in most cases, to be heterosexual. We, as a society, do not erroneously lump all heterosexuals into the pedophile category just because most pedophiles are heterosexual. That would be the height of idiocy.

The other day I was eating lunch in the teacher's workroom where I

103

sometimes substitute and one of the teachers started talking about how a new rule at a certain school in another city has made it possible for bisexual and transgender individuals to enter whichever restroom they feel more comfortable in using. In this particular incident, based totally on rumor, a male individual dressed in female attire entered the girl's gymnasium and observed several students in the showers for a length of time.

I pointed out this was not a gender problem. Any time a person spends prolonged time watching others in a shower, the authorities or police should be called. This is an obvious situation of a voyeur at the very least and a pedophile at the worst and needs to be stopped. True bisexuals and transgenders have enough on their plate of life, everything from unacceptance and hatred from others, to their own struggles with self-recognition and resolving how to accept their life in this cruel world. To automatically throw them into the malignant world of the pedophile without actual proof or reason is sinful. If this scenario referred to by this teacher actually took place, who is to say this wasn't some heterosexual male who has figured out how to work a new system to his advantage, claiming to be bisexual or transgender so he can enter the girl's locker room and look at all the nude young girls he wants? That is as viable a possibility as anything else people dream up.

This teacher is not a mean person, but this situation accurately reflects how uninformed the majority of people in our world are about the truth surrounding the lives of sexual and gender diverse people. Having an advanced education doesn't mean one automatically has a thorough understanding of the difficulties and complex issues bisexual and transgender individuals must deal with. To label LGBTQs as pedophiles is a disgusting and unconscionable act by ignorant people who don't think they have anything more to learn about a particular group of people whom they don't want to accept or recognize as equal. To label LGBTQs as pedophiles is as idiotic as labeling all heterosexuals as pedophiles.

Born of God – Still Sinners Or Not?

Let's use the incident above, in the teacher's workroom for a moment. We have a situation of good people, even Christians who make heartless assumptions or repeat damaging rumors that not a single person who was present in that workroom was witness to. Perhaps 1 John 3:9 can help us make sense of our love for God and our sinfulness, even if John seems to be saying just the opposite. "No one who is born of God will continue to sin; because God's seed remains in him; he cannot go on sinning because he has been born of God." It is absolutely essential that we understand what this verse is telling us, especially after talking so much about original sin in our lives that we continue to act upon daily. In its proper context this verse says so much; gives so much hope to us all.

"To this extent the Son of God has already destroyed the devil's works in everyone that has been born of God, that by regeneration has been born into a new life, has become a child of God, and has God as his Father. Everyone who is so born 'does not go on sinning'…He keeps purifying himself, is constantly busy sweeping out sin." 4 Lenski. John explains more fully that the seed, the living Word born in our hearts is from God, and in God's eyes there is no more sin to be laid at the door of that individual's life.

Yet the reality we need to cling to is that we gladly seek purification in that we are constantly to be about the business of sweeping out our sin. The sin is still there, as we observe in each and every Christian person, but the desire in our hearts is to realize, with God's loving help, that each day we need to be about the business of sweeping our hearts clean of sin. What a beautiful picture of God's children sweeping out the sin in our lives by God's hand, purifying ourselves on an ongoing basis. The work of Satan has already been put to death! We are born of God – but still act upon our sinful desires.

So even though we read that a person born of God will no longer sin, we can't view this with human logic. We must understand scripture as a whole to come to the proper understanding that after the Holy Spirit has worked to bring our hearts to God, that while God no longer lays the penalty of death from sin at our feet, sin indeed does exist in our everyday lives and for this reason, every day we are to be about the task of sweeping away these acts alien to God's love. This is the ongoing work of sanctification as we live out our lives.

Whether homosexual or heterosexual, a child of God, welcomed into His family through faith alone, not because of anything he did or did not do, is a Child of God. I cannot attempt to explain how God determines the purity of heart in any single person's life, only that He does because He has told us so. If Holy God claims the life of any man or woman who is an active homosexual, then they have the seed of "true life" within them. Any sin in their lives are no longer laid at their door, and they desire to continually sweep out and purify their heart each and every day from any sinful imperfections in their lives. That is the promise of Holy Scripture, not a false hope. God does not make mistakes.

One Defining Moment

I want to share something called "Defining Moment" from the book unChristian. "I believe that almost every man who deals with homosexuality has a defining moment when he realizes that everything that is going on in his body, in his mind, and in the secret place of his heart is what is called 'gay'. It is an extremely frightening moment that is usually never forgotten." At fourteen this young man had been kicked out of school, tried twice to kill himself, "and no one knew how to help or love me." During a session with his youth counselor at his church he recognized his sexual diversity. "The result was that I realized I was gay, that it was something really bad and as much as I loved church, I would never be accepted here." 5 Kinnaman/Lyons.

Afterwards followed twenty years of depression, twelve of drug addiction/dealing, and several more suicide attempts. The problem, in opposition to what some prefer to believe, is not that this young man could not accept his own sexuality. The problem is that those in the world he knew, loved and trusted could not and would not accept his sexuality. He could not resolve the complex puzzle of who he understood himself to naturally be versus the churches accusation that he chose to reject God by his choice of sexual diversity and actions.

Today, this man is safely in God's loving protection of grace. Whether as a heterosexual or a homosexual I don't know nor do I care. When he most needed help, as a young, confused teenager, no one was *equipped* to handle the situation. What do you think would have happened if he had experienced a loving support system and acceptance in his church? Would he have ventured down that same self-destructive path for so many wasted years? What might he have accomplished in that same time period with the assurance of God's grace in his life? And the collective Church on earth, might she have grown stronger against the evil manipulations of Satan who continually urges us to lay a cruelly divisive wall between ourselves and homosexuals?

The forward motion of our lives continues to be fueled by ignorance on this subject. Far too many of us are not spiritually equipped to understand how God wants us to live in a world where gay men and lesbian women are our neighbors. "...the hardest things for me to overcome were the hateful words and rejection that came from people who called themselves Christian." 6 Kinnaman/Lyons. When Jesus commanded us to love our neighbors every bit as much as we love our selves, He didn't add any stipulations such as, "But you might want to hold off on that love of your neighbor until he stops sinning or doing what you don't like." He didn't ask us to judge them before we start loving them.

Our children watch us, hear us, and mimic us. "How did they learn that" we ask, amazed at the drama our child just entertained anyone in hearing distance with. How? Where? They learn it from us or something within our lives believe it or not. Every nuance of a mother and father is a little secret trinket our children put into their memory pocket to play with later and assume for their own use. So instead of teaching our children, who have been entrusted into our care, to follow the world's biased hate, what if parents could be honest with their children by saying, "We actually do not understand how or why people are different, but because we are all part of God's creation, He loves homosexuals and heterosexuals equally and wants all of us to love Him. And because it is God's hope that all people can learn to live with, love, and respect each other, *our* family will do just that. There is a lot in life we don't always understand, but God does and He is capable of taking care of each and every one of us." Do you think a child could understand that? Do you think if people stop detesting homosexuals and calling them horrible names in front of children that those children might learn not to act in hate?

Without knowing it, there are men and women that you have met, perhaps do business with, possibly see and talk to every day who are gay. You may even like and enjoy them. You don't realize their sexual identity because they are just like you and me. They go about their lives in a perfectly unassuming manner, working, bringing home a paycheck, paying the bills, doing the shopping, and even raising children. I am still amazed when people use the term "lifestyle". I want to ask what is it about a gay "lifestyle" that bothers them? Is it buying a home, a car, contributing to the world through a job, shopping, cleaning and yard work on the weekend, going to church, because it is sum total of these actions in all our lives that define our lifestyle. They are turning a very harmless word into a malignant cliché to describe a very small, private act that takes place between two loving people in a bedroom which is none of their business.

But the world, the media, and the church doesn't necessarily see homosexuals who are living average lives like you and me, but focus on the more flamboyant ones. They have not been taught that some men and women are still on the long, difficult road trying to process the sexuality they have tried to deny for so long; their "coming out" made all the more harder because of a majority that rejects them. As life opens up new possibilities, they embrace ideas and actions, styles of clothing and body language that they may later discard. That would be no different from teenagers or young men and women who graduate and are moving into a college life with much anticipated freedom. Who hasn't gone a little crazy after certain restrictions have been lifted? That is no different from each and every one of us who have worn differing personalities in our search for who we are as we crossed into our early adult years.

Some gays have a naturally flamboyant personality that is easier to recognize, and it's possible they make you uneasy. Maybe you think you just cannot personally deal with lifelong flamboyant homosexuals. Can I ask you, how do you deal with lifelong flamboyant heterosexuals?

Do you recognize those with tattoos plastered over 70% of their bodies as being flamboyant? How about fifteen body piercings you see, and you don't want to think about the ones you can't see? At the stop light when the car next to you pulls up and you start vibrating to their bass beat, aren't they announcing give me attention – I am so cool? Isn't it also flamboyant for a total of two people to occupy a 20,000 square foot home? Green hair, blue hair, purple hair, a wild top and a skirt hem only scant inches below the panty line that has at least some of us praying she won't bend over – at the communion rail – flamboyant!

Perhaps it really is merely the new normal rather than flamboyant. What have you tried that was over the top and who knows how annoying to others? It is a problem only if you choose to let it be a problem. God loves us all, flamboyant or not.

If all you know about the gay community is what you see on TV you have an impoverished education about a large, thriving, interesting group of people. You do not have the full truth, and when have you willingly settled for not being completely informed? Why now have you given up your right to know the whole truth? Having a great education does not mean you know the whole truth about many subjects.

If your life was on the line and the only person available to help you was gay, would you be happy to accept them and their help? Would you be grateful they were in your life at that moment? A husband, a wife, a child needs a bone marrow transplant to survive. The willing person with the exact tissue match is gay. Does your heart burst with gratitude and allow it to change your mind about people you made jokes about and refused to talk to? Let's say you are $200 short for your mortgage which is due this week because you helped purchase the cancer medication for your mom. Your lesbian co-worker who you have not always treated nicely offers to loan you the money. No one else has bothered to help in any way. Would you take it? Your soldier son is alive today because of the quick response of his gay ally and comrade. Where does that leave your heart? They, the lesbians, gays, bisexuals, transgenders and queer are just like you and me.

Have you ever heard a person say, "I refuse to go visit my lesbian daughter, my gay grandson, my bisexual niece, or the person who used to be my son but is now my daughter, because she/he will think I condone their "lifestyle"? I've given this a lot of thought. Who started this idea as a truism and what did they base it on?

My question is how much intelligence do you attribute to your loved one that you assume they could not be objective about how you honestly feel? Who in the world do we think Jesus would be ministering to if He walked the earth today? For starters – our children, our grand-children, other loved ones and friends who struggle with their sexual identity. And those who have been cheating them, withholding love, compassion and the respect of equality, you and me – those with a heterosexual identity, would Jesus perhaps visit us as He once visited Zacchaeus, saying give to them what is their due? Is it time to reverse our lives, repent and heal our selfish, sinful attitudes?

It doesn't have to be difficult to approach our family member and say: "I love you, I always have, I always will. Homosexuality (bisexuality, transgender) has been a confusing, even troubling issue for me, but I want you to know I am trying to work through my feelings and beliefs. I am still uncomfortable about certain things. I also know Jesus loves you so much and If He can love you with grace then I think I can try to do that too. I don't understand everything about your life, but if I stop and think about it you probably don't understand everything about my life either.

Perhaps it's time to help each other, start forgiving each other, and begin to move past our pain. I am positive that God's grace chooses to overlook the difficulties in our lives so we can feel safe enough to approach Him. I'm not sure I know right now what God wants for your life any more than I know exactly what He wants for mine. But I do believe He wants to help us discover what that is. Tell me, what would you like from me? It's time to sit and talk and learn to live our lives together again."

Do you realize how powerful words of love are? Do you understand when you initiate a conversation like this one you finally uncurl your fist and offer the beauty of God's grace that He placed in your life to share with others. And maybe high in the heavens our Brother, our Lord, our Messiah raises a fist and cheers us on because we have finally gotten it! Jesus relishes every simple act of love and grace that we pay forward in His name. Another life has a chance to be rescued from the grief of being tossed aside by the ones who were trusted to be there, to love, to support unconditionally.

"Faith is a living, daring confidence in God's grace, so sure and certain that a man would stake his life on it a thousand times." 7 Luther. With words like these you've taken a first step in the life of someone important to you. With it you will find the confidence to take the next 999 steps in the lives of others.

CHAPTER 8 THE SINNERS PERSONAL JUSTIFICATION OF FAITH

"There is No One Righteous, Not Even One."   Romans 3:10

Come little one, crawl onto my lap and rest your head against my heart. Today the lesson is long. It requires focus and patience, but I will be with you. For my sake, become like a little child. Empty out yourself before me and start with a clean page.

It is finally time to come face to face with that super-text on the "sin of homosexuality", Romans one. I need to understand for myself, my son, my family, and my friends. I need to be convicted on what I truly believe in my heart and not live my life on borrowed words that aren't really my own.

For me, it is important to define, in my own way, what I mean when I say "homosexual". And if my definition is not exactly like yours, at least you will understand where I am coming from. A homosexual is one, male or female, whose natural gender orientation leads them to desire someone of the same sex. The "why" is an unknown but has apparently been present from birth. The desire for a same gender relationship is anchored so deeply within the very core of their being that to try to separate it from their life is exactly like forcefully removing heterosexuality from my life and yours.

Perhaps you have Christian books or commentaries that you use. God works in miraculous ways, but He also works in the day-to-day reality all around us. Lenski's commentaries have been in my possession for years. From Bible to commentary and commentary to Bible, I relied on that reality around me that God has blessed me with. Romans was the most difficult for me to process in learning where I stand in a world where homosexuals and heterosexuals are at times bitter enemies.

For starters, I have been taught Romans chapter one, is the definitive chapter against homosexuality. In previous pages we have talked about man's natural inclination to sin from which we cannot escape, a result of the fall, which Jesus has taken upon himself to redeem us from. For believers, our sins are no longer credited against us. I've also spoken of the sin of eternal consequences – total rejection of God. This is the sin I call willful godlessness.

The title choice for this chapter came from R.C. H. Lenski's commentary on the book of Romans. He defines the entire theme of Romans with these words, *"The Sinners Personal Justification of Faith"*. Lenski says, "Sin excludes no man from being declared righteous by God." 1 Lenski. This is an amazing statement of grace the Bible backs up through its entirety. It's godlessness, not sin in and of itself that moves God to totally withdraw from a person's life. And that is where Romans chapter one will take us. Sin? Yes. Godless sin? Absolutely.

The Truth Exchanged For Idolatry

I don't want to spend a lot of time on the introduction of Paul's letter except to say Paul humbly puts himself on equal footing with these people. He is writing to the church in Rome – Christians. Who are these people in this church? They are Jewish and Greek converts. For the most part they are educated and may use the books of the Old Testament prophets to guide their faith. Paul calls them saints, but he does this with the understanding that even saints are sinners. This is a letter about judging others.

"The wrath of God is being revealed from heaven against all the godlessness and wickedness of men who suppress the truth by their wickedness, since what may be known about God is plain to them, because God has made it plain to them. For since the creation of the world God's invisible qualities – his eternal power and divine nature – have been clearly seen, being understood from what has been made, so that men are without excuse. For although they knew God, they neither glorified him as God nor gave thinks to him, but their thinking became futile and their foolish hearts were darkened. Although they claimed to be wise, they became fools and exchanged the glory of the immortal God for images made to look like mortal man and birds and animals and reptiles." Romans 1:18-23.

In the introduction Paul takes us back to the beginning of the world, a time before written text, when God revealed Himself to man, in part, through the miracles of the created world. As man is part of that creation in the image of God, He wrote His laws inside man's heart, not on stone or papyrus. These laws are God's laws and therefore laws of pure righteousness.

God says the works of His hands reveals enough for men to learn about the eternal power and divine nature of God and we are without excuse not to believe. He set His righteous glory before men, but they preferred their own brand of righteousness so they refused to acknowledge God's glory, or thank Him for the gift of life surrounding them. Paul plainly states through man's own wickedness comes the desire to suppress God's truth in their lives. In time their senses were so dulled there was no room for anything but their own foolish thoughts that eventually shut off all light in their hearts, erasing the laws God had placed there. Their seat of purity was now void and dark in God's eyes.

The letter appears to be written to adults. I know there are some "evil" children in our world but it doesn't take long, when one begins to dig, to uncover horrible things these so-called "evil" children have been exposed to and forced to live with that have stolen their innocence making them animals of survival. If we trust the words of Jesus, the natural child is innocent of the sly, conniving ways of adults. I am satisfied we are dealing with adults in these verses.

Unreality is their reality. These people chose the lowest form of idolatry, a thing without life or breath. They didn't even choose to worship real creatures but bowed down before deaf and dumb man-made images and considered themselves righteous in doing so. Man was made in the image of the Creator, but after the fall, man made his own god into whatever image he chose to project onto the Creator God, and through projecting – replaced Him. A quick summation, their idolatry, referred to often in the Bible as adultery to God, was nothing more than a bastard form of worship compared to the legitimate worship of the One Creator God, the only worship He accepts.

God Gave Them Over

"Therefore God gave them over in the sinful desires of their hearts to sexual impurity for the degrading of their bodies with one another. They exchanged the truth of God for a lie, and worshiped and served created things rather than the Creator – who is forever praised. Amen." Romans 1:24-25.

These are godless people. Their hearts extinguished the truth of God. "God gave them over" indicates something more than God giving them permission to fall into sin and something less than God causing them to sin, according to Lenski, and that seems to be the best our human minds can comprehend. The curse of disgrace they embraced in their own bodies. No one did this to them or for them. Men usually seek to honor their bodies in life, especially the way they look and present themselves to the world. But these chose dishonor, and the text is unclear whether they were dishonored as a result of their sin or they chose to dishonor themselves by way of their sins, the second having a more negative connotation. There is a difference, and gives an example of the difficulty of translating Greek and other languages into English, a fact we should not lightly dismiss.

"God gave them over in the sinful desires of their hearts." It is important to understand their sinful desires were many and varied as we see listed at the end of the chapter. This is not just about sexual sin. It happens to be the first one Paul addresses. To make sexual sins in general, and sex between same genders specifically, the single focus of this chapter is to derail your spiritual understanding of the Gospel's intent here. Let the flow of Paul's words guide you through the entire text, and don't stop at a single verse that some people particularly wish to avenge.

"Because of this, God gave them over to shameful lusts. Even their women exchanged natural relations for unnatural ones. In the same way the men also abandoned natural relations with women and were inflamed with lust for one another. Men committed indecent acts with other men, and received in themselves the due penalty for their perversion." Romans 1:26-27. Just as there were more than sexual sins spoken of, there was also more than one type of sexual sin acted on. God gave them over to shameful lusts, plural.

In idol worship on the scale Paul is referring to, their hearts were so black, their minds were so lost, no sexual act was off limits. This brand of "worship" to deaf and dumb images had been practiced for thousands of years. Christianity was a new and small force when compared to the stronger "religion" of temple idolatry available to Romans, comparable to the availability of fast food restaurants in America. Husbands, wives, children, aunts, uncles, cousins, strangers, all in full acceptable worship mode, were bowing before godless images and in so doing destroyed their own lives. They were so swept up in their lustful passions, burning beyond restraint, they had become animals rooting like wild hogs out of brutal instinct rather than sanity. Do you get the picture Paul has verbally painted?

In truth, they could have been having dinner and singing songs, or men having sex with their own wives, but as an act of worship to a false god, the evil intent, the godlessness, would still stand. Whatever act, seemingly "benign" or otherwise, could have no other definition than absolute evil wickedness, because that's what idolatry is, and it is completely rejected by God, as a means of worshiping Him. It is unacceptable in His sight. If we are to study homosexuality in light of Romans chapter one this is a thread we must not lose track of.

God gave them over – heterosexual women. We know they were heterosexual because they gave up what was normal, and burned for immoral sex of all kinds, including same gender relations. And the men also gave up what was normal, heterosexuality, for man to man relations. Paul doesn't give them a word label, homosexual/heterosexual. He describes an action linked directly to godlessness, another important fact to remember, and a strong reason to rid our Bibles of such modern labels today that may adversely affect the truth of scripture.

Lenski tells us that Paul's letter does not smoothly translate from Greek to English and even the single shift of a phrase is enough to throw off Paul's entire meaning. This sheds light on why two excellent scholars with years of education may not agree on certain phrases. That is where your heart and personal seeking of God's will for your healing and understanding takes over. That is why our relationship with the Father is personal, not a group affair. Here at last, you will be called on to wrestle with scripture and engage your own personal risk to grow in your faith, and find satisfaction of knowing *why* you believe as you do. You will be able to claim with confidence that what you believe concerning LGBTQs is what God alone has placed in your heart.

These Romans, beyond a doubt, were doing anything and everything completely out of control to a false god and it offended and angered the

God of righteousness and orderliness due to their "adultery", a word God uses to describe idolatry when in reference to Himself.

Questions That Cry Out For Answers

First of all we cannot overlook the most essential truth of Romans one. These were godless people who chose to reject God and replace Him with copies of dead, lifeless things. And these dead, lifeless things are what they worshipped in all manner of sexual ways, not by just one act that may offend some readers. In their godlessness, the lust that was created is what God gave them over to; a godless lust stemming from a godless life. With this upper most in our minds we can move on.

The verses in chapter one read like the people "abandoned" what is normal and natural to their daily sexual lives like tossing off a jacket onto the floor. My question is, do they pick up that normal sexual "jacket" and resume life "normal and natural" the next day? Do they "abandon" what is natural only during the worship of false gods, resuming heterosexuality the next day? If so, how do we use these verses to condemn homosexuals today, especially those who have a relationship with the God of Heaven? The problem is scripture doesn't reveal whether they assumed unnatural sexual acts of all kinds just during godless worship, or whether the unnatural took over their sexual lives completely from that moment on.

I would say it is unnatural for me to have a woman to woman sexual encounter as a heterosexual who would go back the next day to my husband. Would that act alone mean I am evil, wicked and depraved to the point of God totally turning His back on me? What if I performed a sexual act with another woman because I had learned from the time I was small that this was the way to worship various gods, especially the gods of fertility whose temple priestesses were ministered to, in place of the actual goddess, perhaps even in a sexual manner, by other women?

The Greek poet, Euripedes, wrote of frenzied religious celebrations of the god Dionysus. It is also mentioned under the "Mystery Religions" topic in the NIV Archeological Study Bible, that Dionysian worship consisted of a madness of orgiastic, even gory acts that were for a time outlawed by the Roman senate because they were so hideous and offensive to even them.

I want to stop a moment and give you further thoughts to struggle with. Here we have rich, spoiled, young Roman boys who grew up to be rich, spoiled Roman men of the Roman senate. For their entire lives, it had been totally acceptable and legal for Roman citizens to have *non-consensual* sex with others, male or female, child or adult, as long as they were slaves and not citizens. No one cast a second thought over such actions. And now, we see records of that time in the words of Euripedes that outlawed the acts of "worship" taking place in the temple of Dionysus because even they, the senate, couldn't deal with the gory offensiveness of acts. These hideously, gruesome and bloody acts leave our thoughts of homosexuality today in the dust. There is no comparison. They are not synonymous.

The Bible doesn't allow us to actually pinpoint how quickly after the fall of man in the Garden of Eden these vile acts of worship to a replacement god of man's imagination began. But as historical documents relaying attitudes of worship from thousands of years ago show, from what the ancient voices of old wrote and told, the worst of the worst had a powerful hold on the people of Rome. Paul was not simply trying to slay a dragon of man's invention. His words here in Romans chapter one were meant to destroy a kingdom of dragons where evil had lived and reigned far, far before the birth of Jesus.

We take comfort in the fact that Paul's existence along with the other apostles of Christ show God's grace over everlasting time as He preserves His remnant unto Himself as an eternal witness until the end of time. What was going on here in these temples makes adultery, fornication, deceitfulness, thievery, gossip, envy, arrogance, boastfulness , murder, disobedience, sexual immorality, or any other act, on their own, seem like bad behavior in comparison. I am not trying to say what you or I understand to be sin doesn't matter. I am trying to show a bigger truth of Roman times that we seem to naively misunderstand. Because man boldly turned his back on God, the resulting worship of godlessness became such a deadly acting bacteria that man could no longer escape its clutches because he had severed the power line that God alone provides to protect and to save.

So, returning to my point, wouldn't I be evil and wicked because I chose to worship a godless idol? Wouldn't every bit of my life, "clean or dirty" be an irreconcilable waste? Can we begin to understand it in the context of godlessness? Isn't that a legitimate question in order to understand the godless Romans? It seems somewhat far-fetched to believe all those idol worshippers in Rome were homosexual as we understand the term today that can include committed, loving relationships. Rome was full of heterosexual families – fathers, mothers and children that worshipped in those temples dedicated to wood and stone images from man's own imagination.

So now I ask, is it specifically the same gender sexual act that deserves the blasting descriptions of evil, wicked and depraved, or is it the heinous act of godless worship that deserves the descriptions? Perhaps you believe it is both. It is so easy for people who enjoy judging others to regard my words as "idiocy" or "splitting hairs" if one doesn't take the necessary time to really absorb the "what" and "why" of this question. I have all the time it takes to uncover God's truth. And we continue with our need to wrestle with Scripture.

Again, I wish to throw a stone into the pond of scriptural water and make a few additional waves of thought for you. Daniel Helminiak, Ph.D. raises a credible question about the words "contrary to nature". The Greek words, *para physin* used by Paul in these verses of Romans chapter one are also used in connection to God who also did an act "contrary to nature" by grafting in the wild olive shoot (Gentiles) to the natural branch, the family of God, in Romans 11:24 which we talked about in chapter five. God did not constitute a sinful act by what He did. It was unexpected, it was unusual, some thought it was impossibly wrong, but it wasn't sinful. So why, when Paul uses the same words, *para physin* – "contrary to nature" as applied to the women and men in chapter one do we give them an evil and wicked interpretation and not to God in Romans 11:24? If Paul's actual intent had been to portray the unnatural sexual act in and of itself as evil, could he not have used Greek words with that specific intent in his letter instead of the more benign words *para physin* meaning "contrary to nature"?

What's the correct interpretation? I don't have all the answers. And that is why we need to wrestle with scripture and call on God to lay hold of us while we wrestle, just like Jacob does in Genesis 31. When we allow God to lay hold of us and teach us we come closer to a clearer solution where sometimes things turn out to be different than what we thought they would be, because God's hand constrains the bad and allows the good to thrive.

That's why in the midst of churches, and church leaders, and church members, sometimes the only infallible truth for an individual is fully obtained when the seeking child comes to the Father, and bowing in deep humility asks for His truth. Only then do those answers that God has promised He will forever provide, answers to safeguard and draw His world in forward motion toward Him, finally and faithfully become known and usable for the individual. Then through the individual they flow like the vibration of sound and touch many lives for good.

We have a world of respected scholars with differing opinions that gravely affect how we think and live our lives. Where else should I go but to God with my questions and my heart for Him to fill? When it seems answerless questions persist, we either wrestle with our faith at God's feet or we bury our head in the sand. I personally find sitting at God's feet glorious.

Lenski's wording in his commentary seems to reveal his own feelings toward homosexuality as falling into the category of a wicked act in and of itself rather than recognizing an act as evil when used in worshipping godless idols. I hope you can understand the difference between the two uses. His commentaries were written in 1943, at a time when the label, "homosexuality" was beginning to be recognized and used in the most extremely negative manner. No one regarded homosexuals as anything but disgusting, immoral people and of course zealots added "who are going to hell" to the description. And yet, "Sin excludes no man from being declared righteous by God" are Lenski's own words, a significant truth he found in the Bible.

The two statements run on opposing courses, one toward heaven and one toward hell. The two views as they stand here will never merge as one. Do we support Lenski's view of homosexuality as the road to hell because some humans who are eager to judge others say they are going to hell? Or do we support Lenski's Biblical view that "Sin excludes no man from being declared righteous by God" which is a view of God's grace only He is capable of imparting? When we choose the view that sin doesn't exclude any man from being declared righteous by God, it places the power to judge exactly where it belongs, in God's hands. It is inconsistent to declare this as a truth everywhere in the Bible except when it applies to homosexuality.

Since that date in 1943 thousands and thousands of men, women, and children have been counseled, questioned, "treated and trained" to the extent that today a new understanding of homosexuals has emerged.

"There is one thing of which I am convinced, and that is that homosexuals do not choose their orientation. Whatever the causal factors may be, I am sure that the imprinting of the orientation occurs so early in the biological/social/psychological development of the person that he or she can never recall having made a conscious choice." 2 Campolo. Campolo has spent countless hours in prayerful counsel with abused, hurting people who are gay. His belief is that they absolutely do not choose their sexual and gender orientation. Equally important, the "why" of that orientation is not available to us. His voice is just one among many now risking their reputations in the world to show that God's love encompasses all people equally, that homosexuality isn't something to fear or ostracize. The back lash from the Christian community has not always been kind or worthy to leaders such as he.

It's Not Just About Sex

Now Paul moves us from immoral sex to those other sins equally destructive – every kind of "wickedness, evil, greed and depravity". "They are full of envy, murder, strife, deceit and malice. They are gossips, slanderers, God-haters, insolent, arrogant and boastful; they invent ways of doing evil; they disobey their parents; they are senseless, faithless, heartless, and ruthless. Although they know God's righteous decree that those who do such things deserve death, they not only continue to do these very things but also approve of those who practice them." Romans 1:29-32.

Maybe it's just me but I see sins in these verses that I have at times participated in during my own life, a life dedicated to the one true God; some I still fall into that need sweeping out of my heart. They are not considered wicked, evil, greedy and depraved by God toward those He counts as His children, because as His child whose heart fights against those very sins, they don't exist when I or any other believer stands before Him.

The difference between me today and the Romans Paul wrote to is that these sins were attached to their godless society and they took over the lives of these people. Paul was warning the church to be vigilant and on guard against being drawn back into godlessness, for it would become a man eating bacteria that would infiltrate their spirits until it would began to eat away and destroy each victim. Without God, these were malignant acts taking on a life of their own that enjoyed being the destroyer of human lives.

Perhaps the most difficult for us as Christians to understand is Paul's last observation in verse 32. On some level they knew their actions deserved God's judgment, which results in eternal death, but they didn't care because they rejected God as their enabler for righteousness. They embraced their downfall and enjoyed the same catastrophe in the lives of their friends. We wonder how they could fall so far.

It is amazing though, the strength we get from the herd mentality and the downfall that can result from it when we ignore thinking and acting by what our heart tells us is right. For instance, envision yourself at a restaurant having a great time, but suddenly your conscience begins to prick you due to the conversation. But you push it aside because you are with all your friends, good people, and yes, maybe you've all had a little too much to drink. The jokes going around the table about the gay waiter aren't meant to hurt anyone, and everyone stops when he comes around your table, so what's the big deal?

The big deal could be the lady at the next table who suffers so much in her life that she cannot face coming out of the closet. She catches your dribble of conversations floating her way. Arriving home she weeps because once again her spirit is crushed. She pulls out the drawer next to her bed and takes out the razor. She keeps it in the drawer now because some nights it's just too far to go to the bathroom shelf to retrieve it. Slowly she draws the blade up her arm, over and over again. This pain she can control. And sometimes it releases that other pain deep inside. *You know I didn't ask for this, God. Why do you let them do this to me? I don't know how much more I can take.*

It could be a thirteen year old boy eating dinner with his unsuspecting family and he goes home once again to his prayers pleading for God to take away his desires for the same gender because he can't bear the shame he endures from jokes and conversations of others, sometimes the supposedly "innocent", "good intentioned" others.

Maybe the gray haired gentleman goes home and wonders when if ever he will be able to let down his defensive guard in public. He is so weary and he has an early surgery scheduled. They love him when he removes the tumors from their child's brain, but he is not worthy to sit at the heterosexual table and eat a meal with them.

Nor the policeman, the teacher, the fireman, the lifeguard, the funeral director, the store manager, the nurse, the physical therapist, the pharmacist, the vet assistant; all are unwelcome at the heterosexual table. How much pain we release into the world and yet go home each night deeply self-satisfied with our day and sleep the sound sleep of the ignorant and uncaring. Could this be you? At one time it was me.

It seems we spent an extraordinary amount of time on verses 26 and 27 compared to verses 28 to 32. I guess that would be necessary because the world has spent so much time identifying these verses as the justification for hate or indifference for LGBTQs.

However, our story doesn't end here. Paul's letter continues into the next chapter and the two cannot be separated if it is to achieve Paul's purpose, explaining judgment and personal justification of faith for sinners. These two chapters are conjoined twins that share one heart and must stay connected.

I know this may be difficult for some, but this is a truth in our Bibles, and if Romans chapter one is the final hurdle preventing you from totally accepting and reconnecting with your child or loved one, or making peace with anyone who is gay, please stay with me today. This is too important to give up on. You are smart enough to follow this.

Normally I would make a chapter break here. But because I so strongly believe chapters one and two of Romans are conjoined in such a way I will not. I will simply refer to this next section as Part Two.

Before I launch into Romans two, Lenski brings several verses into his commentary here to expand the understanding of his lesson.

John 8:15 & 16 says, "You judge by human standards; I pass

judgment on no one. But if I do judge, my decisions are right because I am not alone. I stand with the Father, who sent me."

1. Our sin filled human standards are not sufficient to judge *anyone* as good or bad. Not my words, God's. Then Jesus says He passes judgment on no one! It's not His appointed job any more than mine or yours.

John 3:17, "For God did not send His Son into the world to condemn the world, but to save the world through him."

2. Take condemning others off your agenda. It's the same as judging.

Luke 19:22, "...I will judge you by your own words, you wicked servant!"

3. Who and how you judge can and will be used against you by God. Or as St. Frances of Assisi said, "It is in pardoning that we are pardoned." 3 Assisi.

Matthew 7:1-5. "Do not judge, or you too will be judged. For in the same way you judge others, you will be judged, and with the measure you use, it will be measured to you. Why do you look at the speck of sawdust in your brother's eye and pay no attention to the plank in your own eye? How can you say to your brother, 'Let me take the speck out of your eye', when all the time there is a plank in your own eye? You hypocrite, first take the plank out of your own eye, and then you will see clearly to remove the speck from your brother's eye."

4. Just don't judge!

Most of us don't focus on verse one of Matthew 7 because we think we understand it. We quickly slide down to those words about first removing your own plank and then you can remove your brother's speck. I'm going to give you something to put in your new wineskin I hope you found for yourself after reading chapter six. Based on so much scripture about our inability to fix others, I do not believe God is suddenly giving us permission to remove our brother's speck! Do you actually think God is suggesting we could ever remove the plank, sin, from ourselves when throughout scripture we are repeatedly told this is impossible? Why does Jesus say it then? Is it possible He wants to show us how absurd our self-righteous thoughts become. You think you can remove this brother's sin? Fine, remove you own sin first! And don't even try to remove his speck until every last plank of sin has been removed from your own. Verse one, "Do not judge, or you too will be judged."

PART TWO Something Worse Than The Sins In Chapter One? Or, Get Ready For A Bumpy Ride

Hasn't the climax of sin of been reached in Romans 1:32? Paul answers this question in a profound way. No, the climax is only climaxed in the man who does the very opposite! "But here is the moralist – his ilk is numerous – who will fully agree with all that Paul says about this general wickedness, who will even sit in judgment on another man...under the delusion that this moralism and its serious practice...exempts them from an indictment such as this one made by Paul. The apostle turns the tables on them: by their very moralism they seal their own conviction." 4 Lenski.

Paul takes on the moralist. For many, moralism has become their private gospel. I would remind you again that this letter was written and still is written to Christians. We need to know and completely understand this grave message from history, perhaps to our own judgment. Paul is not personally singling out an individual person here. As far as I know Paul never stood in front of another person face-to-face and point blank laid their guilt before them with a moralist attitude except when his name was Saul. The reason I lean toward this belief is because in chapter two Paul tells us he leaves it to the individual to recognize his own guilt, a conviction not even he, an apostle of God can bring about. This is a tool of witnessing some of us desperately need to re-examine in our lives.

The Lifeline Conjoining Chapter One To Chapter Two

"The fact that men have God in their consciousness, know that they are worthy of death and yet do the death-worthy things and applaud others who do them, this fact does not establish the truth that the man who judges, condemns, and seeks to stop them is 'without excuse'." 5 Lenski. All those pronounced immoral and godless in Romans chapter one are not to be judged by others. In the Greek translation, Paul sets a brand of greater guilt upon these people who presume they can judge sinners when they, as humans, exist within the same condemnation as sinners. Once again we wrestle with Scripture.

These arrogant judges say sinners must stop, must completely change their actions. Why is this man worse than the sinners of Romans 1: 26, 27 & 32? Because he thinks to himself, "Why, he is a thousand times better! Certainly all should stop and be stopped. And yet this judge is the worst of all, doubly 'without excuse', not only worse in his person but also in his influence on others. He represents the very delusion that must be destroyed if the gospel is to stand." 6 Lenski. Stop right here. Do you see how we at times, ignorantly and self-righteously push ourselves forward and get in God's way when we think it is our responsibility to "love" others into seeing their sins? It actually translates out to "loving to show others their sins". If true Gospel love is to be rightly represented in our world, we must do our part to destroy this delusion. We step aside in prayer and let God show man his sins.

So what is this delusion that must be destroyed if the gospel is to stand? Doesn't the moralist agree with Paul and God's wrath in Romans one? Only as far as their agreement on what the Law says; all else becomes their disagreement. And that is what the entire Gospel in all its Divine power is bound up in. Paul, in his letter to the Romans, is exposing godlessness and unrighteousness, not by exposing a guilty person face-to-face, but to warn a congregation of people who need to understand the difference between Gospel grace and the moralist delusion that says all we need is to keep the Law.

Paul exposes the godlessness and unrighteousness of men in 1:32, saying their ability to recognize how thoroughly their sins are going against them is possible only through the now miniscule recognition of the righteous teachings of Christ, the prophets and the apostles. Some tiny bit of God's righteousness hovers on the tattered edge of their lives holding the possibility to enter and grow the spirit of truth even at this late date. Without the ability to retain this small understanding of God's righteousness, they would have no way to identify their deeds as deserving of death.

Then Paul slams us with the truth, that this is in fact *God's own chosen tool* to *drive* them back to His righteousness, a pure faith that renders salvation! God's merciful, longsuffering patience will wait for sin to drag the godless into the abyss where in time, the sinner might at last discover that one little righteous kernel ready to be placed in a heart yearning for even one tiny scrap of grace from heaven's Gardener.

For those who have descended into an earthly hell like these in 1:32, "...when, then, God's law and the gospel reach them, it is not a difficult matter to bring them to repentance." 7 Lenski. And please take note, "law" is with a little "L" referring to God's righteous law and not the Levitical Law. Now do you see the single heart of these conjoined chapters that must not be separated? To stop reading at the end of Romans chapter one is to totally miss and never understand "the sinner's personal justification of faith" and totally loose the thread of God's Gospel gift of salvation for all people.

I want to quickly share I was taught in a very prominent national Bible study that those in 1:32 no longer had hope. But set against the backdrop of Romans chapter two and the entire Gospel, I see words teaching something entirely different, and this difference I now confidently speak as my own truth. Paul has not given up on those in 1:32 because God has not given up on them. They have turned away from God and He has allowed it, but until their final breath, we who can't see the heart can only hope, the power of God's Gospel, in and through Jesus, can still turn their hearts to Him. That's a large part of what our job is – hope that finds its strongest weapon in prayer to a Christ who intercedes for us in heaven.

What Does The Moralist Receive In Return?

So what motivates the moralist? This type of judge doesn't just condemn. Paul isn't saying the moralist simply condemns these sinners. "He also acquits, even commends, namely all those who bow to him and obey him. Nor is he a mere denouncer; his denunciations are issued for the purpose of getting men to reform, in order that he may commend and praise them. In 1:32 the wicked applaud the wicked; this judge applauds those who reform. He is a mighty moralist who is acclaimed as 'a power for good in the world' and proud of this." 8 Lenski. How many sermons have you heard to help you understand this seemingly confusing truth?

There was a time I thought what Martha did with hard work was better than what Mary did, sitting at the feet of Jesus. We might think God would find it acceptable to applaud those who reform. And yet, we are forced to ask ourselves, who would our acclaim be going to, the man who "changed" or the man who "changed" him? And for what reason would we be applauding? Because we think they had accomplished some great thing? God miraculously brings about any change in a man's heart and life, and the worship and glory all go to Him. This truth the moralist fails to embrace.

The moralist is guided strictly by the Law and deludes himself into believing he is God's right hand man. God needs him. He performs the task he erroneously believes he has been "called" to do. And then he takes it one step further, he becomes a "god" in his own mind by acquitting and commending the "former sinner". He repeatedly uses Law, Law, Law, to induce guilt and shame for the sinner's need to change their self. Once by "his own works" he is able to get a sinner to change, he acquits them of their sin by announcing them cured, saved. Now the world can see and exclaim what a great and wonderful man this reforming moralist is. God must be so pleased at what he has done.

It is essential for each and every one of us to understand this truth: only God acquits. Only God can pronounce the guilty "not guilty". The Bible concerns itself with who God is and what He can do. It's not about what man can do. How many ways does Holy Scripture have to say this before we finally slap our heads and shout, "I finally get it"?

Moralists aren't just people somewhere out there. They are me and you. They are people in our churches and in our society, in our homes and in our workplaces. So with critical honesty we look in our spiritual mirror and ask, "Am I the moralist Paul is condemning?" How do we answer? I guess that depends on how far our "good intentions of Law" take us and what affect the Gospel has in our lives. The most damning thing is that the moralist doesn't even recognize himself for what he is until he is totally flattened by the Gospel in an act of God's grace!

I freely admit I have acted upon moralist tendencies in my past concerning LGBTQs. Only when I took my inner child before God and begged Him to give me His truth was I broadsided by this humility producing piece of Gospel. I pray God ties me up in His yoke and never lets me go.

The moralist knows all about the judgment of God, His censoring and reforming others. Therefore, with all his knowledge, this man makes the assumptions that his "holy" attitude and actions are enough and that he doesn't even need to investigate his own need to repent. He is quite fit and right in his life and others will be also if only they heed his words. And when others heed his advice on the Law and what they must do to make their lives right with God, this deadly deception continues because the "newly saved" now follow that same example to "save" others. Because of who he is and what he does in his own eyes, the moralist is satisfied in his own mind that he will escape any judgment from God.

Salvation By Reform?

God's riches of His kindness, tolerance and patience are scorned by the moralist because he does not see these as God's way of bringing men to Him. In truth, God allows men to heap their sins day after day upon His holy shoulders giving all men time for the Gospel to come alive in their lives. The moralist refuses God's patience because he doesn't work within a framework of patience himself. He denounces and constantly provokes God's judgment and even arranges God's judgment to suit himself. That patience could have anything to do with repentance never enters his mind.

When man envisions he can use the Law in any form to change people he is going down a lost road. "To regard it (law) as the last word is to turn the law into just what the moralists make it, as offering salvation by reform, the very thing Paul shows to be impossible." 9 Lenski. *Salvation by reform!*" That very thing the Apostle Paul knows to be impossible and wants to show us so we can understand its grave error.

Reading through this chapter just screams reparative therapy to me. For those unfamiliar with this term it is an intense, guilt induced, hounding, sanitized by the word "therapy", to change a homosexual into a heterosexual. The man or woman who suggests to anyone who will listen that reparative therapy is a must in the lives of LGBTQs is hard at work on their own moralist agenda using a majority misconception to boost their own careers and concerns. Politicians, pay attention. Those thousands of smiling faces and clapping hands who rally around this one and his agenda are no less guilty by refusing to investigate this lie.

Constituents, pay attention. "The business of every moralist is the reformation of others." 10 Lenski. Reformation their way.

Paul doesn't confront the moralist with head-on declarations of his sin. His own letter recorded in chapter two verifies that Paul never rubbed men's sins into their faces. His reason is sound. That would only allow the moralist to dig in and deny anything Paul may be trying to get him to see. It would produce the opposite effect of Paul's desire.

Instead, Paul uses questions that need an answer to begin to stir this man's mind in relation to truth, God's righteous truth. Paul disarms him by first declaring all the good things this man thinks he has done: a guide for the blind, being a light for those in the dark, preaching to others about stealing, disobedience, lying, gossiping or sexual immorality. Then he exposes the true sin in this moralist's life asking him if he has ever dishonored God by breaking any of God's Laws? As he is such a formidable man of the Law the moralist must answer truthfully and admit his own sin, otherwise he will be forced to recognize that nothing he has said has any validity. Wham! And there is the truth upon him.

Then Paul begins to confront a mournful truth saying, "As it is written: 'God's name is blasphemed among the Gentiles because of you.'" Paul wants any possible moralist in the church at Rome or in our churches today to see himself as God sees him. God cares about His name. Ezekiel 36:20-23. "Salvation is found in no one else, for there is no other name under heaven given to men by which he must be saved." Acts 4:12.

"In the case of the moralist judge, this inner self-conviction is Paul's aim, and in the case of his Christian readers, the purpose is that they shall see man's self-conviction, see that moralism, so far from saving even its highest exponents, convicts them, yea, unless they repent and drop their moralism, destroys them." 11 Lenski. And we wrestle with Scripture.

"For out of the heart come evil thoughts, murder, adultery, sexual immorality, theft, false testimony, slander." Matthew 15:19. The evil heart produces evil, not to be confused with the heart of God's children who long to produce righteousness which the body cannot always follow. "No moralism has ever been invented that could free the heart from lasciviousness." 12 Lenski. "For out of the heart", that place once considered the seat of purity, can only project the lascivious darkness of godlessness when it is hardened against God, void of Christ's Gospel grace.

In truth, there is nothing left but the Gospel! "Solo Fide", faith alone is left when works are shown in no way to affect salvation. God does not contradict His own righteousness. Circumcision was God's seal for the covenant and not the covenant itself. And now a New Covenant has superseded the old. "The ceremonial features of 'the Law' were temporary, but its 'righteous ordinances': were permanent. Circumcision, kosher eating, etc., would cease according to God's own will but not fear, love, and trust in God, true use of his name, prayer, worship in faith and the true godly life." 13 Lenski. Notice the righteous ordinances have nothing to do with "thou shalt", "thou shalt not". They have everything to do with man embracing who God is and giving back to Him the true adoration and worship He deserves.

There is no reason even to bring up the moral Laws of old, because the New Covenant of Jesus' priesthood superseded them with two new Laws that cover all the old, and they are in the spirit here described by Lenski, fear, love, trust, prayer, worship in faith, a godly life.

"The Gentile has foreskin but has it only 'due to nature', and thus not as involving a base attitude of heart toward God who brought him into the world with foreskin." 14 Lenski. This Gentile mentioned is brought into the world by God with his "foreskin", which, during the old covenant, became the symbol of man's separation from God. Paul explains, it does not automatically indicate a base or faithless attitude toward God under the new covenant. This Gentile man symbolizes homosexuals and heterosexuals brought into the world by God with sin "due to nature", and who is not found faithless when through Gospel faith he is found to fulfill the righteous law through the ransom of Jesus Christ. His sins that cry out daily to heaven for punishment have secured his release because Jesus has paid the ransom price. The moralist, even if he has circumcision and the entire Old Testament lessons, stands guilty before God if he does not have the Gospel of Jesus.

All delusion to following the Law for salvation, for Jews, Gentiles or Christians is destroyed. Not only will the moralist not be a judge, he will neither serve as an accuser or as an accusing witness before God. And as he stands unrepentant before God, the things he used to judge others God will now use to judge him. "Someone worse than a homosexual a spiritually complacent world asks?" The moralist brought down by the Gospel truth of God is humbling in the extreme, especially to realize it could be me – it could be you.

So Where Do I Stand?

Only the "Heart Seeker" has the key to all the knowledge we desire. We cannot fully understand God's relationship to sin. But I do know this much, every single book in my Bible points us to a personal faith relationship with the Father because of what He has done and continues to do through His Son, not what I can do. The sinner can be assured of a personal justification through faith. The book of Romans and the entire New Testament assures us of this. Today's homosexual, bisexual, transgender whose heart is in God's possession has no sin in God's mind. It has been removed as far as the east is from the west, just like the sin of heterosexuals. We are equal; we are the same.

There is no man-producing action resulting from guilt or shame under any law that can save a man. Salvation by reform doesn't exist. Only God can circumcise the heart, the seat of faith that says, *I declare thee righteous.*

135

So let me ask you a critical question. Whether one is born a homosexual, or through some mechanism when they are so young they cannot remember moving into its influence, or a choice they make for whatever reason, will you officially label them incapable of faith and salvation even as they live the remainder of their lives in the only way they are capable of, as LGBTQs loved by God, covered by Jesus blood, now and forever restored by a circumcised heart to God's kingdom? Covered by the new covenant of Jesus Christ, will you deny them the equalities you take for granted every day due to some moralist objective?

I want to share a quote by C.S. Lewis. "Finally...I want to make it as clear as I possibly can that the center of Christian morality is not here (found among our sexual desires whatever they may be). If anyone thinks that Christians regard 'unchastity' as the supreme vice, he is quite wrong...All the worst pleasures are purely spiritual: the pleasure of putting other people in the wrong, of bossing and patronizing and spoiling sport, and back-biting; the pleasures of power, of hatred...That is why a cold, self-righteous prig who goes regularly to church may be far nearer to hell than a prostitute." 15 Lewis. Lewis' literary style reflects the decencies of his day as *Mere Christianity* was first published in 1943. But he makes his point quite clearly, I think. "All the worst pleasures are purely spiritual." And here we thought our spirituality absolved us.

Last night at church my pastor asked, "If you could be present for one event in Jesus' life which would it be?" I thought about it off and on during the rest of the sermon. Shaking his hand at the door on leaving the service I told him I would chose to be at Levi's (Matthew's) house with the prostitutes, tax collectors and other sinners so I could watch Jesus' every facial expression and movement, and hear every single word from His mouth. I'd do this so I could learn to love sinners exactly as He did. "For Jesus' pure heart could see God in all people, even enemies." 16 McCollough.

"In modern times it is scarcely possible to appreciate the scandal caused by His table fellowship with sinners…it was legally forbidden to mingle with sinners who were outside the law." 17 Manning. Jesus willingly broke the law of man to serve the higher laws of His Father. Jesus spent as much time as possible with the lowly, the poor, the invisible, the unwanted.

At one point his own brothers came asking for him. Jesus was teaching and when he heard they were there Jesus responds, "Who are my mother and brothers?" He looked at those poor and spiritually hungry seated near Him listening to His words and holding out His hand indicating them, His audience, Jesus says, "Here are my mother and my brothers! Whoever does God's will is my brother and sister and mother." Mark 3:33-35. "By challenging his blood relatives and thus the patriarchal system, Jesus was subverting the whole structure that held this society together." 18 McCollough. And by calling God His Father, it was a direct refusal to honor the Roman system where Caesar called himself "Father of the Fatherland" (pater patriae) reveals McCollough.

Knowing we are all sinners, do you treat LGBTQs worse than you treat your personal friends who are also sinners? Are your sinner friends your equals? Do you love and respect your sinner friends and family members? Do you go to your sinner friends weddings? After all, they are sinners and if you break one law you've broken all the laws. Does Jesus tell you to discriminate on choosing which sinners you should treat like yourself and which ones you should cut yourself off from?

Jesus ate with, talked and laughed with, rubbed shoulders with and slept beside sinners. He risked His life to love the sinners everyone else hated, and He loved them with a purer love than we even love ourselves with.

When God's Holy Spirit goes into the homes of LGBTQs to dine with them are you going to stay outside on the porch and miss life? When God's Spirit goes to a gay or lesbian wedding because He loves them, died for them, and no longer counts their sins against them, are you going to miss the celebration and sit outside e-mailing your sinner friends and bad mouth what's going on? If Jesus loves sinners so much, the ones you choose to "righteously" ignore, maybe it's time to reconsider what exactly your relationship is with Him. Perhaps you are not the friend to Him you thought you were. You don't seem to trust His judgment much at this time.

"The point to be noted here is the fact that sin, excludes no man from being declared righteous by God...Here we see how far the promise of the gospel extends; as far as sin extends, over the whole world." 19 Lenski.

For whatever reason, you may never, in your mind, be able to get past your belief that homosexuality is a sin. But you can choose to understand what the Bible lays out very clearly for even the simplest minds, even the mind of a child to understand: sin, once placed in God's powerful hands with total believing faith to be covered by his omnipotent grace, no longer exists in the spiritual realm of God. Isn't it time we start living our lives under that precept?

There will always be people who don't choose to live their life with faith in God's promises. Not every homosexual is a believer nor is every heterosexual. We give them over to Jesus in our prayers and never approach them as a moralist to fix them so we can say look what I did. We love them as Jesus loved sinners when he walked the earth, as His equals in the Kingdom of His Father, a Kingdom freely given that can't be bought.

Saints will always be sinners; but sinners can always become saints.

CHAPTER 9 WHAT DO WE SAY TO THE SILENCE?

"This is the confidence we have in approaching God: that if we ask anything according to his will, he hears us. And if we know that he hears us – whatever we ask – we know that we have what we asked of him." 1 John 5:14-15.

I'd like you to meet some people. This first is a man named John Stanger who works with youth in New York. Through his work, John hopes to guide young men and women toward a loving relationship with their Father, even if they don't recognize Him as such yet. John made an insightful comment once, powerful in its impact, that I feel the need to share with you. Here is what he has to say. "So many gay children grow up terrified of who they are. They begin to hate themselves because they learn quickly from their peers and adults through Bible based bullying that who they are is unlovable by God. I can remember being as young as twelve and praying through tears that God would change me. When people compare being a lesbian, gay, bisexual, transgender to sins like adultery, they inevitably get it wrong. An adulterer does not lie awake at night at the age of thirteen crying and praying to God to change them." 1 Stanger.

And his prayers were met with silence.

I'd like to examine John's words for a moment. I don't know what sort of childhood you had growing up. I've already shared mine was safe, loving and secure. So it breaks my heart to think of a child who can become terrified of *who* he is. I do remember one time I had to walk down what seemed to me a long, dark hallway to get to my Sunday School class. I imagined "things" were there I couldn't see that were waiting to frighten me or maybe hurt me. But John's words, "terrified of *who* he was," is beyond me. Compound that fear with the belief that he is unloved by God and I wonder, how did John turn out to be the loving, caring, intelligent, God-fearing man he is today?

We see John Stanger, a thirteen year old with all the insecurities and embarrassments that naturally come with being a new teenager. But that's not enough tension. Here he is, a young teen, with tears of pain and desperation, and rather than spend a lifetime of emotional torture at the hands of insensitive people, he begged God to hear him and answer his call for help. He begged God.

Does that make you stop and question what this is all about? What is really going on in the world we thought we knew? Is it just possible there is a new reality and we very much need God's help in processing this according to our faith, the one we have always held onto? How much do I, do you really understand about people of diverse sexuality and gender and God's relationship with them? God, if we ask you as little children will you help us find an answer for what this overwhelming silence means?

I'd also like you to meet Justin Lee, who founded the Gay Christian Network in 2001. From what I read He seemed to always be the happy kid who never met a stranger and always had his Bible handy in his backpack, ready to share Jesus with another. In Jeff Chu's book, *Does Jesus Really Love Me?*, Lee shares, "There's comfort and fear in the fortress of Faith that you build around yourself, and there's excitement and terror in the weakness that you – and only you, or so you think – see in its walls. Invariably, at some point, you have this epiphany: that those walls you imagined were built of emotions and psychological

Jerusalem stone were actually made of plastic, or Legos, of things that can quickly be dismantled or obliterated." 2 Lee.

Justin's safe world fell apart when he could no longer deny that he was gay. He did not want this diversity and he tried to change. He wanted to remove himself from his homosexuality. On the day he came out to them, his parents told him they were "going to help him beat this." "I would have done anything to become straight." 3 Lee. He attended one ex-gay group after another, went to ex-gay conferences, and kept appointments with counselors. Eventually he went back to God. "I stopped praying, 'God make me straight,' and I started praying, 'God, show me what you want me to do.'" 4 Lee.

Why God's silence after each and every prayer, "God make me straight"?

Finally, in *God vs. Gay,* Jay Michaelson shares an excellent point. "For years I prayed for God to make me straight...Certainly celibacy may well be part of a spiritual path for some people, but not when it is compelled by shame." 5 Michaelson. Obviously his search for help was met with the much used advice to live a celibate life. Stop the act; then you will be acceptable. We are taught to embrace the myth, it's what you do, not your faith.

Once again, why did God remain silent to Jay's prayers to become straight?

I'd like to stop a moment and ask you to consider a hypothetical situation that many have faced in reality. You have been raised in church and understand scripture to deny homosexuality as acceptable. Your twelve year old son comes to you one evening and begins to describe what his nights and days are like. He is being teased and bullied during the day by so-called friends and at night he cries out to the God he loves to change him. He says he knows he is naturally drawn to boys and not girls and it is a part of him. He struggles to explain his feelings to you. He begins to cry as he tells you how often he has pleaded with God to change him. This has been going on for a year now. He always thought if he asked God something that God approved of, his prayer would be answered. God hasn't answered his prayer and he is scared. He wants to stay home and hide rather than go to school where he can hardly function anymore. He needs your love and help. What do you say to him?

"Again, I tell you that if two of you on earth agree about anything you ask for, it will be done for you by my Father in heaven. For where two or three come together in my name, there am I with them." (Matthew18:19).

Why are you being silent God? We cling to your promises that what we ask in your will, knowing you hear, you will answer us and grant our petition.

1 John 5:14-15 is worthy to be quoted once again. "This is the confidence we have in approaching God: that if we ask anything according to his will, he hears us. And if we know that he hears us – whatever we ask – we know that we have what we asked of him."

Why are you being silent God? What about your promise?

John, Justin and Jay are not three unfortunate and isolated individuals who happened into the same experience. There are Johns, Justins and Jays everywhere who are being met with what seems to be silence from the Father.

So I ask a worthy question that cries out for an answer – if homosexuality is not in accordance with God's will and thousands of frightened, tear filled voices continue to beg God day after day to take away this sexual feeling and replace it with feelings for the opposite sex, why hasn't God answered them like it says in Matthew 18 and 1 John 5?

There will always be smug individuals who profess to have all the knowledge, who will answer that God did try to change them only they didn't try hard enough. Hopefully you can see what a careless, cruel, hard-hearted response this is when you read it on this page. That's not compassion. That's self-righteousness. Countless children are living this nightmare, children too young to have made a choice concerning gender orientation, a topic still underdeveloped in their maturity range. They are scared and anguished and you would dare to accuse them of not trying hard enough to please God?

Thousands of prayers are seemingly being met with a silence that sadly echoes off the walls of troubled spirits who are earnestly seeking God's voice on this. Where is the answer? Am I overstepping my bounds by suggesting they deserve some kind of comfort and closure – an understanding they can spiritually wrap themselves around?

Who Sinned Rabbi?

Remember the man who was blind from birth and the Apostles asked Jesus, "Rabbi, who sinned, this man or his parents, that he was born blind?" Jesus answers neither sinned, "...but this happened so that the work of God might be displayed in his life." John 9:2-3. I wonder if as a child this man prayed and pleaded with God to give him sight. If so, were his prayers met with thundering silence? Did he go through life hurt and confused? Was he ashamed that he had to beg?

As we see from scripture, during Jesus' day, society clung to the superstition that to be born blind was the consequence of a sin in ones' life. It seems odd that the Apostles would include the man himself as one of the possible sinners since that would mean they believed the man sinned even before his birth, "...that he was born blind?" Either that or they assumed God looked forward into this man's life, saw his future sinfulness, and decided to punish him from birth, before the sins were even committed therefore making him blind. Neither scenario makes sense, nor are they Biblical.

No doubt the blind man's family was at times looked at questioningly, maybe by the superior stare of a close neighbor. Was the stare closely followed by the neighbor's smug thought that thankfully he is not such a sinner because his wife gave birth to healthy, normal children?

Forgive us, Father, but your children seem to have a need to know who the "sinners" are so we know who to blame when things go wrong in a world that we don't understand. Even this simple story reveals what we are all capable of. Perhaps it lays in the unconscious drawer of our minds, but none of us can escape the human need to at times feel we are a little better than others – that we have accomplished something right in our lives where others have failed. It allows us to sigh deeply with self-approval, something we all need, but perhaps look in the wrong places to fulfill.

The "work of God was displayed in his life" that very day. Onlookers stopped to watch. They'd heard this man Jesus was known to produce miracles. Would He do so today? Yes, He would. Jesus spit on the ground, gathered the mud made by His saliva, and put it on the man's eyes. He told the blind man to go wash in the Pool of Siloam. That very day the man could see.

With newly opened eyes, the man's life dramatically shifted that day. We don't think about his life after this encounter. I would suppose when the news spread, people came just to look at him, ask him questions, maybe tested his vision to see if the rumors were really true. But what about the people of the town, did their lives change? What about the neighbor, thankful he had never sinned because he had healthy, normal children, how do you think he viewed the miracle? Perhaps not wanting to believe, he attributed it to sorcery, an acceptable avenue to explain the unexplainable in that culture of complex "religions".

Miracles. We wish we could witness such amazing things. Perhaps we do, often in fact, and fail to recognize them because they don't measure up to what our little minds color as miracles.

Let's throw open a private door and view the life of not all, but many LGBTQs. They have been rejected, ignored, mentally or physically spit upon, and joked about on the street, in work areas, in classrooms, from the pulpit (yes it happens) and the TV. They endure shouts of obscenities, are physically harmed, some have been murdered, their private possessions stolen or destroyed. They are asked into God's house so they will see truth and change their "lifestyles" although they can't really participate nor have a role because they are too sinful. "We can't have sinful Christians in leading roles in the church" and yet that only leaves perfect Christians to assume the positions. Some, who have been raised in church and baptized, once sang in the choir or directed music, taught Sunday School classes, and who finally find the courage to come out with their sexual and gender diversities are rejected from the House of God, a house for sinners. They were good enough before and loved by their church family, but instantly are not good enough now. "Homosexuals are beyond what God will endure, their acts are an abomination and God will not accept them until they deny who they 'believe' themselves to be and change their 'lifestyles' back to heterosexual".

"Gay people are invited to be kept in a perpetual state of sin consciousness." 6 Edser. I cannot live that way. You cannot live that way. Judas, who realized beyond a doubt his act of betrayal was such a fatal sin against the Lamb of God, couldn't live that way so he killed himself. But our gay brothers and sisters guilty of those sins we all have in common are told they must live that way. They must be daily reminded "they" are not equal to "us".

Yet, there is the LGBTQ man or woman who personally knows God and loves Him. He or she never stops looking to find ways to deepen their relationship with their Father. They know God created them and loves them because they have heard the Holy Spirit call out their name. They have gladly surrendered their heart, that seat of purity, to the Father and call Jesus Christ their Savior and Brother. They refuse to be beaten down or succumb to the hard hearts of others who don't know the first thing about the complexities surrounding just living their lives day to day.

Now, tell me this is not a miracle. Tell me you see nothing of God's amazing grace at work to inspire virtue in this faith filled heart. This is not a tale. It's not a silly little character sketch. These people exist and love God with all their heart, soul and mind, trying each and every day to forgive the onslaught of never-ending pain hurled their way. Why shouldn't I listen and believe what they have to say? They are the authority of their own bodies, not me. So, do I, the lowly clay pot who cannot see or judge any heart, stand before the Potter and debate that this LGBTQ heart could not possibly belong to a Christian child of God?

There seems to be some unspoken belief that the church can never be found to have misinterpreted or incorrectly taught even the slightest part of scripture because the whole structure of God's church will come tumbling down. However, through all the changes we've witnessed throughout history, including the Gentile dogs grafted into God's family, the church continues to survive. Not just survive, but grow stronger through a surer theology all consistently directed and guided by God's living presence and His will. The church doesn't stand alone any more than a single lesbian woman seeking God stands alone. Our greatest weakness as human beings is not calling upon and using God's strength in our times of need, and this includes the universal church.

The Apostle Paul lived with a "thorn" in his side. Maybe it was because of the great heavenly revelations given directly to Paul from God that Satan was allowed to torment him with an irritant, possibly a sin, definitely a weakness, nonetheless, useful to maintain Paul's humility. 2 Corinthians 12:9. God does not always give a specific why, and yet He gives us what we need to understand the story and move forward. Paul was told it would not be removed because God's own strength would be revealed through Paul's weakness.

Why are you silent God? Maybe there is nothing in all the requests from His hurting children that God feels the need to change. Maybe He hasn't left you without an answer after all; He is just patiently waiting to reveal the full story so mankind can move forward relying only on Him. "God determines voluntarily what and whom He will create, times, places, circumstances, of their lives. He makes out the path of all His rational creatures, determines their destiny, and uses them for His purposes...God has reasons for willing as He does, which induce Him to choose one end rather than another, and one set of means to accomplish one end in preference to others. There is in each case a prevailing motive which makes the end chosen and the means selected the most pleasing to Him, though we may not be able to determine what His motive is." 7 Berkhof. We can't discern the mysteries of God's will when He chooses to keep them hidden from us. But we do not have to fear God's will. "Where there is charity and wisdom, there is neither fear nor ignorance." 8 Assisi. We do not have to succumb to fearful confusion as God moves among the circumstances or disorder created by each new generation. Yes, let's not forget it is always ourselves or others or things responsible for creating the disorder in our lives. Never God.

Jesus said He would be with you always and never forsake you. No matter how high or how low, you are always mine, He said. Jesus never had bitterness in His heart. He never gave up on other people. You shouldn't either. If you are a sexual and gender diverse individual and just want to live your life with all the possibilities and freedoms other people enjoy, don't give up. If you are a heterosexual Christian and have doubts about what you have always understood to be true about homosexuals, and you now have questions and are looking for answers, don't give up.

Jesus asked for help (a drink) from the very men trying to kill Him. It is a hard thing to understand, even harder to do, but Jesus prayed for them even as they gambled for His only possessions. Jesus is the Divine DNA that holds us together. While there will always be some people against you, not everyone is. If you are gay, there will always be bands of people against you throughout your lifetime. If you are straight and are finding healing and a new compassion for gays, those same bands of people who insist their way is the right way will be against you also. There, you now have something in common with each other. God is not against you, even in His silence. "I thirst". Jesus understands your humanity. Jesus, the living water who gives us life won't force His gift – He offers it to us. Drink deeply until the satisfaction flows over you, and from you, leading others to also freely drink. Whether homosexual or heterosexual, you too have a gift to give. Don't wait to use it.

CHAPTER 10 WHEN THE POWER OF GRACE INITIATES HEALING

"It is Good For Our Hearts to be Strengthened by Grace…" Hebrews 13:9

Have you ever wondered why Jesus didn't come to earth sooner? Or why didn't God just deal with Satan then and there in the garden? Knowing after the flood mankind would eventually follow his own way right back into sinful self-destruction, why did God destroy everyone except Noah and his family? God hates idolatry. Why was Aaron's life spared for fashioning the golden idol in the first place? And why a little later did God specifically instruct Moses to fashion a serpent of bronze, an image, and place it high on a pole for the people to look upon and be healed from the bite of poisonous snakes in the desert? I bet a few Israelites were confused by that, being unaware at that time that one day Jesus would also be lifted up to save mankind.

Human beings have questions. It's normal. I get excited by questions and have learned digging in my Bible for answers sometimes leads to great spiritual treasure. Others may raise their eyebrows over questions, but when their head hits the pillow at the end of the day not having even one question answered isn't a problem for them. In fact they may have forgotten what the questions were in the first place.

Clearly we all have different personalities that we are born with. God deals differently with one man from another. We don't all learn the same so we must be taught by different methods and God accommodates us in this. You can't read through the Bible very long before that becomes evident. It partially explains why at times my perception of God differs from yours. But this need not polarize our lives. And it doesn't mean our uniqueness prevents either of us from being whole in Him or holy in Him.

Our personalities manifest themselves in different ways, but a central truth is that we are all created in God's image – not just a few of us – all of us in equal measure. It should be reasonable then to agree that even though our personalities vary in many ways, in the essence of our created selves we are the same. So how might this work to our advantage to heal our hearts and relationships with sexual and gender diverse individuals?

Let's See.
You need food, I need food – we are the same.
You need water, I need water – we are the same.
You need air, I need air – we are the same.
You have a skeleton, I have a skeleton – we are the same.
You communicate, I communicate – we are the same.
You have thoughts, I have thoughts – we are the same.
You learn, I learn – we are the same.
You are sexual, I am sexual – we are the same.
You bleed, I bleed – we are the same.
You love and hate, I love and hate – we are the same.
You have feelings, I have feelings – we are the same.
You hurt, I hurt – we are the same.
You are a sinner, I am a sinner – we are the same.

You are made in God's image, I am made in God's image – we are the same.

The essence of our humanity is the same which binds us together.

Now I have a variance list that I want you to go through.

You are short, I am tall – we are the same.

You have facial hair, I have hair on my head – we are the same.

You have red hair, I have gray hair – we are the same.

You are blind, I can see – we are the same.

You are young, I am older – we are the same.

You are vegetarian, I love meat – we are the same.

You love sports, I love reading – we are the same.

You speak Spanish, I speak English – we are the same.

You sink, I swim – we are the same.

You have autism, I do not – we are the same.

You live in a mansion, I live in a moderate house – we are the same.

You have taken a person's life, I have not – we are the same.

You don't go to church, I do – we are the same.

You are male, I am female – we are the same.

You have a yacht, I have a picture of a boat – we are the same.

You are married to one of the same sex, I am married to one of the opposite sex – we are the same.

I used to work at a florist shop taking orders and assisting the public. My friend, Crickette, who still works there is a floral artist. We are the same. She once told me a very important fact about her work. When putting together floral arrangements you first have to know the rules and have practiced them with understanding before you can begin to break the rules and still achieve quality work. Another way of saying this is until a person understands the lay of the land and what the parameters are, you can't really be successful when you move outside the parameter or outside the box and expect to be successful.

Until you and I understand who we are as human beings, who we are at the essential core of our humanity made equally in the image of God, we will never be able to fully relate or see our sameness to each and every other person on the planet, or in our country, down the street, or in our home. And we won't master the ability to turn out beautiful, high quality relationships with consistency. Do you see that I am placing the first and most important step in this process with myself and with yourself?

When you went through my first list did you have any trouble agreeing with the statements? What about when you went through the variance list, could you agree with all the statements? If you didn't, I'd like you to take a moment and go back over that list, stopping by each one to determine whether you agree or disagree. If you disagree, I'd like you to ask yourself, "In comparing my essential humanity to your essential humanity, where God created us both in His image, why are we not the same?" You need to be brutally honest with yourself. Did you consider yourself superior or inferior? Then ask yourself, "Do I or do I not believe in my heart the words of God when he said all men were made in His image?" I'm not asking you to define what the word "image" consists of, but to use this exercise so you will understand there is a core of sameness and equality on us crowned by the hand of God the Creator.

At first you may rebel at this idea. I can't see you after all, and you can just as easily keep reading and forget the lists. But sometimes healing is very difficult and takes a huge toll on our energy, our bodies, and our emotions. The question then becomes, exactly what am I willing to do to initiate healing among myself and those I have been taught are extreme sinners?

My children were in high school before I went back to school to earn a degree as a Registered Nurse. Early in my nursing career there was one patient in particular that will forever stand out in my memory. She was a fairly large woman who had spent a great part of her days laying around, perhaps watching TV and eating. I know this because she had spent so much time on her back that she had developed huge pressure sores around the lower rear pelvic area, near the lowest spinal bone, with a smaller sore on each heel.

She couldn't see how bad they were. She didn't understand the healing that needed to take place. My job each night was to remove the saline packing from the approximately four inch diameter by one to two inch deep wound. I had to pay particular attention to what I was doing because the wound was also tunneling beneath the skin surface where you couldn't see for at least three inches and maybe more. I would ease the packing out and throw away every dirty item I had used. I would then thoroughly wash, re-glove and set out a sterile field in order to repack the wound with sterile saline gauze to hopefully promote healing so she could eventually heal enough to return home. This was not a quickie job.

My patient would get frustrated and complain about how long it was taking me. It was tedious work and her remarks were discouraging so I began to time myself to see if I could complete the job quicker each successive night and hopefully reduce the tension it was creating for her. As I recall, the first night took me around forty minutes to complete my work.

About the third night a doctor came into the room and informed me that the woman's sister was there. He wanted me to call him when the pack had been removed because he planned to bring the sister into the room and show her the extensive damage to her sisters' body. You see, the lady visiting that night didn't believe there was really too much wrong with her sister and she wanted the hospital to release her so they could go home. Well that was going to ruin my nightly race against the clock, but this lady needed to see how badly her sister's body needed healing.

I pulled off the tape and protective covering and begin to pull and pull and pull out the gauze until the wound was completely exposed. The doctor brought the sister into the room to inspect the ugly exposed layers of muscle and tissue and she immediately broke down crying. My patient still couldn't see the sore, but the reaction of her sister had a sobering effect on her that night and afterwards was less inclined to whine about her treatment. The decision was made that they wanted her to heal.

Healing is sometimes harder than we think it should be. Sometimes we just have to learn things are worse than we think they are in order to be willing to accept the work that must be done. It is essential that each and every one of us find a way to discover the sameness between all of us so the quality of our relationships with all people, from the relationship with ourselves down to the relationships with those we at first want to pull away from, will eventually reflect God's love within us.

Two weekends ago I attended my niece's baby shower just outside of Dallas. On Sunday I went to church with my childhood friend, Patti, the same Patti I talked about in chapter one. For grins I asked her mom if Patti could come home with me after church just like we did so often as little girls. Mrs. F. laughed and said no because she knew Patti was coming to central Texas to visit me for a couple of days.

I enjoyed worshiping with my friend and during the sermon these startling words caught my attention and I want to share them with you. The preacher said, "We can't stand next to each other if we can't stand each other." I like that. It fits a lot of situations and it certainly fits if you can't stand homosexuals. So what's the big deal about standing next to each other? Because Jesus asked us to in John 17:21.

Jesus' prayer will not see fulfillment as long as we refuse to let God heal us. There really is a necessary healing that needs to take place. I know not all diverse people are pleasant and friendly, but neither are all heterosexuals. But what I am talking about doesn't rest on one's sexual and gender differences or even one's friendliness. It rests on each of us asking ourselves, "Am I personally willing to give this dark place in my heart into God's hand and let Him wash it red with Jesus' blood?" Can you do it every day? When you and I are finally willing to once again surrender our willful hearts, just as we did at our baptisms, into His

154

hands so He can remold them, we will be able to admit our sameness and be a step closer to oneness in God. We crucified Him – can't we at least help answer His prayer? If you do you will discover a life focused by grace.

Are You Sin Focused Or Are You Grace Focused?

Quick, without thinking, how are you inclined to answer this question? Do you consider yourself a sin focused or grace focused person? Now let's think about it in a little more detail.

When you read about a particular sin in the Bible does a name immediately come to mind that fits the sin and it's almost never your own name?

Do you spend more time during the day thinking about how others need to recognize and repent of their sins rather than focus on your own sins?

Do you hate sin more than you have compassion and love for sinners?

Do you believe your hate accurately mimics and reflects the idea of God's purely righteous hate that is rarely spoken of in the Bible?

Do you hate someone's sin yet find it difficult to list the specific ways you love the person; and are your acts of love easily recognized by others?

Do you believe you personally are supposed to "do something" about another's sin and does it always involve going to your own self-appointed lengths to show them how sinful they are?

If so, then you are Sin Focused in your approach to life.
Now lets' switch our focus.

Can you acknowledge each day the good and the ugly, the light and the dark of who you are and how it puts you on equal footing with all others God has created?

Do you spend more of your time grateful to God that He has done all the work necessary to cancel out your sins and you want to build relationships with others based on that same unmerited grace?

Understanding your failure to earn a place with God by any act you do or don't do, do you finally forfeit your claim to heaven through your own abilities and let your life rest solely under the unmerited, unearned grace of God?

Is it more important to you that others understand grace, accepting that God's Spirit will help teach others about their sins as He sees necessary and in His own timing?

Are you content to step aside, resume the role as a follower – a disciple, and let God be God?

If so then you are Grace Focused in your approach to life.

Once again, healing requires you to take a fearless, honest and if need be, brutal assessment of what you believe about yourself and when you're done, share it with God. The first reflects the focus of the Moralist. The second reflects the focus of a humble heart resting in God.

The DNA Of A Disciples Heart

Most of us want to believe we know how to be a disciple. But if you're like me, you've attended more than just one church in your life and have listened to sermons from more than one individual, and perhaps attended different denominations in your lifetime. You have had multiple Sunday School and Bible teachers and read books by all types of authors. So if you pull it all together into one portfolio, is it wrong to question whether we clearly understand discipling according to Jesus, especially if we tend to be more sin focused in our lives? Maybe it won't hurt to have a quick look to compare our discipling with Christ's own example.

First, Christ humbled Himself and left the realm of holiness, absolute oneness and perfection with the Father, and took on the skin of humanity with its various degrees of humiliation, and we call it humility. That is what you and I hopefully have been striving toward, humility. Next Jesus entered an intense time in the desert in need of the Father's presence as He repelled the temptations of Satan. Yes, He modeled for us, how to ask for the Father's presence knowing what He would need most as He prepared for His ministry. It is important to recognize our own need to rely on our Father daily in our ministry to others.

Immediately afterwards Jesus went to the people who needed Him, the outcasts, the rejected, those outside the Hebrew Law through no want or desire of their own. Imperialist Rome was an iron fist on the Jewish leaders who walked with sly caution to preserve themselves and their safe lives to the selfish exclusion of the monetarily and spiritually poor. Ninety-seven present slaved, bent their heads and wore out their bodies to serve the three percent nobility. No, they did not choose their lifestyle no matter who might try to convince them otherwise.

Jesus first encounters Simon (Peter) and his brother Andrew and invites them to come be with Him. Jesus then creates a vision of joy when he speaks in a way they understand, "I will make you fishers of men." Matthew 4:19. This was something they loved, fishing. Jesus invites us to Him with the good He has to offer. The same happened with James and Zebedee. Fishing for men – how intriguing and exciting it sounds. Jesus went from city to city preaching the "good news" and demonstrated His love by touching people, talking to them as equals, feeding them, healing them and listening to them.

He asked Levi (Matthew) to come with Him and together they went to Levi's home where there were other sinners and Jesus ate dinner with them – where He risked his life and reputation by breaking the Law of the day, by associating with the lowest rejects of society. That's not something our Bibles tell us. Like many other ideas in scripture, we can only comprehend a more accurate meaning of verses by learning about the culture of that time.

The writers of the Bible didn't always explain their thoughts and dictations or writings in detail because they knew the people they were writing to at that time would automatically understand due to the oral traditions that had been handed down to them through the generations. They wouldn't need to repeat the details that had been a part of their verbal history for thousands of years, so why waste expensive parchment and precious time repeating it?

They weren't thinking about us in the twenty-first century, trying to decide whether or not their words and phrases would be sufficiently understood hundreds of years later. Our generation puzzling over the most accurate meaning of their words and meanings never entered the minds of ancient scribes.

With Philip the invitation is the same. Come and walk by my side, and Philip saw something in this Man that caused him to drop everything and go. But first, he was so excited that he found his friend Nathanael and tried to explain the wonderful thing he saw in Jesus. *"Here is a man not like others who pretend to be what they are not. He speaks words that compel me to want to know more. Come and see."* Nathanael, not easily persuaded by what he hasn't seen in person goes with Philip. Jesus doesn't throw Nathanael's reluctance up in his face. Instead He presents a vision. "I tell you the truth, you shall see heaven open, and the angels of God ascending and descending on the Son of Man", John 1:51, words that many still are unsure how to accurately interpret. Could it be that this predicted part of Nathanael's life was omitted from the Gospels and we will never clearly be able to understand Jesus' words here?

Jesus tells Nicodemus He didn't come to condemn the world, something we can't afford to forget as followers. And of blind Bartimaeus, Jesus simply asks, "What do you want me to do for you?" Jesus was here to serve. When Jesus sends out seventy-two disciples, he sends them out vulnerable, with only their robe, sandals and staff. They are dependent on the strangers they meet in towns and villages to help them survive with the hospitality of food and shelter. They don't become power Disciples building mega-churches. Jesus has taught them to approach the people in such a way of honesty and compassion that a trust is newly born and the humble are willing to listen. Jesus talks about a "Harvest" here, not condemnation. And at the end of the visit, if the town refuses to listen, they don't pray curses down upon them. Jesus tells them to symbolically shake the dust off their feet and move ever onward to the next field of people waiting for good news. We step aside, and we move on.

Christ had a "Grace Focused" mission in this world. He has now returned to glory to present our prayers in daily intercession before the Father for His mercy.

Do we have the DNA of a disciple? Yes we do. We get it from our Father and our Brother. Do we know how to use it? Yes. Many of us have had a lifetime of hearing just what to do, Sunday, after Sunday, after Sunday, Christmas through Easter and everything in between. However, it is possible we haven't recognized that all those inspiring words of love, help, care, involvement, and compassion applies to all men on the earth whether or not we understand each other, agree with each other, travel the same road as each other, or perceive God the Creator in the exact same way. And when sitting in church, every time I hear how we are to love our brothers and sisters, I find I want to stand and shout, "Does this also apply to my lesbian, gay, bisexual and transgender brothers and sisters?"

Sermons Bursting With Grace

"To be a slave of God is freedom. Blessed to be a blessing. Whose life have you touched in blessing?"

"How can we touch others with the same blessings we have received from the Father?"

And we pray, "Lord, we like so many others who have called

ourselves Your people for centuries have a way of taking Your salvation for granted. We use the Good News of Jesus to make ourselves appear to be better than others with whom we disagree...Teach us instead to do justice and to love kindness and to walk humbly with our God."

"The grace of our Lord was poured out on me abundantly, along with the faith and love that are in Christ Jesus. Here is a trustworthy saying that deserves full acceptance: Christ Jesus came into the world to save sinners – of whom I am the worst."

"It is good for our hearts to be strengthened by grace."

"Jesus Christ heals you. Get up, take your mat and go home."

"But God has shown me that I should not call any man impure or unclean."

"Take heart, daughter, your faith has healed you."

"Lord, how many times shall I forgive my brother when he sins against me? Up to seven times? I Tell you, not seven times, but seventy-seven times."

"Where do you see where God's plan has fallen short? Step out of your comfort zones. And SALT.

Stop, Ask, Love, Touch".

We have been hearing the plan for years. We just need to direct it into our lives with the understanding these words also apply to the sexual and gender diverse individuals in our lives and neighborhoods. When we do, healing will truly incubate and lives will begin to change, including your own.

CHAPTER 11 DID JESUS GET WHAT HE PAID FOR?

"May They Be Brought to Complete Unity to Let Them Know That You Sent Me and Have Loved Them." John 17:23

Jesus paid the price for our sins. He alone understands perfectly the wrath of God and God's "hate" for sin. Some believe that because I, and others like myself, believe God's grace, and acceptance includes LGBTQ men and women, that we are watering down the power and strength of God's feelings about sin. In truth the closest any of us come to understanding this side of God, His perfectly righteous "hate", is to not understand it at all. We certainly don't understand with any accuracy the depth of God's holy love, so let's not kid ourselves we understand with any accuracy how God "hates" the few times it has Biblically been linked with His name.

As humans we can only project our distorted image of hate onto God, and believing we are accurate, react accordingly when we feel justified to "hate", on God's behalf, someone or something that is sinful. We imagine His hate through the malignant lens of our lives, so we think God's hate for sin is also malignant. I believe nothing could be further from the truth. We can't begin to comprehend let alone act on the completeness of God's pure love and we can't comprehend let alone act on the pure order and righteousness of His hate.

However, I believe we have a limited view of the severity of God's wrath during an isolated incident by viewing the crucifixion. One perfect Son of God, spit upon, slapped, two inch thorns crushed onto His head, a cat-o-nine tails whipping and ripping His skin until it hangs in shreds, nails driven into hands and feet, arms spread so wide the lungs can't fully operate, and all of this took place before death. I would never envision such a price on my head. It's a lot to take in some days.

But it also moves me to ask, did this supreme sacrifice satisfy the demands of God's hate of our sins? The Bible says, yes, paid in full. Which leads to my next question, did Jesus get what He paid for? Getting what we pay for is very near and dear to American hearts. Obviously Jesus is not here to give us His verbal answer. How then would you answer this question on His behalf?

The petition, that mankind be brought to complete unity so the world will know the Father sent His Son and Loves them, will be recognized by many as part of the "High Priestly Prayer", which I mentioned in the very first chapter of this book. Jesus begins by praying for Himself in relation to the Father, that they both be glorified by His obedience. I believe that glory has been accomplished even though that fullness is yet to be revealed to us.

Second, Jesus prays for His Disciples. "Now they know... For I gave them the words you gave me and they accepted them." (John 17:7&8). Scripture and the actions of the Disciples after Jesus' Ascension would verify the truth of this accomplishment.

Third, Jesus prayed for you and me; for all mankind. You and I weren't born yet, but pray for us He did. "May they be brought to complete unity to let the world know... that you sent me and have loved them even as you have loved me." John 17:23. I'd be lying if I said I believed this part of Jesus' prayer has been satisfactorily answered. We Christians are not the unit that we may see ourselves as being in our own eyes. Ask an impartial person (perhaps someone not in a church), and they will probably verify this for you. Could it be through our unconscious, selfish desires as a "religion" or "denomination" to be right and therefore all "others" must be wrong, we fail in unity as Christ's followers and we prevent the "world" from knowing Christ's words, "that you sent me and have loved them even as you have loved me"?

Is there some way we can begin to move into a better position to help answer Jesus' prayer before He returns?

Not Thinking Is Not An Excuse

To some extent, it's a rude awakening when a daughter starts to sound like her mother. But there it is. When I was growing up this one phrase of my Mom's, "Not thinking is not an excuse" really took seed in my fertile young mind for some reason. Or course, the older I get the more forgetful I get and can only plead with others to accept that forgetting isn't really an intentional not thinking, right?

But her words carry a lot of gold in them. To believe we aren't responsible for certain actions or reactions in life because we didn't think it through, because we didn't use our God given intelligence in situations is simply not a good enough excuse when things go wrong, when people are cruelly hurt, and lives devastated. When I hear a religious lesson taught and little blips start to erupt inside my spirit and cause me to ask myself, "Does this mesh with what my heart is saying?" it is not wrong to question what has been taught. However, most of us, in our need to avoid conflict, ask ourselves, who are we to question? In fact, many times we are encouraged, by our "group", not to question because it creates conflict and no one wants to deal with conflict.

The longer a belief or idea has existed, the more protective we are of not allowing it to be turned or adjusted. We don't like to risk and we don't want to be wrong so we don't like going out on a limb by ourselves with our questions and doubts. In the end we take the road most traveled, fearing to take the road less traveled, and sometimes not thinking, turns out to have detrimental consequences for some people. In this case, a whole group of people who are different from us in their sexuality and gender are suffering in various ways that affect their daily lives, and even though we don't see it, affect our own lives. And when the desire of Jesus' heart, that all men should know how much He loves them runs into a road block of man's good intentions that lead some men to believe Jesus hates them, we have a mega faith/intelligence problem that we cannot ignore, for Jesus' sake.

If you fear the risk of raising questions against such a huge obstacle as your religion, and the less traveled and unknown road about homosexuality creates conflict in your life, please know you are not alone. But your God given faith and your God given intelligence weren't created to oppose one another. Nor do you need to work through the difficult times alone. God has promised not to abandon us, but to be with us and lead us into His truth. So, we take our faith and our intelligence to Him for the right answers in our difficult times of need. That step of absolute trust in God alone is the first step to reconciling hearts and lives of men and women everywhere, so the world will know God's love for them, and Jesus' prayer is one step closer to being answered before He returns. As far as I know, Jesus welcomed the questions of uncertainty and searching thoughts of the multitudes. And from what I have read, Jesus always gave something of Himself that each and every one could take away with them, to cherish and base their growing faith upon if they dared.

In *You Lost Me,* so many of today's younger generation admit, "...They reject Jesus because they feel rejected by Christians...Often outsiders' perceptions of Christianity reflect a church infatuated with itself." 1 Kinnaman. Rather than concern ourselves over losing them, do we quickly answer, "Well, some people will blame anyone or look for any excuse to leave the church and God" to deflect any guilt or blame from the church and from ourselves?

"One outsider from Mississippi made this blunt observation:

'Christianity has become bloated with blind followers who would rather repeat slogans than actually feel true compassion and care. Christianity has become marketed and streamlined into a juggernaut of fear mongering that has lost its own heart.'" 2 Kinnaman.

The quotes from Kinnaman's book are at times blunt and seem harsh. In truth, they are not meant to slay Christian dragons if all we consider is our personal integrity at stake. His words are meant to produce a spiritual mirror for us to gaze deeply into, so perhaps we can find a new desire to bind up the hurt when we consider others. Kinnaman's words shout to get our attention and heat up the spirit of those long set in their ways. They sound a reveille to open our eyes and ears because the words stirring on the winds today are just as relevant as those during the days of Jesus. Feelings like the man from Mississippi are not owned solely by those who some label as pagans or worse. Many young men and women inside the church are becoming disillusioned with the dissonance between who Jesus was and is and how so many typical church goers express themselves.

Kinnaman tells us that this current generation of young church goers believes the church is not a safe and hospitable place to have questions and raise doubts. In short, they feel the church as an institution has failed them. Their close friends are gays and lesbians, bisexuals and transgenders along-side heterosexuals, and together they have formed a working unit of give and take, love and tears, listening and helping. In their world it works because there are no blistering accusations, expectations and rules. They listen with their hearts, and when their sexually diverse friends say, "I didn't ask to be this way, this is not a choice", those with open hearts accept it and understand it in their souls with the help of Jesus – a help they seek in a quiet, passive, yet expectant way, and listen for in their gut. And God is using their insight and wisdom beyond what the church can recognize because she fails to investigate for whatever reasons – reasons that perhaps resemble a God given faith not wanting to risk "conflict" with God given intelligence.

As the mature generation, we find the questions of our young people difficult and their actions alien to our beliefs. We want a simple church with simple answers that have been given to us. And we pass onto others a "church instilled fear" that today's younger culture is outside of God's will. Taking the trouble to seek God's will and pray with our hearts wide open and vulnerable is simply beyond what we want or perhaps even know how to risk. And if we befriend a lesbian, or transgender, our religious friends will begin to talk about us, maybe ignore us and marginalize us. It is too much to ask us to live outside our comfort zones, even though we demand that very thing of LGBTQs when we demand they become heterosexual. Isn't it just possible that we believe God's wrath might spill down on us if we try to imitate Jesus, and yet get it "wrong", by loving sinners, the wrong people, *too* much? What prospect does that leave for us? If we shouldn't love too much what is our option but to not love some people in certain situations. I just don't find that premise my Bible.

I don't believe we are expected to literally accept everything about a person. No one does that, heterosexual or homosexual. But that we accept *the* person, love another human being, one created in God's image should be our goal. And let's not overlook the basic importance of accepting and loving ourselves for who we are. Until we have an accurate self-portrait, not air-brushed by the hand of good intentions, but one with all the blemishes and sins of who we really are day in and day out, we will be unable to move forward and accept anyone else.

"We'll always be who we've always been if we always do what we've always done." 3 Pollock. At some point we need to ask, "Is who we are and what we've always done still working in our present culture to God's satisfaction?" And if we have a mega faith/intelligence problem by being who we've always been and doing what we've always done, are we obstinately refusing to examine whether God wants to reveal something new to us and move us past our own stagnation? If so, we have no excuse for Jesus but one, "I didn't think and I didn't dare to question."

Do You Understand?

Chapter after chapter, book after book, Jesus attempts to assure us He did exactly what He set out to do. He wants us to comprehend in our own minds the words of the Father so no one can persuade us we are not loved by God or that His truth is not in us. In the book of Matthew alone there are over forty-five verses concerned with our knowing and understanding truth. "I tell you the truth", "Have you understood all these things?", "listen and understand", "Do you still not understand?" In all these verses Jesus is pointing us toward the Father. The pinnacle of our lives has always been to reach up to touch God in a real and intimate relationship. Nothing has changed.

Have we understood all things? Do we still not understand? It is my heartfelt belief, based on my last three years relying on God's help to listen to Him and understand with my faith/intelligence, that God with His Spiritual presence that fills 100% of our world, is making Himself known in the same way He has always made His presence known. It is with His righteous hand alone that God desires to move men in forward motion to Him, and moving us to *be* more than we have been up to this point in life and to *do* more than we have done. Regardless of what or how homosexuality has been viewed or received in any other generation, I believe God, in faithfulness to His Godhead, once again chooses grace to cover mankind – homosexual mankind and heterosexual mankind – so we will begin to understand just how important Jesus' third petition is in His "High Priestly Prayer".

I don't share my beliefs as one claiming to have some "inside track" or a level of theological acclaim superior to others. I have no PhD's or any other letters beside my last name. My beliefs, laid out before you here, are the result of that child that trustingly laid her nothingness at the feet of Jesus in a "no man's land" and patiently received what he chose to fill my soul with. When all is said and done, I've simply decided to just take Jesus as His word as I believe God has attempted to clearly imprint it into my heart.

He is opening the eyes of so many Christian men and women who lovingly want to lead the church in a new direction of gleaning, so we can learn and move forward with God. In their conviction to be obedient to what they feel God's Spirit is saying, contemporary writers and speakers are committing their lives to spread this real life-altering inconvenient truth. "Your job is not to anesthetize yourself with congratulatory prose about the state of the world or the church, but to deal with reality even when it is embarrassing or hurtful." 4 Barna. George Barna's words to the church and society at large, about the state of Christians and our response to this next generation exiting the church, leaving us with the unanswered question of where are they in relationship with the Father, is meant to send us into crises risk mode, trusting God every step of the way, for Jesus sake.

God desires each one of us to be certain in our own minds, where we stand and what we believe, about so many things concerning the future of His church. He wants us as individuals to know in our hearts and in our minds how we can become lovingly and compassionately involved in the lives of sexual and gender diverse people. Jesus asked *everything* of His followers. And while He simplified our lives by removing the barriers that prevented our freely giving our hearts to the Father, He didn't minimize the individual effort, the prayers, the time it would take from our private, fun obsessed, self-absorbed lives to learn a new love for Him and all people.

Traditions Or Traditionalists

"Most Christians will tell you that their faith is a relationship with Christ, not a laundry list of duty-bound obligations. That's 'religion.' Our approach to sexuality should take the same view. The purpose is relationship with each other and with God. Any rules we put in place, rather than keeping people 'in' or 'out,' like the rules of the traditionalists, are to help relationships thrive – and we stay on guard against rules taking on a life of their own, multiplying, and expanding for their own sake." 5 Kinnaman.

Kinnaman tries to help us understand that there is a difference between traditionalists and traditions. Whereas the tradition of chastity and fidelity are significant acts in the spiritual lives of all people, "Traditionalism, on the other hand, is an idealogy that seeks to replace a thriving, grace-filled relationship with Christ with human-made rules and regulations." 6 Kinnaman.

Jeff Chu took a year out of his life to tour the country, talking with heterosexuals and with LGBTQs, and observe real lives in motion. "What I never found was unity in what Jesus taught. If the church is supposed to be the body of Christ, then what I saw on my trip were our Lord's dismembered and terribly dishonored remains." 7 Chu. We can change this. Those who undergo a healing process with their diverse brothers and sisters can start a personal campaign to give Jesus the desire of His heart by daily renewing their effort to fulfill the third petition of His High Priestly Prayer, "May they be brought to complete unity to let the world know that you have sent me and have loved them even as you have loved me." John 15:23.

In Philippians, Paul is telling the church at Philippi that he presses toward the goal to win the prize for which God in Christ Jesus has called him to. "All of us who are mature should take such a view of things. And if on some point you think differently, that too God will make clear to you." Philippians 3:15. Our citizenship is indeed in Heaven. We have an omniscient God who can and will make our paths clear to us. We do need to ask Him, though, and we may need to spend some time, borrowed from our amusements, to really study His Word.

For a time homosexuality may seem like a thorn in the side of the church. But if you believe God's grace is truly sufficient for you, and God's power is made perfect and complete in our weakness, then the church has the opportunity to rise to a new level in the history of God's earth. It may require you to start with a new understanding of what homosexuality is all about, razing to the foundations any and everything you have thought it to be or have been erroneously told about it in the past. Life is not static. You can let God help you blueprint and build a life that is fair and honest in its equality for all people everywhere. And like it says clearly in the promise of Philippians, "God will make clear to you" all those things you need to know on your heavenward journey.

CHAPTER 12 STRAIGHT TALK ABOUT GAY MATTERS

"If you do away with the yoke of oppression, with the finger pointing and malicious talk...your night will become like the noonday sun." Isaiah 58:9&10

How could these words written thousands of years ago be so perfect for today? Because our magnificent Heavenly Father oversees His creation and is our greatest help in times of need until the day we see Him face-to-face. It's safe to say there has always been a yoke of oppression of some type in our world, since the beginning of time. Why else would God mention it? God gave us a valuable solution for those oppressed – meet their needs.

God didn't say change everything about them; make sure they become just like you and me. He simply asked that we meet their needs. How intelligent yet profoundly simple is that. Once again the heavy bound tomes of theology pale in comparison. Some needs are readily obvious to us, those of food, water, clothing, shelter. Others needs remain almost invisible at times, the needs of the emotion and soul of a person, human companionship, a listening ear empty of judgment, someone to share your pain and ease its weight.

Reality – A Step Forward Into Understanding

"Homosexuals in the church are not only the most marginalized groups, but are often victims of violence or driven to suicide because they cannot make sense of their sexual feelings in light of what they believe or are told their Bible says." 1 Cannon. I am quoting Cannon because until we fully understand and learn to appreciate all the emotional contortions, the mental gyrations, the spiritual grief and the physical abuse that results, we will never grasp how it will be possible to want to "stand beside them" because we still "can't stand them".

LGBTQs are caught in a drag-net of polar opposite feelings (what I am in my own mind verses what I "should be" as the constant haranguing by others demand) competing for equal importance in their lives. Like the opposite ends of a magnet, these feelings do not attract and merge into a happily ever after. They are polar opposites that repel and rip apart real people just wanting a safe place to live their lives.

It is a mistake of grand proportion to blame drug and alcohol abuse, promiscuous acts, even suicide on the inability of the sexual and gender diverse to accept their sexuality because they know in their hearts it's wrong. Unfortunately, this exact claim can be found in certain Christian and social circles. Yet, when you finally empty out your prejudices and open yourself to listen to gays, they will tell you they were undisturbed during their early years when their diverse sexuality was still innocent and undeveloped. It was only after the taunts of insensitive children, youth and adults that they felt threatened by the voices and acts of hatred. They became confused and their lives in many ways became dysfunctional, and all they wanted was to make the pain feel less, or go away completely for a time.

I want to briefly revisit that afternoon three years ago when I met my new sexual and gender diverse friends. My first question that day was, "When did you first realize you were lesbian or gay and did you know what it was at the time?" I want to share Brandon's answer with you. "I think it's like when you grow up and you hear words and you don't know what the definition is. Like, I know I always was (gay) but didn't know what that meant. And I didn't know that word (gay/homosexual) was assigned to it. You always just act that way. It's a part of me. I was attracted to guys always. But I didn't know (what it meant) when someone talked about someone being 'gay'. I thought they meant 'stupid' like we still kind of use that word. Somebody was telling me a story the other day. Somebody does something they don't understand, like what he did was in elementary school. Somebody got in trouble throwing spit wads but he didn't know, (that it was bad or negative) and somebody says, 'You just threw a spit wad.' And you say, 'Oh, I didn't know what that was. I didn't know not to do that.' I didn't know to be any different. It's not something you learn either. Cause in my environment, there's no way. I knew I 'was', but I didn't know I was 'gay' because kids don't think in terms of sex." 2 Brandon.

If children could be allowed to grow up believing in and accepting themselves just as they are without a verbal diet of how negative, wrong, and shameful they are, their chances to grow into the beautifully confident people God created and celebrates would no doubt increase a hundred fold. Let's face it, our omniscient Father is not surprised by the path our lives take. Only we are surprised when after our innocent childhoods, we are taught to believe the gender path can only go one way.

You are no doubt aware of reparative therapy programs, some that operated nation-wide, that have worked diligently to "help" LGBTQ men and women who are wracked by guilt and confusion to find help through their spiritual faith. Some used words like "change" to attract hopefuls to their programs.

Alan Chambers the past president of Exodus (no longer a working organization) asked if he could be on a panel at a Gay Christian Network Conference, started by Justin Lee. He astounded people when he admitted of all the men and women who attended Exodus over the years, "...the majority meaning ninety-nine-point-nine percent of them have not experienced a change in their orientation..." 3 Chu. Reorientation has not happened. But instead of accepting the possibility that sexual orientation takes place during the amazing growth of an unborn child, people continue to look for the next best theory that supports their belief that homosexuality is a choice, forever ignoring the words of those who know far better than any others what's going on inside their bodies and lives.

There are currently groups as I have already mentioned that work on a strict accountability program. It would be unfair not to mention that some of these procedures may have contributed to bringing a change for some people. Some who previously identified as homosexuals are now in happy heterosexual marriages and have children. Others have confided that after years of living a heterosexual life they re-experience a pull toward the homosexual life they left. Whatever their personal story, I have absolutely no doubt most have lived with enough tension, confusion and possibly anguish for a lifetime and I would not add to that. I respect each and every one of them and they have every right to continue their present lives in peace.

However, to turn around and judge others for failure to change their sexual and gender diversity is also an injustice. Do not make the mistake of believing every lesbian or gay feels the same way as their ex-counterparts. Do not dare to assume the belief that one young woman hangs herself or one young man gets heavily into using, buying and selling drugs, all because they don't accept their diverse sexuality – that it's a problem too overwhelming for them to live with. We who have never even once in our lives experienced the hate or disgust from others because we are sexually different, we who have never once understood the desire for a same sex relationship, cannot possibly claim to understand why those who are homosexual, bisexual, or transgender sometimes turn to self-destructive behaviors, *not to self-destruct,* but to anesthetize themselves, and through anesthetizing find a small measure of relief for a short time. In the case of suicide, it is a clear marker of absolute hopelessness and a need to stop the pain at any cost.

People inside and outside the church make their demands on LGBTQs to change. If they try and fail, try and fail, try and fail, what price then becomes the value of their lives in their own eyes? Perhaps it is worth nothing more than to dangle suspended from a beam with a rope around the neck. Perhaps it is worth nothing more than the destruction of the body through drugs and alcohol. As least the oblivion ends the pain in a world that doesn't want them; of the "God who doesn't love or want them." No, we do not understand!

Again, from that afternoon three years ago comes the story of another who chose his own way to deal with the world's cruel reactions to his true self. After one of the participants had shared that for her, rather than alcoholism, work was her "ism" Joran shared his coping mechanism. "The thing she (Shirley) was saying is her "ism", Josh (his therapist) recognized it early on. You have to put balance in your life. It was like, I don't want balance, this (constant study and no social life) was for me. It keeps me from having to deal with the homosexual side of me. And I think God put him (Josh) in my life when 90% of my life was school, and getting some kind of balance (was needed)." Brandon asked him if he ever left his apartment for anything other than going to school. "Yeah, I left my apartment when they (roommates) were having parties. That's how bad it was. It was my "ism". It wasn't drugs or alcohol. I didn't do those things because I had a different upbringing. For me, that (compulsive study) started when I was abused as a kid. Now, I don't have to deal with abuse anymore, I have to deal with the fact that I'm gay." 4 Joran.

Please hear the words of a young lesbian woman. She told me due to her religious upbringing, drugs and alcohol were not an option to numb her through the pain. If she had not had help from compassionate gays she would have "disintegrated". Because of the unyielding attitudes at church she was beginning to slip away from God. She shared with me the moment she was finally set free. It was late one night in bed and as she had so often before, was once again wrestling with her questions about what to do when suddenly she felt Jesus silent voice fill her head. He spoke plainly with His gentle admonishment that He did not die a brutal death on a cross so she could slip away from Him. She did make a choice that night, not the one we accuse her and others like her of making. She made the choice to let Jesus be her protector and mentor from that moment on. Today she freely lives and enjoys life as a lesbian. With Jesus' help she is securely living and celebrating her life, the life she was born to live.

I thank you for this intimate sharing and I love and respect you.

The Stress Of Living A Lie

In his book *Being Gay, Being Christian: You can be both,* Edser talks about the stress of living a lie. He relates how often those policemen who do deep undercover work suffer when day after day they are forced to act in ways in direct opposition to their moral and/or faith beliefs. After what can amount to months or even years, many must spend an unexpected amount of time in counseling, emotional therapy with the assisted use of medication from living the lies of who they were not. They emerge from undercover work on the brink of exhaustion that may take years to recover from.

Edser draws a correlation between the anguished lives of these police men and women and the anguished lives of the diverse who for years have lived in fear of being found out, who continue to live a daily lie scrutinizing their every word and action, afraid of being "found out" by a heterosexual world. And there is a cost, one of heartbreaking spiritual and physical damage.

When a person is repeatedly told the only way to be acceptable to

God is to change the person they believe God created them to be, to change the most intimate part of their lives, their sex lives, the strongest natural impulse God has given us, it creates an unbearable tension in their lives where that destructive exhaustion trails in its wake.

This tension has a professional name: Cognitive Dissonance, which is when "...two or more thoughts, attitudes, beliefs are competing and are therefore incompatible. Such dissonance also causes such an uncomfortable physical state that the individual tries to reduce the tension. The severity of the tension depends on how much importance you place on each." 5 Edser. Do you see how the young man or woman who recognizes a difference in their sexuality from others, one who is raised to believe in God's unconditional love, faces the destructive thought that God's love *is* conditional when it comes to their own life and their faith foundation disintegrates beneath them? Does this reality hurt your heart even a little?

"When we interpret scripture in a way that is hurtful to people, we can be sure that we are not glorifying God...No interpretation of Scripture is correct that leads to or supports contempt for any individual or group of persons either within or outside the church...Any interpretation of Scripture is wrong that separates or sets in opposition love for God and love for fellow human beings." 6 Rogers.

If church members have no idea what their church leaders even believe, if they have not one single idea about how to live their lives in a culture where homosexuality is not going to disappear, if the average church member believes homosexuality is an abomination, which gives them the license to ignore or treat LGBTQs with contempt or worse, the church needs to sit up and take notice. The Scripture based authority in your institution is broken. To teach that God would have all men come to Him and yet prevent that very thing from happening based on what *we* believe God wants rather than let God be in control of spiritual saving grace is a shameful deed, leaving another negative mark against the history of the church.

"What are we doing to facilitate conversations...If we cannot set aside our holy values roadblock long enough to quietly and respectfully listen, we will never understand them, never gain the trust and friendship that opens the ears and hearts of those Jesus may want to give a part of himself to." 7 Kinnaman/Lyons. This isn't just advice concerning sexually diverse individuals. It includes all people, gay and straight, our children, who the church doors slam behind them on their final exit because we have failed to recognize their own right to be in a mission field of their own choosing, one we stubbornly refuse to approve of or even validate as real. But it is far too often a mission field that follows the footprints of Jesus that the "old guard" can't reconcile. We fail to understand the need for risking our lives to share God's unmerited and unearned grace with those who need to hear. But our children, they have somehow grasped the threads of risk priority.

The Effects Of Deprivation

The more you educate yourself, the more successful you will be in forming your own, solid opinion of living in a diverse world and the quicker your fears will vanish. They will be replaced with a competent voice where sharing your ideas and decisions with the world will plant a much needed seed for healing in others. Like the undercover police men and women mentioned earlier from Dr. Edser's book, sexual and gender diverse individuals also suffer from deprivation. I'd like to explore these areas with you.

The first is Nurturance – the deprivation of affection or caring. It may not be in every relationship of their lives, but a parent, a sibling, a few friendships, snubs from one's church, neighborhood, or school all add up and can leave one feeling alone and uncared for. God created man to be in relationship with Him and with each other. Loneliness can happen even in a room full of people when you know they are judging you; when there is no one emotionally available to help you and be there for you; to cheer you on and support you on the tough days.

Second is Empathy – the deprivation of listening or understanding. How often do you think it occurs when a teen or a young man or woman finally gathers up enough courage to come out to a loved one only to be told they don't know what they are talking about and they have a choice not to be gay? It certainly happened in my family and it continues to be the knife that cuts the line of communication in other families. How many times can one ask, "Why is no one listening to my heartfelt pleas? How can you say you love me and never really see or understand me?" Everyone needs someone to really see and accept them and to really hear what they have to say. And that's just the beginning.

The third is Protection – the deprivation of a strong insulation against the outer world. We don't come into this world knowing everything and needing no one. We need that person who can set aside their personal doubts and step up to the bat to protect and defend us whether they agree with every little difference in our lives or not. This person has the wisdom to understand unconditional love and the courage to demonstrate it before the eyes of the world.

"Deprivation in one or all of these areas sets up a way of dealing with the world that is maladaptive and repetitive in adulthood. Emotional deprivation is the direct opposite of the vision of God that Jesus tried to show us. He is not a God who is distant, uncaring and cold, but a God who is like a loving father. He wants to give his children the sense that they are loved and cared for and wanted. He wants to give them the sense that He is always on their side." 8 Edser.

Each Of Us Discover Life Is A Process

Homosexuals are like you and me. Just as I am unique in my life, my likes, my dislikes, my dreams, my wants, my desires, the foods I love, the movies I want to see, the clothes I wear, and the people I want to be around, the gay community revolves around equally unique men and women. There is no single set of descriptors that captures the way all diverse people think, feel and behave. And just as my life has been a journey that is still opening up to new possibilities, so is the life of the homosexual, bisexual and transgender.

They are individuals with individual talents and individual needs. If you can find your way past the one small difference between you and them, how wide and how interesting is the ground left to discover and build upon. You will never understand just how small the sexually diverse difference is until you become a true friend. You will only have the inaccurate words of others who don't know either, guiding you in the wrong direction from what might have been. I urge you to put this difference out of your mind once and for all and allow God to take care of you, your world, and your new friend.

I have heard many well intentioned leaders question the validity of same sex orientation from birth because many homosexuals are adults before they recognize who they are and come out to the world. There are so many books available to anyone who wants to learn more about homosexuals. Anyone who understands so little about the process gays go through, not unlike the process heterosexuals go through in their own self-actualization process, should find some and start learning. The three deprivations mentioned by Edser go a long way in explaining the obstacles faced by gays, whatever their age.

"It is a process. You don't wake up one morning and understand everything about your sexuality." 9 Edser. Our entire world is by majority considered heterosexual, and virtually everything said, done, and offered is taken for granted to be heterosexual in nature. Greeting cards are a good example and baby gifts emphasize "I love my Dad" or "I love my Mom", but never "I love my Dads" or "I love my Moms". We take it for granted a wedding ring symbolizes a union between a man and woman. But it doesn't, not any more. The sensitive little things make a huge difference and will begin to help you understand what being an ally to LGBTQs can mean.

So the individual who silently suffers and fears the reality of their differences, no matter what their age when it first reveals itself, discovers a cracked foundation masquerading as a safe life, and deprivation begins. And after it begins it grows and the starvation of needs grows with it. The reaction to ignore, to deny and bury this new understanding of their sexuality can begin as a conscious or unconscious endeavor so early in life, that it is years before the individual begins to trust herself or himself enough to finally peep out and begin to examine the truth of who they are and learn how to safely adjust their lives accordingly.

Edser continues to state the growing same-sex awareness in an adolescent is like a prism through which they continually view their world. Their journey begins to unfold in their lives and the success of it is greatly affected by how well they move through the stages of identity. The following are the six areas of identity formation theory from the studies by Vivienne Cass, a researcher and theorist in Australia.

First is Identity Confusion, feelings of a sexual awareness that create confusion and can be disruptive.

Second is Identity Comparison and depends a good deal on the feedback of others to his behavior.

Third is Identity Tolerance which becomes that time of making contact with other homosexuals to see if the experience is positive. The person may come out to a trusted person or small group of people in the homosexual community. This is a time of mixed identity as they juggle the heterosexual expectation versus the homosexual reality.

And as I have just recently learned, some take on the identity of bisexual at this time because of the confusion. For these, identifying as bisexual can present a temporary, safe stepping stone to a full lesbian/gay identity. It initially allows them to keep one foot in the heterosexual world until they are sure about the homosexual world their mind and souls tell them to move toward. They are not playing games nor are they "choosing" to be different from others. They are searching for a truth to rest their lifelong battles on, and while they are doing so, they still need a place of refuge they are familiar with to protect their weary and fragile state of mind. None of us as humans should misunderstand the need for protection in our vulnerable states in life. We have all been there whether we want to remember or not.

Fourth is Identity Acceptance where the experience in the gay community has been positive and disclosure to certain family and friends begin.

Fifth is Identity Pride where there is a division between heterosexual and homosexual and there is a growing pride in their sexuality. This isn't an unrighteous self-pride as I heard someone express recently. It is a recognition pride of finally belonging. We all experience that in our lives.

Sixth is Identity Synthesis where they become fully integrated in their self-identity. Homosexuality becomes just one aspect of identity in a long list of identifiers, where peace and harmony finally fill a previously empty place in their lives. Thank you Dr. Edser and Vivienne Cass for helping us understand this complex and human journey.

(For those of you who may be wondering what are "identifiers", they are those names we call ourselves as we interact with the people in our lives. Rarely do we start our list with our sexual identity if we mention it at all. I don't, because it does not define the total me. I am a daughter, sister, wife, mother, substitute teacher, author, reading enthusiast, child of God. My son might say he is a son, brother, husband, Licensed Professional Counselor, friend, traveler, reading enthusiast, and child of God.)

Those with sexual and gender diversities are as unique to one another as heterosexuals are – in how they see themselves and how they determine to live out their lives. In Chu's book he quotes Wesley Hill, "...at a time in my life when I was feeling especially lonely: The love of God is better than any human love. Yes that's true, but that doesn't change the fact that I feel – in the deepest parts of who I am – that I'm still wired for human love." 10 Chu.

Gays feel that irresistible need for an intimate relationship with another human being, close and personal. They want to wake up each morning next to the same loving individual. They want a soul mate to share God with, and all His glorious creation and blessings. Many long for children, a home, a yard, even a dog, to surround them with their being and purpose. It's simply not all about sex. It's about life – the life each of us longs to live.

Do you know how to satisfy the needs of the oppressed or lessen the yoke of oppression weighing down so many today? How do you live and interact with homosexuals? What is your *own* solid opinion in your Spirit filled heart about homosexuals, not someone else's opinion? Do you know the name of one lesbian, gay, bisexual or transgender? Do you know where they are from, where they work, what they like to do in their spare time? Have you ever sat with them long enough to share your life with them? How about a meal? A movie? A book? Been to their home? Do you laugh with them or cry with them? Do you laugh and talk nonsense with them one time and debate deep mysteries another?

It's called a friendship and it is normal. You have them every day with people who have all kinds of sins in their lives. In fact, that's the only type of person you can have a friendship with. It's not our place to determine the spiritual lives of others whether they are homosexual or heterosexual. So, how about it? Don't know a single one? Do you kind of see how you could be considered a hypocrite? Do you begin to see how you might think you are a hypocrite?

Tonight in the heavy silence of your room is it possible you might understand why the lesbian, the gay might be a member of AA, due to the overwhelming obstacles and hatred in their lives, and now repent that you judged them? Do you wish you had been their friend in their

183

dark and sometimes desperate search for reasonable answers so maybe your shoulder could have carried the tiniest bit of their anxious load? And in sharing the pain heaped on them by uncaring others, who have never bothered to really understand the complex layers of their lives, perhaps you could have been a small light of hope in their darkness? Would you have set foot in that gay bar to be their quiet pillar of strength as your friend's gut churned with the anguish of his unsettled life?

This is the reality of getting involved in the dirt and grit of life that Brennan Manning wrote about in *The Ragamuffin Gospel.* We have too often been left with the idea that Jesus only went to clean places during His ministry – that somehow even Matthew's house with prostitutes, tax collectors and thieves was an acceptable environment. Look at the Biblical art of these stories. We see Jesus surrounded by men and women, but the tension and threat, the darker level of feelings, the shattered lives don't show through the paint and canvas to give us an accurate picture of the dirt and rawness in the lives Jesus ministered to. There wasn't anything He sheltered Himself from. He knew about the worst life had to offer and many times He was in the midst of it with grace and mercy.

Is there a chance tonight before sleep claims your body that you can thank God for the chance to be challenged in your spiritual walk? Do you feel the least excited to begin a faith walk that will let you pass through the confusion of society and hold out a hand to someone who needs the kind of care only you and I can give if we dare?

Yes, it is called friendship. It is totally non-judgmental and it's okay with God to have homosexual friends. And if there are those in the gay community who seek to serve God through marriage rather than live outside of it, do you think you can step aside and let God take care of the lives of those involved?

"There are still moments when I wonder whether my homosexuality is my ticket to hell, whether Jesus would love me but for that, and how good a Christian could I be if I struggle to believe that God loves me at all." 11 Chu. Will you take a silent moment and imagine this is the voice of your child, tormented about his place in the Kingdom of God. Ask yourself, what would you do to help him find his rightful place in life?

What God made at creation was wonderful and still is; man created in the image of the Godhead – man adding a new dimension in God's life. Do we dare entertain the beautiful idea that our Father longed for us as much or more than the angels and the creatures of heaven? Could the God of everything long for you and me and all of us no matter our sexual orientation? I find that a humbling, but exciting thought!

13 WHAT YOU CAN DO AS A CARING PERSON

"Make every effort to live in peace with all men and to be holy...See to it no one misses the grace of God and that no bitter root grows up to cause trouble and defile many." Hebrews 12:14&15

Why should we not believe that the desire of God's heart is to bring every last one of His created children into a deep and satisfying relationship with Himself. God's goal, His will, His plan does not need man to improve upon it. We just need the strength to follow His example. We can live in peace with all men, and for our love of God, we can be sure that we, as well as we are able, do our part so no bitter root rises up to cause trouble or defile others.

And that love of God, "...demands that we reconsider that which we think we understood." 1 Michaelson. In his book, *God vs. Gay* Michaelson asks each of us to consider whether we can see the life of a homosexual not by our own personal values but in a way that lets us examine our values by *their* experiences. "Can I open my heart to the possibility that love may require something greater than what I can presently understand?" 2 Michaelson.

This is not beyond what you can do. You have help. "In the same way, the Spirit helps us in our weakness. We do not know what we ought to pray for, but the Spirit himself intercedes for us with groans that words cannot express. And he who searches our hearts knows the mind of the Spirit, because the Spirit intercedes for the saints in accordance with God's will." Romans 8:26&27.

"Who will bring any charge against those whom God has chosen? It is God who justifies. Who is he that condemns? Christ Jesus, who died – more than that, who was raised to life – is at the right hand of God and is also interceding for us." Romans 8:33&34. What more perfect help could we want or need? If you are still unsure in your heart about exactly what to do, then begin in prayer. The Father, Son and Holy Spirit will guide your prayers, your heart and your footsteps. And one step at a time is the best place to start.

First of all, there is hope. Just as accepting oneself as a homosexual isn't a process that happens over-night, so is the softening of your heart toward LGBTQs through these ideas you are being introduced to also a process. It will take patience, it will take prayer, it will take meditation and Bible time with God. And as the days and months unfold, take heart. You are free to examine Scripture and move forward in a way that is right for you according to what the Holy Spirit reveals to you. And as many of us have learned, "Past practice is not necessarily a recommendation for future faithfulness." 3 Rogers. Sometimes we must let go when non-productive acts have kept us from growing in a healthier direction.

Second, we don't have to all see perfectly eye to eye. I have not written this book expecting you to accept every detail I have offered. I will say everything I have written is right for me and I must live my life accordingly. Let this book be a guidepost for your journey with God.

Third, it helps to be honest seeing yourself as a true sinner. There are some of us who hide behind religion so we don't have to unveil our status of "sinner" to ourselves, and never to the world. It is beyond what we are willing to risk. In truth we have to expose our wounds and imperfections and thrust our way into and beyond the pain to the goal line before we can stand by another in compassion born of confidence. But trust me, it is a weight thrown off to know you are no longer bound by the rules of self-righteousness.

Fourth, you can work toward your discernment of homosexuality. This is between you and God alone. You do not have to subject yourself to the prying eyes of others who might try to dissuade you from going where your heart may want to take you. When it comes to God and the real world, "Discernment is transparent about the hazards of being human and teaches the full witness of Scripture, which is messy, complex and ultimately, wonderfully true." 4 Kinnaman. I like that phrase "the hazards of being human." We are all complex as God has made us and sometimes there are just no easy answers or answers we understand. To learn to be teachable and yet know when to completely let go and give it back to God is an act of faith you never need to be ashamed of.

Fifth, you search out God's grace in your own life to find the compassion you need to begin a relationship with someone who is of the gay community. You begin by acknowledging they are no different from you. "I know that many people think God's love is expressed precisely by curbing our sexual desires and eradicating all sin. But homosexuality is not a sin; it is an inclination of the heart that can tilt toward holiness or perdition, health or depredation." 5 Michaelson. You can train yourself to forget about their sexual life which has nothing to do with you whatsoever. Your very own heart tilts toward holiness or perdition. We are all people with complex lives, so different in personality, yet so alike in the need for acceptance.

Sixth, you don't need anyone's approval to initiate a friendship with a homosexual. "...the church is uniquely called to be the community of God – and true, authentic community vanishes isolation, loneliness, and alienation and replaces them with love." 6 Kinnaman. You have God's blessing. Go back to your Bible if you have any doubts. Then you initiate a sincere conversation. You find a common bond, something you both enjoy, something you want to discover and you experience it together so you have a place of common ground from which to grow. Common ground builds honesty between two people and brings strangers into the comfort of friendship.

Seventh, enjoy yourself. You are not trying to "fix" this person, only to love them. If they say something you disagree with, you are not required to launch into a verbal sermon. You can actually choose to say nothing. The greater sermon will be your act of unconditional love. Disagreement does not end the life of a relationship. It should challenge it, stretch it, bring new levels of thinking forward, and instill growth, not barriers.

Eighth, when you are unsure, look to today's youth for guidance. They have grown up with the structure of family defined all sorts of ways and learned that whatever the dynamics, life goes on. For our children who love God, they have learned to forge their own paths understanding they are not their parents, and the culture in this generation has taken a dramatic shift from what was. They have also learned their distinctive way of loving others for God is not a betrayal of Him but a new way to serve Him. Now, if only that gift can be passed around.

It Helps To Live In "God Space"

When Doug Pollock wrote the book *God Space* he knew a good definition was needed to show us his intent. I'd like to share his definition with you.

"God Space is where…

…God is felt and encountered in the tangible ways that addresses the longings and cries of the heart.

…we come to the end of our own finite resources and experience the infinite resources of God.

…the natural gives way to the supernatural.

…seeds of faith are planted, watered, and nurtured.

…gentleness and respect are present, judgment is absent, and divine dialogue flows naturally because trust has been established.

…the invisible principles of God's kingdom are made visible in ways people can see, touch and feel.

…friends of sinners – in other words, *our* friends – dwell.

…the topic of God can be explored freely without agendas, biases, and personal convictions getting in the way.

…cynics, skeptics, scoffers, and spiritually curious people alike can raise their questions, share their doubts, voice their concerns, and even vent their anger toward God and the church.

…the "unworthy" feel safe enough to bring their real selves out into the light, and to journey, one step at a time, toward the magnetic pull they sense deep in their souls.

…spiritual curiosity is aroused, and the message of Christianity becomes plausible." 7 Pollock.

What a beautiful place to live out our lives. But for some of you, the more you identify with a certain group of people whose beliefs edge out any sense of new discovery in what the Living God can and might do that is different from those tightly held beliefs, the harder it will be for you to exercise your freedom to live in "God Space". The possibility that old beliefs need to be replaced by new is too threatening to experience and your insecurity to risk on your own may hold you prisoner. But it is not impossible to enter your own "no man's land" with your God and I pray God's strength will carry you past any weakness on your part.

One Last Word About Marriage

I'd like to cover one last idea with you about marriage between two men or two women. "In a culture of 'non marriage', it is ironic that we are spending great amounts of money and energy in trying to prevent people from marrying who want to do so in a way that would contribute to the stability of society." 8 Rogers. If you don't know any gay or lesbian couples who have been married, you won't understand Rogers' sentiment. I am acquainted with several and they have as good and solid a marriage as any heterosexual couple I know and an even better marriage than others I know. They lead happy, secure, and productive lives. I am not saying homosexual marriages are only blissful. That is not true. Like heterosexuals, some find they cannot continue on together for various reasons. A marriage that does or doesn't work is not distinctive to either group.

If you were to ask me if I personally believe when two men or two women choose to marry is the union blessed by God, I can respond in all honesty "yes I do", whether in a civil setting or overseen by a minister of God. I rejoice for the couple and wish them as much happiness as I wish for any heterosexual couple getting married.

You know, when I fell in love, I wanted to get married because Jesus said marriage is good and He blessed it. I cared about living a Christ-centered life then and I care about it now. I can understand if two people of the same gender who are Christians fall in love and want to get married. That is human nature. It is also human nature to crave someone to share our lives with, to not have to live alone forever, missing out on intimate companionship.

Sin Focused Or Grace Focused

The Bible says a sexual relationship outside of marriage is a sin, yet most couples cannot be bothered with such "outdated" and "trivial" religion today or we would see more couples exchanging their sacred vows. Let's take this and follow it through. Let's assume that a same gender sexual relationship outside of marriage is a sin equal to an opposite gender sexual relationship outside the sanctity of marriage.

Let's look at two scenarios and determine what they mean. Your child is a homosexual. He has been in a relationship with another young man for over a year but they don't feel comfortable continuing without the benefit of marriage. Will you disown him and banish him and his partner into a world without the benefit of your Christ centered love, support and protection? The Prodigal son chose to leave home. His father did not cast him out.

In the second scenario your daughter comes home and tells you she has been living with her boyfriend for the last year. You over-look this sin hoping they might eventually change their minds and get married. You tell yourself they are adults and can make their own choices and continue to include them in your family in every way. And when your first grand-child appears without the benefit of married parents, well that child will certainly need your love and support, so you can't turn your back on them.

The first reaction is sin focused; the second is a response of grace.

When God overlooks our sins with His astounding gift of pure grace, we can be sure restoring us to Him is more important than punishing us. As long as He has something to work with He does. He knows when the dark has consumed a person's life and that soul will no longer respond to Him. But until that day if He sees even the tiniest mustard seed of love in our hearts for Him He lets it grow, in spite of who we are or the mistakes we make.

I am not saying God never cares about admonishing or correcting us or that we can do anything we want in life without regret or a need to repent. We who love God understand that is not what I mean when I say God overlooks the sins of man. Discipline is also part of His grace. But it is not for us to determine what His discipline is or when it is.

Luther said, "God in punishing, does not give up all sinners in like manner, even though they might sin in like manner. The reason for this is to be sought in his hidden divine judgment... At any rate God stops every arrogant mouth in order that no one might prescribe to Him any rule according to which He should punish sin or reward virtue."9 Luther. Only you know whether your own arrogant mouth needs to be stopped as you pursue headlong into setting rules to punish sin or reward virtue that you expect God to follow.

It is my conviction, if I err in what I believe to be true, I'd rather err on the side of an innocent child's heart full of love and mercy toward others, trusting that God has led me, rather than err on the side of harsh judgment and lack of grace. Somehow I can't imagine God saying, *"You are loving others way too much. Please stop!"*

"The Story" in the following chapter is in no way meant to denigrate the men and women in the armed services.

From my own beloved father who served God and country in the U.S. Army - WW II, To an Army nephew who served in Desert Storm, a Marine nephew, and a Marine family friend who came home from Afghanistan without his leg, my heart is with all of our soldiers and I salute you, especially the fallen who have been lovingly carried home covered by our Red, White, and Blue.

14 "A STORY"

In a rugged land there lived a Nobleman who everyone said was a brave leader, who fought wars to protect his people and their homes. His Wife was obedient to her husband and kind to family and servants alike. They had a handsome little son, the Prince, who strutted and marched around the castle proudly imitating his great father. Sunny days would find him ordering his invisible troops across the noisy battle fields of wheat and barley to the distant sounds of goats and sheep bleating out orders of their own. The young Prince was always lovingly watched over by his father's Loyal Servant.

The rough fields, crudely plowed by oxen, left behind chunks of hard dirt and rocks unfriendly to skinny little boy legs. Every day after long battles were fought and won, the little son would limp back to the great hall to boast of his latest conquests to his father. The Nobleman, eyes as shrewd as a hawk, narrowed his focus on that limp each night.

One evening at the end of summer the Nobleman calls for his Wife and announces their son is crippled and for this reason the nation cannot respect the Prince as a future leader or conqueror in wars. So, he calls for his Loyal Servant and orders him to take the little Prince across the valley and drown him in the big river. It is best for all.

The Loyal Servant cries as he carries the little Prince across the valley because he understands the true cause for the limp is the hard land, not from any weakness of the firm little body.

In time another son is born to the Nobleman and his Wife, a son he is proud of. Great care is taken to raise him to be the New Leader of the land.

The seasons change, the people plant, they harvest, they take their wares to town to sell or trade. Every few months a peasant couple comes to town to trade and purchase essential supplies for their daily lives. The child they bring is always covered; a bright scarf covers all but the eyes and a shawl always drapes the head and falls below the knees. Many families suffer as children struggle against disease and the strains of life to stay healthy. But this couple and their daughter are indeed odd. No one dresses their family that way. Warriors and their families cannot fight if their over- abundant garments hinder them.

Some begin to make snide comments about the poor family. Whispers flourish and turn cruel. As the years pass whispers turn to bold comments that result in boisterous laughter. Citizens of the town arrogantly try to engage the humble couple in vain conversation. But no one talks to the child. She is invisible. The people spread their gossip; she is not right in the head or her face must be hideously scarred. At the end of the day they go home to their families and forget the little threesome.

The tower bell wails the news of the old Nobleman's death. His son is now the New Leader. It is a quiet time in the land. Crops are grown, herds are raised, and businesses are built.

The New Leader has a Noble Son who grows up enraptured by the tales of war and mighty soldiers from years passed; of those who rode strong stallions and killed and maimed and came home with their plunder in glory. Inflamed by the passion of stories night after night, Noble Son dreams of the power and the glory and yearns after them. Look how proud the old soldiers stand, their chests puffed out, their faces shining as they relive the radiant glory of yesterday.

But there are no enemies to fight now, so the Noble Son and his friends grow up wielding their wooden swords against bitter, imaginary armies of another land. They always win. At night as they drift toward sleep they are proud of their achievements and dream of more.

During these years of peace the old peasant couple dies. Their child, now grown, still comes to town with the bright scarf around her face, the shawl hanging below her knees. The Noble Son and his "warrior" friends, growing broad of shoulder and longing for manhood yell and laugh at the old woman who never talks -the crazy old woman - a freak of nature. That's what everyone calls her, after all. Once in a while they get caught up in their own frenzy and nudge or push the old lady aside. She is not like them. She is not one of them. She is the enemy who comes to their town and makes them ashamed to have to look at her odd person. The healthy sons are offended by her presence - by her looks. She is nothing. She is not right. She needs to learn not to be with the people of this town. Her place is across the valley. She should stay there! It is best for all.

For those who long for power and for glory, sometimes planting crops, raising herds, and building comfortable homes for their families are not enough. There is nothing in these to make you stand tall, puff out your chest, and shine with glory the way returning home after a successful battle would make you feel. That is what you have always been told so it must be true.

Younger sons grow up and manhood takes hold, and when you are a Noble Son of a New Leader equally noble, it is possible to create an event that will bring you the power and glory you crave. And as everyone knows, that is the best for all.

So they exchange their wooden swords for steel, harness mighty stallions and cross many valleys to find other noble sons who long to find their own power and glory. And the wars begin again.

Many are maimed, many are killed, and all that remain are weary and hungry. The proud fire that once filled their minds is replaced by shadowed uncertainty that silently lurks and haunts their once proud dreams. The blood of comrades has washed away their hopes of a victorious return home. The thunder of horses slamming together in combat, the cries of the maimed and dying cutting through the dust and the pestilence echoing over the battleground at the end of the day is the mournful music that serenades the moon. Soon there is nothing left but gaunt specters struggling against the heat, and the land parched but stained, on the long, churlish road home.

Through the haze of the morning a Strong Man tends his gardens as his lazy sheep graze, their stomachs rounded and full. On his dirt road are three young men, sluggish in their uneven gait, once bright uniforms now dusty and hanging from bodies much too thin, dressed not by medals of valor but by patches of dried blood, all in need, body and soul. The two drag their badly wounded friend and beg for help. The bleeding warrior is the Noble Son of the land. Today there is no power - no glory.

Inside the humble but comfortable house his friends lay him on a pallet. The two friends are assured the Noble Son will be taken care of by the Strong Man and his Friend. The two warrior sons promise to return for the New Leader's son.

Days pass and the wounded young man finds rest for his weak body and soul. He is fed and his wounds are cleaned and wrapped and he begins to find new life with his returning strength. The worse injuries will take longer to heal but they are cleaned and attended to daily and will eventually close.

The Noble Son begins to notice his two helpers surrounding him, the gentleness as they attend to his hurt body and soul, the respect in their kindness. He feels compassion flow out from the strangers. They give all and ask for nothing.

One day the healing warrior begins to long for a closer relationship - he wants to talk. He longs to fill his mind with pictures other than cries, blood, death, hunger and destruction. So the Strong Man of the humble home begins to talk, easy at first, letting life and words take a calm pace. He sets a steady, comfortable rhythm.

I'm the only child of an old peasant couple who are no longer living. We went to the town of your noble family for our needs.

The Noble Son is puzzled that he never met this man before. He has had much time to observe and study the life on this farm and is impressed with the knowledge and the level of work to sustain it. There grows an abundance of food, more than adequate herds, and a comfortable home with a deep and plentiful well. But what amazes him more is the Strong Man has an ability to heal the body and ease the soul that is remarkable.

One morning the healing warrior awakes and the Strong Man is not there. The Friend tells him it was time to make a trip across the valley to the town for supplies. The Noble Son anticipated the Strong Man's return all day. He had begun to look forward to the time spent with these two strangers now becoming real companions.

In the shadowed evening the Noble Son looks expectantly as the door to the home creaks opens. What he sees makes his body weak and sweaty. He trembles and finds it difficult to breath, for at the door is one with a bright colored scarf that covers all but the eyes. The shawl that drapes the head falls below the knees. The healing warrior is confused. The crazy old lady has come to the home of his companions.

The shawl is pulled off and folded away. The bright scarf is unwrapped and folded away to reveal the Strong Man of the house who turns to see how the healing Noble Son is doing. The Friend enters the room and begins to set out their evening meal.

In shock, barely finding his voice the Noble Son tells of his years growing up in the noble family in the town where an old couple brought their daughter, always covered with a bright scarf and shawl.

The Strong Man sits and begins his story. As long as he can remember his sweet old mother told him he could never go into the town if people could see him. It would be their secret. So she lovingly covered all but his beautiful eyes with a bright scarf and draped a shawl over his hair so the townspeople would not recognize him. She told him he was the love of her and her husband's life and she never wanted him hurt, because there are those who would indeed hurt him if they discovered his presence. So it became a way of life for him. During the cold winters the coverings added warmth on the long journey. When he was in town and people shoved and laughed at him, he took comfort in the scarf and shawl because they had been tied by the loving hands of his old parents and he knew it was to protect him. As an added comfort when the cruel words and mean acts would sting his heart, he could nestle down and draw in the familiar smells of his home, the odors of his safe and loving world that were caught in the bright threads. Within the folds he could bury the pain he received from the uncaring people.

As the strong boy got a little older his parents told him of a Nobleman that ruled the land - who one day sent his Loyal Servant away with the instruction to kill his son, the Prince, because it would be the best for all. They recalled the servants' sorrow and indecision because he had loved the Noble Prince since birth and could never kill him, but he had to go home and tell the Nobleman his orders had been obeyed. In this distant valley by the big river he found a poor man and woman who desperately wanted the child and promised to raise him as their own. They would cover and protect him and no one would ever discover that the Loyal Servant had let the Noble Prince live.

The years continued and his parents did all they could to give him a happy home, and a normal life where he would feel secure and loved.

But as he grew older and began to dwell on the strange story of his past he felt a dark spot take root in his mind and in his heart for the Nobleman father who didn't love him. There were hours and days when he needed to be helping plant the garden but his hands would suddenly grow still. His eyes would narrow, focused on nothing, his shoulders would hunch and he would brood about this information.

Years passed. He grew stronger and so did the darkness that he now understood was not pain but hate. The hate built and required more of his attention. Jobs were left undone and the old couple worried about their son. They shared all they could from their one special *book* and from the love they had inside themselves hoping it could be enough to save him from this hate. But they could not uproot the deep emotion. And they died, their hearts still grieving for their once strong son.

The hate grew and every day the man hoped his Nobleman father would die. He worked his fields hard with the need to destroy. At night he would lay awake with his punishing thoughts, until eventually he began to stoop and cough. He would lay curled on his bed and not get up. He would not eat food – his hate fed him, fed at least his dark soul, but there was no nourishment for his body and it began to suffer greatly.

There came a day when a man knocked on his door, a man who traveled looking for work because he had no family or land of his own. Receiving no answer he slowly pushed the door open and saw someone who needed his help, so he stayed. He used his own knowledge and strength to help the owner of the house find his way back to life. And the owner of the house began to respond and get well. The two formed a strong bond and stayed together. Their need for togetherness, someone to touch, to talk with, to laugh and cry with was as important as food and water is to nourish the body, as rest and work is to strengthen the body. And a love grew; a mystery too difficult to define how it comes and goes, but a love so necessary to humans. The owner of the house became a Strong Man again. The hate was gone - no longer eating him like worms on a rotting corpse.

The healing Noble Son heard this story to completion, but could not talk or hear anymore. He asked to move his pallet to the barn for he needed time to think. He was very grateful for all the two men were doing for him. But his heart was numb, his mind in turmoil, and his body felt awash with shame. He needed to be alone.

Days and nights passed and the healing Noble Son tossed and turned on his bed, wrestling with alien thoughts. At times he cried silent tears of disgust while his stomach twisted with revulsion. At other times a fear he couldn't name took over. He was sick at heart for all kinds of different reasons.

He had started out with his fellow warriors to find power and glory, the best he could dream for himself. But the fire stoked dreams of glory had too quickly become cold ambers of disillusion. Now his nights and days were filled with a different kind of agony, doubt and indecision. Who can help him? He felt grateful to these kind men who had brought him to healing.

But he has only known one way in his entire life. It is the way of his Noble Leader Father, of his Nobleman grandfather before him – and this is the best way for all. Certain things alone are right and the others can only be wrong. Who can change the order and rhythm of what should be? But his thoughts confused him and only brought more questions. Is it glorious to kill and shameful to love? Could it be shameful to kill and glorious to love? Are there any answers?

Inside the house Strong Man and his Friend waited patiently on the healing Noble Son. They would not push for acceptance, they would not defend themselves, and they would not trespass upon the younger man's feelings and privacy.

One evening as mutton stew filled the air the younger man, now fully healed from his battle wounds, opened the door on the humble home. He stopped and stared. With newly opened eyes, he no longer saw the Strong Man, but the man who was his Noble Uncle and the Friend quietly eating their meal. At their invitation he joined them. They shared their food and talked long into the night and also into the next day. They would take food, drink, and short rests, and talk some more.

Man hates, kills and is killed. The Noble Uncle explained to his Noble Nephew that the day he discovered his Nobleman father had died from disease, he knew somewhere deep inside that he, the disinherited son with all his hate, had somehow killed the Nobleman rather than disease. Every dream at night, every day dream he experienced was of him, the Strong Man, killing his father, the Nobleman, over and over again. And it began to kill him also. This was not what his humble parents, the peasant couple, had taught him. He knew the death he had sought in his heart and mind was a grievous wrong, yet he felt powerless to halt the destruction rising like the waters of a broken dam inside his heart and mind.

The Noble Nephew thought about the death and destruction he had grown up idolizing, that was supposed to bring power and glory, the validation of manhood he had been longing for.

And man loves, his Noble Uncle continued and sometimes that love is the only way to survive. No, it was not the type of love his humble parents had. But when you grow up invisible to people, when you are hated and pushed around, and later when you are all alone, season after season remembering the voices that said something was wrong with you – that too brings a death as sure as the hate of war does.

So where do we find life between hate and love? How does one, hurting and all alone survive? Where is the middle ground that can nourish our souls? Perhaps I have exchanged one wrong for another. I do not have all the answers. But I did need life – I wanted to feel again, to be seen, to matter when I wasn't hidden behind the scarf and the shawl. There was only one that cared for me. My Friend who has loved me and asked nothing in return.

The Noble Nephew looked deeply into the eyes of his Noble Uncle and the Friend. He looked deeply into the eyes of his own heart. Nor did he have any answers. The hate of war had not brought glory. The hate of the people had brought destruction to his Noble Uncle. He could not hate these men who had given so much of themselves for his healing. He would leave here with much to think about.

As the years passed the Noble Nephew and his Noble Uncle grew in friendship, and respect. It wasn't always easy, but it definitely was not always hard. They found common ground to share and build a trusting relationship on. And they worked at it.

One morning the Noble Nephew crossed the valley, the cold winds blowing against his back. Arriving at the small home he had grown so fond of he found his Noble Uncle digging into the hard ground. Silently, he took the shovel from his tired Uncle and completed the work. Together they tenderly placed the Uncle's Friend in the dirt and solemnly, gently placed the covers of soil around one who had been deeply loved and would be greatly missed.

The next day the Nephew wanted to help his Noble Uncle with words to mark the new grave. He quietly pondered in is mind all the many loving things his Uncle might want to carve on the cross.

At the clank of the old barn door closing the Nephew rose from his pallet and looking through the window, was surprised to see his Uncle holding the carved marker ready for placement. The simple words read, "Beloved Brother".

After the quick chore of securing the beautiful wood into the ground, they returned to the house. Drawing close to the fire the Nephew admitted he was puzzled by the words on the marker. His Uncle settling in close by began to explain. In the years after my parents died Friend became my whole family until you came along. Today, I give him the highest place of honor in my heart, that of "Beloved Brother". And it comes from a higher love than I can give.

A heart of hatred is never fertile ground to receive the truth of rights and wrongs. My humble parents had tried to teach me of love, the greatest love, but it couldn't take root in my dark heart. Later when the love of Friend coaxed life out of this destroyed body, the hate began to crumble and healing began. This new life was so precious to me it became my air, my blood, and it was all that mattered, and it was enough.

During the early years of my anguish and hate before Friend came, I took up the only *book* my parents had ever possessed and I tried to read and understand the words. But all I felt was a fear that the book was describing its hate for me. I cried and only wanted to get rid of it. So I made a small coffin for it and wrapped it up in so many layers, cotton, paper, whatever I could find, so they would muffle the sounds of it calling my name, and I buried it beyond the garden.

Then, my Nephew, you came along from the people who never saw me, never talked to me, wanted me to vanish from life, not caring if I died, because it would be the best for all. But in time, you brought a change. It was a gift of grace - you listened without condemning, a gift of mercy - you touched me and looked into my eyes with caring, and a gift of compassion - you ate at my table, and no one had ever given me that from your town. My soul which had begun healing by the love of Friend and the bridge of trust you and I had built between us created fertile ground in my heart, and for the first time I remembered that little coffin buried so long ago. I felt safe enough at last to dig it up and try once more to read and understand its words. My mother had loved them so. Perhaps there was something I had missed.

This time it called my name in a different way. I was no longer threatened to see the mistakes in my life, the wrong choices I had made, and I finally owned the sin of hate that had nearly destroyed me. Sometimes the lessons lifted my spirit, other times I had to stumble off on my own, with an ache so deep I couldn't talk, I couldn't eat, I could barely breath. One day I felt a desire to talk to this Father I had been reading about for so long. My Nobleman father had only taught me hate but this Father was more like the kind man who had taken me in and raised me as his own, sparing none of his love for me.

I felt a little shy at first because I didn't know exactly what to say. So I just started talking to him like I had talked to my peasant father. Out by the river I sat, the sun was warm on my back, a light breeze stirred the trees edging the woods. I can't remember everything I said, but afterwards I felt good. It was probably a week later that I tried talking to this Father again. I told him about my week, my garden, my sheep, my Friend. I talked to him about what I might want to do in the future and that the next time I went to town I would not wear the scarf and shawl. I was tired of hiding and I finally felt strong enough to be myself.

I asked him about his Son, wondering if maybe he could help me understand why he had to suffer like he did. Pretty soon I was talking to the Father every day, and one day while planting spring seed in the garden I knew that he heard me. I can't explain how I knew he heard me, but it was there, warm and real. I was learning about a love even greater than that my old peasant father had given me. And I began to understand something so big called forgiveness and how it is a part of that love. I began to share all this news with Friend. Our lives became steadily fuller and richer because of it; because we had a new Father, a new Brother, and a Spirit to help us.

Nephew, for so long you and Friend have been my only family. But there is a family that is loved by the Father and in it we are all "brothers." In my entire life, this is the best gift I have ever received. Today I buried my "Beloved Brother". Soon you will need to dig my place in the ground next to him. You are a strong man now. You've been searching so long for that which gives life true meaning. Take my mother's book with you and make it your own. In it you will finally find that truth you seek. Read the words and talk to this Father and he will help you understand. Because it is the best for all.

There are two crosses now. Both say, "Beloved Brother", and we are, all three of us now beloved brothers of the Christ. I read his mother's book about his Father's love and sure enough I found the truth I had long been searching for. I'm glad, because before he died, I told my Noble Uncle how much I loved and respected him, because, after all, it was the best for all.

CHAPTER 15 A TIME UNDER HEAVEN FOR PARENTS TO FINALLY REACH OUT

"I Urge You Therefore to Reaffirm Your Love for Him" 2 Corin. 2:8

It's time to take a breath. We've studied a lot of scripture and worked our way through some complex issues. Perhaps some of what you have read is new and maybe even difficult or confusing. Give yourself some time to sit with the Father and rest. Let your mind and heart relax by His side for a time.

If you are reading this book there is a good chance you have a homosexual, bisexual, or transgender child or family member. My son is gay, so now there are two of us. You are not alone, ever again. I don't know what your journey has been like, but I hope and pray that as of today it gets better. This chapter is just for you.

For me, it was at times extremely depressing to be surrounded by sincere Christian leaders and friends who had no specific plan for living with a homosexual loved one; no answers for the difficult questions. I encountered my share of good people whose "rules" were made of steel reflecting nothing, as far as I could see, of Christ's example when He walked on the earth. There were lots of "good intentions" but that's about all.

Most of all I was disillusioned with myself, that I was so ill-equipped, initially, to trust my own ability to prayerfully study God's word and know he would lead me. This is my child. This is your child. We do love them in spite of what feels like the world falling away beneath us. First, we have to be involved in our own decisions. And second, we need to be secure that when we take them to God, the questions we ask will be answered with His truth and blessing. It's that important. And it's as simple as deciding to just take Jesus at His word. Once you feel satisfied that both criteria have been met you will be ready to move forward.

An essential starting line is for us to begin to understand our sons, our daughters, or whatever relationship your loved one is to you. For the sake of brevity I'll refer to them as our sons and daughters. There is a very good chance that you have felt deluged by pain and confusion and your focus has been on you, which is natural and understandable. You may or may not have sat down and begun to have any open and honest conversations with your child. You may feel at a total loss when it comes to your knowledge about homosexuals, their feelings, their wants and needs because you see them as so different from yourself.

First of all, if you haven't heard from or spoken to your child in a while that suggests to me you possibly haven't been able to think of him or her in positive or endearing ways. Perhaps you are afraid to accept them because you have always believed God would disapprove of your love for them. I hope by now Scripture has begun to assure you that Jesus' mission and our purpose is love for all people.

My original two step plan fell short. Since those years God has helped me find "enough" to heal the pain in your life and your child's life. Let's go.

Step 1. I want to encourage you to start right now and admit that deep inside of you is the love, Jesus calls it unconditional, for your child that desperately needs to be acknowledged. For the first time in however long, give yourself the luxury of saying, at least in your mind if not out loud, how very much you love your son or daughter. Say it over and over until it fills you up. Let your emotions take over and roll with your words. This is your time for some intense healing to begin. Don't short change yourself. This is between no one but you and your Father.

The next step may be a little tougher, but with God's help you can do this. I've been where you are and I support you and encourage you to work through the challenge.

Step 2. Admit, again in the quiet of your mind or out loud, that your child is lesbian, gay, bisexual or transgender. The more you finally begin to use "the word" the more you will become accustomed to it and the less it will threaten you. It's not some frightening, monstrous, dangerous thing. It is simply a word that defines a *small* part of your daughter or son's life. You need to begin to assign it to a less significant area of your thinking, and not let it eat away at you any longer.

I understand how it has grown to such proportions in your mind. Homosexuality floats alongside a whole boat load of myths, faulty logic, and even lies, in our present culture. But sexual and gender diversity is a reality and it is not going away. I want to assure you that your child has many more areas in her or his life that are deserving of your attention. They are human beings with full and active lives exactly like you and me. Stop thinking of them in terms of "sexuality" only. In fact, stop thinking of the "sexuality" at all! I get so tired of people going on about this intensely private issue they themselves would never allow others to interfere with or manipulate.

You and I don't want people thinking of us in terms of our "sexuality". That's an invasion of privacy and it really is okay for you and me to turn it off once and for all. This word, "sex", needs to be relegated to its proper place, into their lives and out of ours. You are doing great harm to yourself and a dreadful disservice to this wonderful child of yours if that is your focus.

Step 3. The flip side to this relationship is your child's perceptions of you. This may be something you haven't thought about. Have you given up on them? An equally important question is have they given up on you? Do they believe that you hate them? Were you instrumental in their leaving home and moving to another location? Maybe you can't even answer that question because you honestly don't know the answer. What were the last words you exchanged with them? Eventually these questions will need to be dealt with. But for now it is enough to understand there is a good deal of hurt inside your child, even as you have experienced and lived with pain.

In the book, *unChristian,* Gary Haugen shared his thoughts on compassion. He believes that the heart is required to involve itself in the rough and difficult venues in our world and assures us this is neither easy or natural. He encourages us to set out with the intention to be compassionate that allows us to stand with people who are hurting. "Compassionate" comes from two Latin words, *cum* and *passio*. *Cum* is defined as "with" and *passio* means "to suffer". Compassion means "to suffer with".

What a beautiful definition and yes, some of our children have suffered at the hands of who knows how many people and in how many ways, and may even now be suffering, just as we are, as our most intimate parent/child relationship is cracked and broken. Let's you and I put our hearts together. We can heal this. Above all, when we finally learn "to suffer with" we will be blessed, because we will finally be walking in the footsteps of Jesus!

Learn to feel compassion for your child. When you begin to suffer with their pain you will want healing in both of your lives.

My journey as described in this book began with little more than frightened loneliness. The burden I carried could not be set down. My only option was to move forward. The only companion I could find to rely on was my Father, Son, and the Holy Spirit. I was required to dig deeper into Scripture than I could have imagined, requiring hundreds of hours and over three years of days and nights spent with God. When I hoped change would come in my life it was not left unfulfilled. The change, however, was in me, in my heart, in my spiritual awareness of a truth I believe God wanted to reveal to me. It no longer matters to me if scoffers can't accept. God is alive and moving in an active and changing world and will carry His plan through to the end His own way.

My personal conviction, although it is unproven at this time, is that homosexuality exists from birth. I believe that gay men and women can be Christians equally as effective in the world as heterosexuals, and being equal with all children of God, all of their sins have been forgiven through their faith in Him. It is also my personal belief that the homosexual who has laid his heart into the hands of Christ is not judged on his sexual orientation, that his relationship with God is in no way lacking in integrity by his imperfections, whatever they may be, any more than the heterosexual.

When that little boy, my son, was placed in my arms after hours of laboring to give him life, my will for him was to protect him and raise him to love God and be a good, responsible man someday in our world. My job was to set the example and launch him on his way to solid, wholesome, decision making in his life. He did and he has. But it certainly wasn't because I was always the shining example I had hoped to be. I see God at work in His life. And that is enough for me to dismiss those who believe LGBTQs can't be Christians. Seeing the work of God is believing!

My son displays a sincere love, care and sensitivity to others. He has a master's degree in counseling and is now a Licensed Professional Counselor where he uses those wonderful attributes to help others. And in his freedom of will he has accepted to live the life he feels is a part of his being. Since my Father doesn't love me any less just because my will doesn't always fall in line with His will, as C.S. Lewis reminded us, who am I to turn around and disown my son if his will does not fall in line with mine in a specific area? When we look at free will in this light does it help you to feel less threatened about your child?

Step 4. Ask yourself this simple but important question. If God can do that for me, if God refuses to love me any less when I exert my free will, sometimes in ways He may not always approve, can't I also love my child in this same way? Allow a little time for the significance of this question to resonate within you. Surely if God can I can!

Perhaps every morning or any other time of day when you think about it, as long as it takes you to believe it, tell yourself, "If God can, I can."

If you have been carrying a heavy burden over your child's sexual and gender diversity, it's time to set it down today. If there is anything that needs to be shouldered, God will shoulder it because that is His job, okay? Remember, "Come...you who are weary and burdened, and I will give you rest...For I am gentle and humble in heart, and you will find rest for your souls." Matthew 11:28-29. Do you trust Him to do it? I do and at last I'm enjoying a freedom I haven't known in years. I encourage you to set the weight of your heart down. You can do it. God will even help you by taking it from you and placing any burden on His own shoulders. He does it every single day. We just never visualize this truth.

Our Father is so amazing. First He creates us. With our free will we listen to Satan and make a proper mess of our lives and our world. So now, God times His plan and sends a Savior to us to do what we cannot possibly do. And that's not all. Then He calls us by name and teaches us how to respond to Him. Does He love us or what! He does all the work. And there is so much more He wants us to have that we can't even envision.

Are you starting to feel a little lighter in heart; a little healthier in your mind? If not, please don't rush ahead. Take all the time you need to pray and work through these first four steps until you feel strong enough and ready to move forward. Just mark your spot in this chapter and come back when you are ready.

Step 5. This step is to take you back through the scriptures and Bible lessons we've covered so you can begin to pray over them. God will lead you where you need to go if you are willing to give yourself into His protective hands. As the Lord begins to work in you give yourself permission to let go of all the false beliefs that have taken hold and deeply troubled you for so long and accept God's truths as He reveals them to you so you can find your way back to your child. This is just between you and the Father – *no one* else. If past thoughts try to insert themselves back into your mind, and they will, they can prevent God from blessing you as fully as He intends. Keep pushing destructive suggestions away and the Holy Spirit will enable and support you to be strong.

At this time you are covering yourself with the protection of prayer and scripture. You are building your own "inviolate room" of protection from anything profane or evil. If you get stuck on certain verses and you need time to decide how you feel about them don't worry. Do not stress out. You have carried enough stress for too long. Put those verses aside for a while in a little pocket of your mind with the assurance that God will bring them back with His wisdom for you and your situation when He knows you are ready.

The next two steps you will be working on more or less simultaneously.

Step 6. As you go through the days and weeks hopefully discovering a haven of relief from the past, begin to imagine what you would like to say to your child. Start a list as ideas come to you and jot each one down. What you are beginning is a possible letter to your son or daughter. You may not use all these thoughts when you finally do write your letter, but it is good to begin getting ideas on paper.

It was a long and agonizing year of feeling a need to resolve my pain before I finally began my study of the Bible one April morning. I spent hours of the day and often continued into the night reading, researching, praying and meditating for answers. After two full months of this I was finally ready to open myself up to my son. Until reading this book you might not have ever anticipated contacting your daughter or son. In sorrow maybe you have given up hope of restoring any sort of relationship. So give yourself plenty of time. Do this at your pace, not mine.

The day I finally sat down to compose my letter, scratch out, rewrite, change my mind and rewrite again, it took several hours. At last I had my letter written on stationery. Phone calls and e-mails were not going to work for me. This was my way to give something of me back to my son. After signing my name I was emotionally exhausted. However, I was also emotionally exhilarated. There was also some fear and uncertainty about what the outcome would be. But I realized that was out of my control. It was a monumental day in my life – one I'd do over in a heart-beat.

Step 7. At the same time you are jotting down your thoughts for your letter you are also going to begin preparing yourself for the person your child is at this time. This is especially important if neither of you have talked to each other for an extended period of time.

You need to face the possibility there is a partner in her or his life. Just like heterosexuals your child will feel a real affection for this person. They may use words of endearment, "honey" or "sweetheart" when talking to their partner or referring to them. When you meet them in person there could certainly be intimate contact between them – hand holding and hugging, a kiss. If you have only talked by phone or e-mail it would be a good idea to ask for a picture of the two of them, especially if you anticipate a visit to them or from them in the future.

In the privacy of your home you have a chance to visually reconcile the truth that may still be hard to accept, your child has a same sex partner. Put their picture in a place where you will see it. That is your child, the one you love so much and are working hard to reconcile with.

If the picture is at first difficult to look at, please be assured as you continue to read back through the Bible and pray, it will become less of a problem. This picture is to help make their relationship as acceptable a part of your life as is possible, with God's help, even if you still may not totally agree with a same sex relationship. And put the picture among other family pictures. Don't isolate it. Your child is part of your family.

Maybe your son or daughter has gone through a commitment ceremony with their partner. How do you feel about that? Or there is a real possibility they have had a marriage ceremony. One important reason they may have chosen marriage is to be able to receive certain benefits to help them live and take care of themselves, such as medical or other insurance and legal problems that could arise in the future, just as we in heterosexual families need to sustain our daily lives and secure our futures. After all, civil rights are for all humans, based on humanity, not sexual identities.

There is another possibility concerning marriage I'd like you to just think about. Many lesbians and gays attend churches that in recent years have "reconciled" and opened their doors to them. They study their Bibles, attend Bible class and church and love God. Marriage makes sense to them, to vow to love one person in a monogamous relationship. And perhaps they wish to honor God through their marriage vows rather than just living together. Again, their feelings are not unlike any heterosexual couple in love. You and I don't have to understand everything. God has never required this of us.

What if they do have or are going to have a child? How does this make you feel? This will be your grandchild. You know what? Whatever you think and feel right now is okay. You and I have been buried under a lot of pain, misconceptions, and extra stressful trash for a long time. It won't go away quickly after reading one book. You must give yourself time to acclimate to any and all possibilities. That's what preparation time is for. But another truth for you to eventually accept is that this is your child's life, not yours. Yes, it affects you, but it is not yours to own.

This is your time to be honest with yourself. I can't say that enough. If you are stunned and heartbroken, this is obviously not what you wanted for your child. For your daughter you may have visualized the beautiful wedding dress in a church with her groom waiting at the altar. For your son you may have anticipated a lovely daughter-in-law to have your grandchild. But this is not where our lives have gone. You may need to take the time to actually mourn this loss, all the more so if your child has only recently revealed his or her life to you. If that is what you need, it is your right and a healthy one. But remember, there is a life waiting to be lived. Don't stay in perpetual mourning. Let it cease with God's help after an appropriate time.

This is still new and foreign to everything you have possibly been taught. Just know that spiritually I am wrapping my arms around you, and I will sit quietly by your side. If you need to cry go right ahead. As a mother I understand. My spirit will accept your pain to comfort you, and God's Holy Comforter who understands all our pain makes three of us. If you are a father, you have every right to express your feelings to God in whatever way is necessary and appropriate for you in the privacy of your home. When you are ready, you can move on. And as sure as I breathe, let me convince you there is a reason to move on.

That is why this step runs concurrently with step #6 because you want to think all of this through before committing to write a letter to your child. You need to know in your heart what you are ready to accept, what may still be difficult for you, and what you personally cannot condone, at least at this time – or maybe never. There is no cookie cutter mold for personal advice. Maybe you can accept a partner but need more time to internalize that any type of a commitment ceremony or marriage has taken place. Or you may never be able to emotionally and spiritually accept a marriage that your child has chosen for his or her life. That is between you and your Father. But I ask you to spend some time trying to resolve in your mind that this relationship is between your child and their partner and God, if He is part of your child's life.

But that is not all you are offering to bring to this new relationship. Be honest about this. Your private limitations do not need to destroy your desire for a loving relationship, blessed by God, with your child. And when you finally write your letter, allow yourself to be vulnerable through your honest explanation that you are trying earnestly to understand and love them. Be *tenderly* open if you aren't entirely sure how comfortable you are about certain aspects of your child's relationship, but above all else assure them that you do love them and want and need them back in your life, and that includes accepting their partner in your life, because they also, are a person created by God and God wants them to be a part of His life if they are not already. You are accepting and loving people in Jesus name, not condoning what some believe is a sin. There is a big difference. And you are learning to live with compassion.

You may be wondering what to do if your spouse can't make the same commitment as yourself. That is okay because it is something only they can come to terms with. However, this should not alter the fact that if you are ready to go ahead their reluctance should not stop you. You and your spouse are two separate adults. Perhaps someday as your relationship improves with your child your spouse will begin to find their own way back to his or her child also on their own terms.

During the wait for your daughter or son to receive your letter, spend some time loving yourself because your Father loves you. It may take some time for your letter to arrive and then your child will possibly need their own time to digest its contents and decide how they feel before responding back. This is one reason I strongly recommend a letter rather than a phone call. A phone interview makes it dangerously easy to impulsively say the wrong thing that could destroy in a matter of seconds what has taken you so long to build. Stay busy, because it's difficult not to anticipate what is taking place on your child's end. Depending how long a time has lapsed since you have spoken to one another the letter may be a shock. You can love them by giving them the time they need to process this.

I could never tell you what might need to be said to your child, but I think it is important to share a few thoughts at this point. It is crucial for you to be honest with them and humble in heart toward them just as God has said He is humble in heart. Your child is a smart person, capable of discerning the truth. This letter is to help you give your heart to them. But it's not about you primarily. It is about the *two of you,* your hurt and their hurt.

I had things to apologize for to my son and that is exactly what I did. I wanted to give love and hope and I tried to do just that. I was as transparent as possible about the changes in my life – the whys, the hows, the whats and I refused to dress them up for the occasion. They were what they were. If I was struggling I said so. Where great changes had come I excitedly shared them. But everything was open, honest, and non-threatening. There were no words to hurt or condemn him, and nor must there be between you and your child. Those days are over. We're done with that! If not, then you are not ready to send a letter. If you use any negative words about them in any way, they will feel threatened and you have given them a false start – a false hope that will only make it harder for them to trust any future attempts to reconcile.

In the end I told my son to hold close with Jesus. If your child is not a Christian and you perceive they may feel hostile toward the church especially if any of their past or present torment is from that source, you may want them to know that this "miracle" of change in your life has come from the love of the Father and you give it as His gift to them. Simply put, they will hear it so there is no need to preach it. They will approach you with their own questions when they are ready. But you have planted a wonderful life-giving seed.

If you feel the time has come, go for it. I stand with you prayerfully and support you all the way. You can do this. And don't forget to ask God to help you write this important letter. See Him by your side as you begin your words and don't forget to also ask Him to go with the letter and be present at your daughter or son's side as they read your words of love and healing.

When they are ready they will communicate back to you in some way. Again, depending on what has transpired previously between the two of you, they may be very reserved, cautious, and even a little suspicious. If that is their honest reaction it's okay to let them have their feelings. Do not tell yourself they are trying to hurt you or punish you. Perhaps a child that has endured a lot of hate at the hands of others might be lashing out from their own pain. But if you tell yourself you should have never written or tried to reach out and "this is the thanks I get", you will be packing up and going to the locker room much too quickly and you WILL regret your haste to prematurely end this important "event".

You've had some time for recollection and healing. This may be a required step in *their* healing. Maybe they feel the need to *test* your love. They may ask you to "own up" to certain things you said or did that hurt them. Do It! Own up to it. Be the parent. Maybe it was an entirely misunderstood situation on their part. Who cares at this epic moment. Own up. Even misperceptions can cause pain. Pointing out their mistake will slam the door – not open the way to reconciling. It is also possible the misunderstanding is your own.

If you are sincerely trying to heal a seriously fractured relationship, let your child tell you his or her hurts, real or imagined, and mentally and emotionally hold them until they can finally start to put the trauma aside. We did it when they were little; we can do it now they are grown.

You don't know everything they have been exposed to or have had to deal with. Let your tenderness for your child see you through to the other side of any torrential storms with God's help. Stand by them with compassion. I'm betting on love all the way and I believe with all of my heart they need and desire yours more than anything else. You're the father, the mother. So be their father. Be their mother. Let your child find her or his way to you the best that they can. After the storm has ended, has begun to clear their own frustrated or devastated emotions, they will be ready to talk, to listen, to receive, and maybe even give.

My son's partner became his husband, my son-in-law, two summers ago in New Hampshire. I love him and he has endeared himself to me by the care and love he has shown to my son. I tell you this so you can share in my hope and joy and so you will see that life can be full and good and meaningful for you also.

If after Bible study, prayer, and time spent devoted to listening to God, you find you can't condone their every decision, then you must go with your heart while still maintaining the decision to healing your lives and loving your child. After all, when do parents with heterosexual children ever condone every decision of their child? Nor do you have to accept the beliefs and expectations of outsiders. This is strictly between you and God. Never, never forget that. No one has the right to prevent you from fully loving and accepting your child. You are free to be a mother, a father, the one you always envisioned being. We are free to love our children just like God loves us and involves Himself in our lives. The day you realize this, how blessed you will be, and how full your life in God's kingdom will become.

CHAPTER 16 A QUIET AND SIMPLE BENEDICTION

"I Urge You Therefore to Reaffirm Your Love for Him" 2 Corinthians. 2:8
"So if God gave them the same gift as he gave us...who was I to think I could oppose God?" Acts 11:17

At long last peace and contentment are settling around me. They have breathed new life into my precious family, some old friendships, and additional friends I am now making who are sexually and gender diverse, some who are in churches and others who are not. My Father casts His eyes on each and every one, sending His Spirit to call their names and to draw each willing heart unto Him.

My God is a jealous God. But He is not jealous *of* false gods capable of nothing, He is jealous *for* us, and He wants every one of His created children to join Him in His eternal home. I truly believe, based on the actions of Jesus when He lived out His physical presence on earth that my priority is to make His loving desire to draw others to Himself easier not harder by my impulsive interruptions. I can't let the things I don't understand or can't conceive become the stumbling block that prevents someone from seeking the love of the Father who sees clearly and weaves all things together for His purpose.

1 Thess. 4:11-12 urges Christians to, "Make it your ambition to lead a quiet life, to mind your own business and to work with your hands, just as we told you, so that your daily life may win the respect of outsiders and so that you will not be dependent on anybody." I'm not so sure any of us lead a "quiet life" any more. Where it is possible, such a life provides ample time to help meet the needs of others and it simplifies what we are to do with our lives. I have certainly begun to make some needed changes in my routines.

And we are to mind our own business, to busy ourselves in such God-pleasing ways that we don't have the time or inclination to boldly interrupt the life of others and take it upon ourselves to "straighten out their faults" (so glaringly obvious to us) so they can become, to our satisfaction, "acceptable" to God. Our daily lives should be designed to "win the respect of outsiders", something we seem to care less and less about as time goes on. We are reminded in a steady barrage of daily input that we are entitled to do and say whatever we want, and everyone else needs to just deal with it, because it's their problem. We are repeatedly being informed that we, as a single entity, are more important than the whole, whether it's a whole family, a whole neighborhood, a whole city, an whole group of people, or the whole world.

Jesus tried to show a bigger picture to us about a positive ongoing walk to His eternity. He preached time and time again, "*Blessed* are they who..." rather than "*damned* are they who...". He personally took it upon Himself to reduce all hurtles by the cross He carried to simplify our journey, and established a new covenant of two laws instead of 600. He approached others with a calm, humble, yet confident authority and He often spoke with terms of endearment. "Do not be afraid, little flock, for your Father has been pleased to give you the kingdom." (Luke12:32).

"Before this faith came, we were held prisoners by the law, locked up until faith should be revealed. So the law was put in charge to lead us to Christ that we might be justified by faith. Now that faith has come, we are no longer under the supervision of the law." Galations 3:23-25. We are no longer to view our lives under a strict supervision of a Law that holds us prisoners. I'm not trying to say change and a penitent heart aren't important. I'm saying it is the job of the Spirit to work this miracle in His own timing. How much more effective could we be in reaching into someone's heart with Jesus' own words, "Blessed are they..."?

One Sunday morning my husband and I could not get to church due to unexpected car problems late the previous evening. I turned on the television and heard about sinners and their sins, rules, and what God does not like. I turned the television off. Where is the positive message of "Blessed" that Jesus focused on? Grace really is God's choice to cover us so we will not be crushed by sorrow, but be able to lift up our hearts to a God who cares about tomorrow's relationship with Him.

"Now instead, you ought to forgive and comfort him (the sinner), so that he will not be overwhelmed by excessive sorrow." 2 Corin. 2:7. (Parenthesis mine.) God is concerned about our eternity settled and sealed in Him, once and for all. Once our eternity is settled, whether we are gay or straight, God will attend to our needs. He will guide us and even discipline us as He sees fit, not as you or I see fit.

I am not a super-Christian. But I do know if I must police my sins, minute by minute, day and night, day after day, afraid to leave God's Spiritual altar for fear I am going to mess up again, I will have no life to extend to anyone else. I will become so overly preoccupied with my life that it will be the only one of any consequence to me. And in my mind that smacks of pride to think that I could even begin to spend enough time on my knees to gain favor with God when Jesus bled and died to gain the very thing I cannot.

Homosexuality is not going away. It has lived permanently on the landscape of mankind's history in one fashion or another. Certainly not all gay individuals are Christians. For every misguided homosexual you will find his counterpart in the world of misguided heterosexuals. But this is not what has eroded the moral fabric of society for thousands of years. Godless men who have their own agenda, whether they are in powerful positions of responsibility or not, who live to see name of the Father, Son, and Holy Spirit erased from the world and men's consciousness, it is these who cause nations to implode. More and more people who simply have no time for God, who refuse to bow before Him as the Creator and Life Giver of the world are extinguishing the light pushing the nations of the world into a downward spiral.

While "Some believed and some doubted", Matthew 28:17, Jesus still put His belief in His apostles and sent them out with what we call The Great Commission, each into his own direction of the world to tell about God's Son, man's Savior. Scripture is silent on what those "doubts" were, but they did doubt. The future work of Jesus' very first followers was not so perfectly, so easily, so completely grasped that they never had to fall on their faces in prayer. It wasn't so smooth that they never worried or questioned what they should do or tell others to do in certain instances. Perhaps God didn't specifically identify those "doubts" in scripture so each of us can fill in that verse with our own doubts. God does not let man's doubts and imperfections stand in His way or prevent what He intends to do in His world. His word will not return to Him empty.

From those ancient historical records that are still available, Philip Jenkins has written his book, *The Lost History of Christianity*. In it he shares that as far as it can be determined, apparently Thomas, "doubting Thomas", went east, eventually establishing the church as far as India. "One 9th century copper plate records the grant of land to one of Thomas' Indian churches by means that would have staggered contemporary Europeans: The boundaries were marked by walking a she-elephant around the grounds." 1 Jenkins.

Even with doubts that sometimes overtake us, much good can be done in the name of Jesus Christ. Through this amusing record from ancient history I'm trying to show that different is not necessarily wrong. A she-elephant is only one way to measure the boundaries of God's kingdom. From India, the Words of Jesus eventually made it to Japan. And this was before Bibles in all languages and theological translations. This was accomplished from the true desire of one man's heart to stop doubting and "be holy as God is holy". He was willing to risk for God.

But new leaders and their warriors come and go, destroying all those religious or otherwise of whom they do not approve. And when time and time again hundreds of thousands in the Christian Church were struck down, God's promised remnant would go underground. The richness of God's church, at times looked strained, impoverished and threatened – anything but holy and glorious.

Throughout hundreds of years, especially at times when the church was "underground", we would find it had little resemblance to either the first church or the church 500 or 1000 years later or even to our ultra-modern church of the 21st century. Let me share a fascinating example from Jenkins book. During the 17th century Japanese leaders destroyed the presence of a great Christian church in Japan. Of those who survived, some resided in a small fishing village. While their exact form of worship looked nothing like our modern day worship, they never hesitated to serve God in their hearts.

As I studied Biblical commentaries I found one writer who was very obstinate that wine and bread were the *only* elements sanctioned when observing the Last Supper or Communion. However, in this little 17th century Japanese village, where these men, women and children supposed themselves to be the only remaining Christians in the whole world, their meal of Holy Communion consisted of rice, fish, and sake (rice wine). I just don't think God said, "Well that won't work. I specifically said bread and wine and I prefer Kosher." Again, what is important about this vignette is that different is not necessarily wrong when the heart belongs to God.

While I believe we must avoid frivolously interpreting scripture, it becomes equally harmful to be so legalistic and literal that we vacuum pack our minds against what God can flex back open when He needs to. If today, at this crucial time when history is ripe for the knowledge, God needs to teach us something new, moving us forward to a higher level of faith and maturity, do we seal our minds too tight for Him to reach us? If so, what exactly is our relationship with the Father?

In truth, God's world from the beginning of time remains vast with uncharted territory in spite of how much our Bibles or history books have revealed. We cannot satisfy our tiny minds from our own shallow place in history with His mysterious plan. How He has ruled and judged or chosen to bless or overlook acts that we would never believe Him capable isn't ours to scrutinize and worry over.

"As late as the eleventh century, Asia was still home to at least a third of the world's Christians." 2 Jenkins. Jenkins continues to teach us that when we draw up a mental map of the earliest Christian churches, we don't include Asia or Africa because we are not taught about them. About one-thousand years of history and thousands of square miles of territory are unknown to us and we are unable to draw from them when forming our opinions of Christianity. Another truth I suppose is that most people today don't want to know or they feel that it wouldn't add anything further to our understanding of God. But in my mind, well, you never know. I will always be curious and in wonder of how God has worked in previous centuries. Actions can speak louder than words, even and especially divine actions.

We perhaps, over rely on the churches of Europe, specifically England, a country where from 1290-1650 Jews were outlawed from entering her borders. Compared to those vastly matured Christian empires of the east, England and France were babies rooting around for mother's milk. "During the later Middle Ages, mass defections and persecutions across Asia and the Middle East uprooted what were then some the of world's most numerous Christian Communities, churches that possessed a vibrant lineal and cultural connection to the earliest

Jesus movement of Syria and Palestine." 3 Jenkins. They were uprooted with so much knowledge having been lost to us.

These were churches with a close lineage with the times of the apostles, and yet their churches, their ways of worship, their ministries if you will, how they acted and responded with their neighbors whose beliefs were so different, is nothing like we could imagine today. And yet, God filled one-hundred percent of their world just as He does ours and His blessings were distributed among all people. There *were* churches before the church of Charlemagne and the Western world. "When we speak of the medieval church we are usually referring to conditions in Western Europe, and not to the much wealthier and more sophisticated Eastern world centered in Constantinople. But there was, in addition, a third Christian world, a vast and complex realm that stretched deep into Asia." 4 Jenkins. And their "Sunday mornings" looked nothing like our modern western worship. Yet, I believe God honored and blessed them.

So why is this important to visualize? Because while the history of the church has many times seemed strange to other generations, perhaps even weird or incomprehensible, God, the one constant, has faithfully connected all of us together under the safety of His plan. So if tomorrow's church doesn't look anything like todays, we shouldn't worry. God will continue to place His hand upon the future history of His church to His glory

The goal, the prize is not necessarily about how we get there, but that we *do* get there to His glorious and heavenly home. And when we get home, we will behold the "Tree of Life" which was once removed for our sakes from that long ago Garden. Its roots will anchor each side of God's eternal river and at last we will hold in our hands "...the leaves of the tree (which) are for the healing of the nations." Rev. 22:2. Can you envision it? Will each single tree have multiple types of leaves demonstrating that in spite of our differences we have at last joined as one family? Finally, complete healing of all nations – complete healing for all God's children. It appears we will still need areas of healing when we first reach heaven.

On Good Friday a couple of years ago my pastor closed with these words; "In the end whatever you believe of man's best understanding of scripture, let it lead you to God."

I'm sure he was not thinking of sexual lifestyles at that time. But for me his words that night were appropriate and comforting. Our best understanding of scripture is all any of us have. And God so knows this. "...let it lead you to God."

Who among us would dare to boast they have made a single righteous choice in life? The answer is none of us. For our Father in heaven has chosen us and only through His extended grace does all righteousness become possible...not through us, but through Him alone.

"Oh, the depth of the riches of the wisdom and knowledge
Of God!
How unsearchable his judgments, and his paths beyond
Tracing out!
Who has known the mind of the Lord? Or who has been
His counselor?
Who has ever given to God, that God should repay him?
For from him and through him and to him are all things.
To him be the glory forever! Amen.
Romans 11:33-36

An Open Letter to Lesbians, Gays, Bisexuals, Transgenders, Queers and Heterosexuals

Dear Child, Young Lady, Young Man,

I don't know your name, your age, or where you live, but I long to reach out to you. Would you come and sit by my side for a few moments? The world is so busy and noisy and stressful. We could spend some quiet, peaceful moments together. I wish you could feel my touch and know I am real. I'd love to look upon your face and smile into your eyes. It is okay with me for you to be whoever you are today, homosexual or heterosexual. We can just enjoy the two of us in mutual respect.

For a few moments in our private time together, if you wish, you can call me "mom" or "friend". My heart reaches out to yours in love and acceptance of you as a person, in all ways equal to me. If you have excelled in your life, helping others, contributing positively to our world,

I am proud of you. If you are just now striking out to find your path, I encourage you, and I am proud of you. If life has kicked you down, broken your spirit, and reduced your self-esteem to ashes, I give you my compassion and encouragement because you do have value and are someone with much to contribute to life, and for that I am proud of you.

In this moment in time, it's just you and me here together. Is there some memory that has left a mark on your soul? Is there a pain that hurts too much to let out? Is there something you need for someone to hear but they aren't listening? Is there a secret too dark and too deep? Is there a cry that has gone on so long there are no longer tears?

These last years have been a long and tiring journey for me, but one of the results I have received is a desire to love others wider and deeper than ever before, without judgment or condemnation. I'd like to share the best love I have with you.

I call him Father. I don't know what picture fills your mind when I say the word "father". Maybe your father has been a source of pain, even hatred for you. The one I call Father is burdened by grief when any one of us are on the receiving end of such destruction. His heart is humble and He would draw you into his arms to comfort you, call you tenderly by your name, and tell you about a love that is higher than either you or I have ever experienced. There are no words really to describe it.

Father wants everyone to know Him. The problem is that the ones who are supposed to be messengers of His love are not always doing their jobs, in part because we don't realize how simple it is because others have tied so many rules to the "how to". I and others have become burdened and frustrated doubting our ability to even be messengers. And I'm so sad and sorry I haven't understood it with the intensity I do now. I'm still not the best messenger. But because I finally took the time to ask Him myself, Father has freely given me a new and powerful love so hopefully I can begin to give it away to others.

And do I have a gift for you. There is a destiny that has been within your grasp since the day you were born. Its glory is beyond our comprehension. Our life as we presently live it compares to the life we are to eternally inherit like a rhinestone compares to the sun. It holds more joy than we can imagine, a never ending supply of perfect fulfillment which of course means no more pain and tears. And it has always been and always will be. It's not mine to give but I know beyond any degree of doubt it is ours for the asking because it is free.

Please don't listen to those who would stand in your way, preventing you from receiving your full inheritance. Those who don't believe will twist and turn Father's words, because they don't really understand His grace. His words make no sense to them and they refuse to study or ask for help to understand Him.

Just believe that when we can't get life right, when our faults take over even when we try so hard to get rid of them, we who still want to be loved and cared for can be! Believe that Father has already made things right for us. But he doesn't want to *make* us love Him. He doesn't want mindless puppets, but real people who can come to love Him of their own free will. He wants people willing to step up and respond to Him as He calls their name and reveals His love for them. It is not any more difficult and it cannot be any simpler.

I don't know if anyone has hurt you in your life. But if you have been hurt I almost wish it had come through me, because now I could look you in the eyes and tell you how ashamed I am for all the mistakes I've made. I wish I could make you well and whole and free from any emotions that would continue to imprison you. I can't. But don't forget my gift to you. Father can do all that and more. All you have to do is just talk to Him and let your own relationship with Him become a real part of your life.

Nothing fancy is required, just something simple like: "Hi Father, it's me, _____. I'm not really sure about what I'm doing but 'mom'/'friend' assures me you do know and you can help me." Then

232

you just tell him anything and everything that comes into your mind and out of your mouth and heart. Tell him you want His love – ask Him for it. After that, you talk to Him anytime you want. Talk with your heart and Father will find you and He will let you know He has found you. The best part is you will never be alone again. His Spirit which I talked about in this book will come and live with you and will guide you as you make decisions in life, even when you may not feel His presence. And like the Noble Son in "The Story", get your Father's book, get a New Testament, and just begin reading and hearing from him. And at some point I believe Father will send a true ally into your life you can trust to help you grow and understand more about what you have read and are learning.

Never, never forget, you are someone important to the Father because He sent His heavenly Son to stand in your place and mine, taking all our sins on Himself so they will never be laid at our door again when we love Him. They are removed from us forever. And here is an amazing mystery. Of all the so called gods in the world, only one, this Father, Son, and Holy Spirit, all three in one, is the only God who loves sinners. All other so called gods require more than we can actually be or give to serve and satisfy them.

You are loved and worthy of love.

Signed,

A mom/friend who loves you

If you'd like to reach out and connect for a quick word or conversation, you can reach me at cindykrueger0402@gmail.com. I'd love to hear from you. Blessings on the next wonder years of your life. I hope you find the "God Space" to give you peace.

Notes

Quote by E. E. Cummings used under the "Fair Use" guidelines.

Chapter Three

1. Brennan Manning, *The Ragamuffin Gospel,* (Multnomah Publishers, Sisters, Oregon, 1990, 2000, 2005), 53.
2. Doug Pollock, *God Space,* (Group, Loveland, Colorado, 2009), 67.
3. Brennan Manning, *The Ragamuffin Gospel,* (Multnomah Publishers, Sisters, Oregon, 1990, 2000, 2005), 79.

Chapter Four

1. Brennan Manning, *The Ragamuffin Gospel,* (Multnomah Publishers, Sisters, Oregon, 1990, 2000, 2005), 111.
2. David Kinnaman, *You Lost Me. Why Young Christians Are Leaving Church...And Rethinking Faith,* (Baker Books, division of Baker Publishing Group, Grand Rapids, Michigan, 2011), 39.
3. Matthew Henry Citations: Listed Quotations - *Matthew Henry's Commentary,* (MacDonald Publishing Company, McLean Virginia 22102, no copyright) Volume V, 187.
4. Ibid., 189.
5. Ibid., 189.
6. David Kinnaman, *You Lost Me. Why Young Christians Are Leaving Church...And Rethinking Faith,* (Baker Books, division of Baker Publishing Group, Grand Rapids, Michigan, 2011), 145.
7. Matthew Henry Citations: Listed Quotations - *Matthew Henry's Commentary,* (MacDonald Publishing Company, McLean, Virginia 22102, no copyright) Volume I, 39.
8. C. S. Lewis, *Mere Christianity,* (Simon and Schuster, Touchstone Book, New York, New York, 1943, 1945, 1952, 1980, 1996), Permission and all rights by Rachel Churchill, The C. S. Lewis Company Ltd., Dorset, England, 48.
9. Louis Berkhof, *Systematic Theology,* (William B. Erdman's Publishing Co., Grand Rapids, Michigan, 1932, 1938, 1996,) Permission under the "Fair Use" guidelines. Part 4, 416.

Chapter Five

1. Louis Berkhof, *(Systematic Theology,* (William B. Erdman's Publishing Co., Grand Rapids, Michigan, 1932, 1938, 1996,) Permission under the "Fair Use" guidelines. Part 2, 219.
2. Brennan Manning, *The Ragamuffin Gospel,* (Multnomah Publishers, Sisters, Oregon, 1990. 2000, 2005), 26.
3. Martin Luther, *Commentary On Romans,* (Kregel Publications, Grand Rapids, Michigan 49501, 1954, 1976, translated by J. Theodore Mueller), 83.
4. C. S. Lewis, *Mere Christianity,* (Simon and Schuster, Touchstone Book, New York, New York, 1943,1945, 1952, 1980, 1996), Permission and all rights by Rachel Churchill, The C. S. Lewis Company Ltd., Dorset, England, 53.
5. Louis Berkhof, *Systematic Theology,* (William B. Erdman's Publishing Co., Grand Rapids, Michigan, 1932, 1938, 1996,) Permission under the "Fair Use" guidelines. Part 2, 248.
6. David Kinnaman, *You Lost Me. Why Young Christians Are Leaving Church...And Rethinking Faith,* (Baker Books, division of Baker Publishing Group, Grand Rapids, Michigan, 2011), 39.

7. Matthew Henry Citations: Listed Quotations - *Matthew Henry's Commentary,* (MacDonald Publishing Company, McLean, Virginia 22102, no copyright), Volume I, 195.
8. Ibid., 195-196.
9. Tony Campolo, *Speaking My Mind,* (Word Publishing Group, division of Thomas Nelson Publishers, 2004), 58.
10. Daniel A. Helminiak, PhD., *What the Bible Really Says About Homosexuality,* (Alamo Square Press, Tajique, New Mexico, 2000), 17.
11. C. S. Lewis, *Mere Christianity*, (Simon and Schuster, Touchstone Book, New York, New York, 1943, 1945, 1952, 1980, 1996), Permission and all rights by Rachel Churchill, The C. S. Lewis Company Ltd., Dorset England, 109.
12. Martin Luther, *Commentary On Romans,* (Kregel Publications, Grand Rapids, Michigan, 49501, 1954, 1976, translated by J. Theodore Mueller), 75.
13. Daniel, A. Helminiak, PhD., *What the Bible Really Says About Homosexuality,* (Alamo Square Press, Tajique, New Mexico, 2000), 38.

Quote by Louis Berkhof, *The Kingdom of God,* (William B. Erdman's Publishing Co. Grand Rapids, Michigan, 1932, 1938, 1996.) Part 5, 568.

Chapter Six

1. R. C. H. Lenski, *The Interpretation of St. Paul's Epistle To The Romans,* (Augsburg Publishing House, Minneapolis, Minnesota, 1936, 1945, 1961), 271.
2. Reverend Steve Chalke, *A Matter Of Integrity: The Church, sexuality, inclusion and an open conversation,* (London, England, 2013), Used under the "Fair Use" guidelines, 1.
3. R. C. H. Lenski, *The Interpretation of St. Paul's Epistles to the Colossians, to the Thessalonians, to Timothy, to Tutus and to Philemon,* (Augsburg Publishing House, Minneapolis, Minnesota, 1936, 1945, 1961), 116.
4. Ibid., 116.
5. Ibid., 124.
6. St. Francis of Assisi, Quotation used under the "Fair Use" guidelines.
7. David Kinnaman, *You Lost Me. Why Young Christians Are Leaving Church... And Rethinking Faith,* (Baker Books, division of Baker Publishing Group, Grand Rapids, Michigan, 2011), 193.
8. Martin Luther, *Commentary On Romans,* (Kregel Publications, Grand Rapids, Michigan, 49501, 1954, 1976, translated by J. Theodore Mueller), 46.
9. R. C. H. Lenski, *The Interpretation of the Epistle to the Hebrews and the Epistle of James,* (Augsburg Publishing House, Minneapolis, Minnesota, 1936, 1945, 1961), 226.

10. Martin Luther, *Commentary On Romans,* (Kregel Publications, Grand Rapids, Michigan, 49501, 1954, 1976, translated by J. Theodore Mueller), Preface xiii.
11. Matthew Henry Citations: Listed Quotations – *Matthew Henry's Commentary,* (MacDonald Publishing Company, Mclean, Virginia, 22102, no copyright), Volume VI, 663.
12. Louis Berkhof, *Systematic Theology,* (William B. Erdman's Publishing Co., Grand Rapids, Michigan, 1932, 1938, 1996,) Permission under the "Fair Use" guidelines. Part 3, 402.

Chapter Seven

1. Flavius Josephus, *Josephus, The Jewish War,* (Zondervan Publishing House, Grand Rapids, Michigan, 1982 translated by Gaalya Cornfeld), Book IV, Chapter VIII, 229.
2. Jack Rogers, *Jesus, the Bible , and Homosexuality, Explode the Myths, Heal the Church,* (Westminster John Knox Press, Louisville, Kentucky, 2009), 113.
3. Ibid., 115.
4. R. C. H. Lenski, *The Interpretation of St. Paul's Epistles to the Colossians, to the Thessalonians, to Timothy, to Titus, and to Philemon,* (Augsburg Publishing House, Minneapolis, Minnesota, 1936, 1945, 1961), 124.
5. David Kinnaman and Gabe Lyons, *unChristian What a New Generation Really Thinks About Christianity...And Why It Matters,* (Baker Books, division of Baker Publishing Group, Grand Rapids, Michigan, 2007), 117.
6. Ibid., 118.
7. Martin Luther, *Commentary On Romans,* (Kregel Publications, Grand Rapids Michigan, 49501, 1954, 1976, translated by J. Theodore Mueller), Preface xvii.

Chapter Eight

1. R. C. H. Lenski, *The Interpretation of St. Paul's Epistle To The Romans,* (Augsburg Publishing House, Minneapolis, Minnesota, 1936, 1945, 1961), 250.
2. Tony Campolo, *Speaking My Mind,* (Word Publishing Group – division of Thomas Nelson Publishers, 2004),59.
3. St. Francis of Assisi, Quotation used under the "Fair Use" guidelines.
4. R. C. H. Lenski, *The Interpretation of St. Paul's Epistle to the Romans,*(Augsburg Publishing House, Minneapolis, Minnesota, 1936, 1945, 1961), 128.
5. Ibid., 130.

6. Ibid., 131.
7. Ibid., 132.
8. Ibid., 133.
9. Ibid., 146.
10. Ibid., 183.
11. Ibid., 186.
12. Ibid., 188.
13. Ibid., 198.
14. Ibid., 201.
15. C. S. Lewis, *Mere Christianity,* (Simon and Schuster, Touchstone Book, 1943, 1945, 1952, 1980, 1996), Permission and all rights by Rachel Churchill, The C. S. Lewis Company Ltd., Dorset, England, 95.
16. Charles McCollough, *The Non-Violent Radical, Seeing and Living the Wisdom of Jesus,* (WIPF and Stock, Eugene, Oregon, 2012), 55.
17. Brennan Manning, *The Ragamuffin Gospel,* (Multnomah Publishers, Sisters, Oregon, 2000, 2005), 59.
18. Charles McCollough, *The Non-Violent Radical, Seeing and Living the Wisdom of Jesus,* (WIPF and Stock, Eugene, Oregon, 2012), 146.
19. R. C. H. Lenski, *The Interpretation of St. Paul's Epistle to the Romans,* (Augsburg Publishing House, Minneapolis, Minnesota, 1936, 1945, 1961), 250.

Chapter Nine

1. Rev. John Stanger, Executive Director of Parity, (New York, New York), Direct Quote.
2. Jeff Chu, as quoted by Justin Lee, *Does Jesus Really Love Me?*, (Harper Collins, New York, New York 2013) 228.
3. Ibid., 229.
4. Ibid., 230.
5. Jay Michaelson, *God vs. Gay? The Religious Case for Equality,* (Beacon Press, Boston, Mass., 2011,) 7.
6. Dr. Stuart Edser, *Being Gay, Being Christian: You can be both,* (Exisle Publishing Limited, Wollombi, Australia, 2012,) E-book, LOC 2883.
7. Louis Berkhof, *Systematic Theology,* (William B. Erdman's Publishing Company, Grand Rapids, Michigan, 1932, 1938, 1996,) permission under "Fair Use" guidelines. Part 1, 78.
8. St. Francis of Assisi, Quotation used under the "Fair Use" guidelines.

Chapter Eleven

1. David Kinnaman and Gabe Lyons, *unChristian,* (Baker Books, Grand Rapids, Michigan, 2008,) 11.
2. Ibid., 15.
3. Doug Pollock, *God Space,* (Group, Loveland, Colorado, 2009,) 34.
4. George Barna, *unChristian,* (Baker Books, Grand Rapids, Michigan, 2008,) 9.
5. David Kinnaman, *You Lost Me, Why Young Christians Are Leaving Church...And Rethinking Faith,* (Baker Books, Division of Baker Publishing Group, Grand Rapids, Michigan, 2011,) 164.
6. Ibid., 154.
7. Jeff Chu, *Does Jesus Really Love Me?,* (Harper Collins, 2013,) 242.

Chapter Twelve

1. Rev. Justin Cannon, *The Bible, Christianity, & Homosexuality,* Copyright 2009, All Rights Reserved. Reverend Justin R. Cannon. Used with permission. E-book, LOC 661.
2. Brandon, Quoted directly to the author, used with his permission.
3. Jeff Chu, as quoted by Alan Chambers, *Does Jesus Really Love Me?,* (Harper Collins, 2013,) 109.
4. Joran, Quoted directly to the author, used with his permission.
5. Dr. Stuart Edser, *Being Gay, Being Christian: you can be both,* (Exisle Publishing Limited, Wollombi, Australia, 2012,) E-Book, LOC 3236
6. Jack Rogers, *Jesus, The Bible, And Homosexuality Explode the Myths, Heal the Church,* (Westminster John Knox Press, Louisville, Kentucky, 2009,) 61.
7. David Kinnaman and Gabe Lyons, *unChristian,* (Baker Books, a Division of Baker Publishing Group, Grand Rapids Michigan, 2007,) 169.
8. Dr. Stuart Edser, *Being Gay, Being Christian: you can be both,* (Exisle Publishing Limited, Wollombi, Australia, 2012,) E-Book, LOC 3436.
9. Ibid., E-Book, LOC 890.
10. Jeff Chu, as quoted by Wesley Hill,*Does Jesus Really Love Me?* (Harper Collins, 2013,) 150.
11. Ibid., 6.

Chapter Thirteen

1. Jay Michaelson, *God vs. Gay? The Religious Case for Equality,* (Beacon Press, Boston, Mass. 2011,) 25.
2. Ibid., 26.
3. Jack Rogers, *Jesus, The Bible, and Homosexuality Explode the Myths, Heal the church,* (Westminster John Knox Press, Louisville, Kentucky, 2009,) 60.

4. David Kinnaman, *You Lost Me, Why Young Christians Are Leaving Church...And Rethinking Faith,* (Baker Books, Division of Baker Publishing Group, Grand Rapids, Michigan, 2011,) 104.

5. Jay Michaelson, *God vs. Gay? The Religious Case for Equality,* (Beacon Press, Boston, Mass. 2011,) 22.

6. David Kinnaman, *You Lost Me, Why Young Christians Are Leaving Church...And Rethinking Faith,* (Baker Books, Division of Baker Publishing Group, Grand Rapids, Michigan, 2011,) 50.

7. Dave Pollock, *God Space,* (Group, Loveland, Colorado, 2011,) 20.

8. Jack Rogers, *Jesus, The Bible and Homosexuality Explode the Myths, Heal the Church,* (Westminster John Knox Press, Louisville, Kentucky, 2009,) 99.

9. Martin Luther, *Commentary On Romans,* (Kregel Publications, Grand Rapids, Michigan, 1954, 1976, translated by J. Theodore Mueller,) 48.

Chapter Sixteen

1. Philip Jenkins, *The Lost History of Christianity, The Thousand Year Golden Age of the Church in the Middle East, Africa, and Asia, and How It Died,* (Harper One-an Imprint of Harper Collins Publisher, New York, New York, 2008,) 10.

2. Ibid., 4.

3. Ibid., 2.

4. Ibid., 5.

www.ingramcontent.com/pod-product-compliance
Lightning Source LLC
Chambersburg PA
CBHW060841280326
41934CB00007B/874